The Secret
of Paradise

Mysteries of the Pacific Coast of Ecuador

Patricio Tamariz & Bo Rinaldi

The Secret of Paradise

Mysteries of the Pacific Coast of Ecuador

ISBN: 13:978-0-9838623-0-7

DEDICATION

To My Family,

In memory of my Ancestors, whose lives had meaningful purpose for our existence today.

To my son and daughter and their future descendants, in hope that my actions during this life strengthen our solidarity and my spirit can accompany them on their paths on this beautiful planet and towards the light.

ACKNOWLEDGEMENTS

I have always wanted to fulfill what I call the "three accomplishments." The first is having a child with your loved one; the second is planting a tree, and the third is writing a book. Now I can proudly say I have completed all three of these.

I have written from my heart about some of the wonderful and authentic experiences I have had during my blessed life, and in so doing I have been able to promote my homeland with all my passion. The hardest part of this book was to begin writing the first paragraph on the first page of the first chapter. Then everything just flowed with rhythm and motion.

This book was born out of my profound love for my wife, Juliana, my daughter Melissa, and my son Patricio Miguel. I thank my parents, Flor Maria and Patricio (†), for their unconditional love and support, and Veronica, my beautiful sister. I send many blessings to my uncles and aunts, Joaquin (†) and Meche, Leonardo and Cecilia, Jaime and Leticia, Clorinda and Marcelo (†), Teddy and Maria, Hector and Rita, and the rest of my family.

My daughter, Melissa

Loving and living in harmony with nature

My son, Pat Jr.

"Hey! What's mí papá doing in there?"

I was born in Bahía de Caráquez and, like many other families migrating to the land of opportunity, we moved to the United States in 1963 when I was 2 years old. When I returned home to Ecuador years later, I was mesmerized by the incredible amount of pre-Hispanic and colonial history present in this beautiful bay city.

Three people opened the door to my ancestorship: my great uncle, Gonzalo Dueñas (†); my great aunt, Bertha Santos de Dueñas (†); and her daughter, my aunt, Carmen Dueñas de Anhalzer. My Aunt Carmen, who has a doctorate in Latin American History from the University of Florida at Gainesville, is a well renowned Ecuadorian historian. She has studied in Madrid and Paris and has many amazing publications to her credit.

My deepest gratitude goes to Bo Rinaldi, my good friend and co-author. Bo is one of the leaders and visionary pioneers of the organic food movement. When he visited me, he recognized my passion and spirit for this paradise and encouraged me to share it with the world. His support gave me the courage to pursue my dream of writing this book about my homeland. I hope *The Secret of Paradise* will entice you to reach deeper into the spirits of my ancestors and of the lands, just waiting to be discovered.

A special thanks to Bo's team of editors and artists for beautifully articulating my love of life, my land, and our past. On this professional team, my praise to Chloe Hallock, an incredible person in mind and spirit, for sharing with me brilliant and quality time on the editing. Praise to all the artists involved; Chino Flores, my good friend, Bob Mack, and especially Ruben Martinez for sharing his incredible painting for the cover of *The Secret of Paradise*, which depicts harmonious life within our ancient cultures and the illustrious trade of the Red Spondylus shell, a symbol in Amerindian life on the Pacific coast of the Americas. Thanks to Carl Wescott, a true visionary and incredible land developer, for introducing me to Bo.

Many thanks to the archaeologists and anthropologists that have helped me at the archaeological site of Chirije, the underwater site of Cara and the Ruta del Spondylus. They are: Javier Veliz Alvarado, Jose Chancay, Karen Stothert, Douglas Ubelaker, Betty Meggers, Johan Reinhard, Jorge Marcos, Jean-Francois Bouchard, John Staller, Felipe Cruz (†), Olaf Holm (†), Richard Lunniss, Mercedes Guinea, Fernando Mejia, Angelo Constantine, Gerardo Castro, Mariela Garcia, Franklin Fuentes, Telmo Lopez, Pierre Usselman, Anne Rose de Fontaineu, and Georges Clement. My appreciation to the Escuela Superior Politecnica del Litoral and their Centro Anthropologico and Arqueologico of Guayaquil for the first modern investigation in Chirije. To the CNRS Centre National de la Recherche Scientifique led by Dr. Bouchard for the second modern investigation held there. "Mi gratitud especial" to Emilio Estrada (†) and Julio Viteri Gamboa (†) who discovered the ancient site of Chirije in the middle of the last century, which was the catalyst for this book and the Ruta del Spondylus.

Creating a global tourism initiative for one's country comes with sacrifice, passion, and teamwork. I wish to thank all the Ministers of Tourism that I have worked with as a team: Rocio Vazquez, Gladys El Juri, Veronica Sion, and Vice ministers Maria Isabel Laniado, Titi Palacios, Maria del Carmen Burneo, Mateo Estrella and Luis Falconi.

My appreciation to the team members of the Fondo Mixto de Promocion Turistica (Ecuador's Tourism Promotion Fund) who intricately helped me execute Ecuador's first tourism marketing plan. The promotion council, the technical committee and the operation technical unit were comprised of now lifelong friends – Andre Barona, Luis Maldonado Robles, Natalia Santamaria, Norma Bock, Solange Garces, Rodrigo Salas, Pablo Ochoa, Nubia Jaramillo, Ilse Tugendhat, Diego Utreras, Fabian Carpio, Patricio Gaybor, Jazmin Campos, Wendy Saltos, Laura Salvador and Mauricio Alarcon, and many more to whom I am truly grateful. Thanks to my friends in the Ministry of Tourism of Ecuador, especially Carla Portalanza. I would also thank the Ministry of Foreign Affairs for their side-by-side help.

To Jose Carrion Ycaza, my special thanks for being confident that I could lead Ecuador's tourism promotion to the world. His strategic thinking led to a more harmonized tourism sector for Ecuador. To Nathalie Pilovetzky, the grand professional in marketing and public relations that helped Ecuador become known in the US and Canadian markets. She always referred to us as "Batman and Robin". A special thanks to her team at Latitude PR, for all their amazing work throughout the years. As the first foreign country ever awarded by the Travel Industry Association of America for a campaign, together we proved that even if we are a small country, hand-in-hand we can triumph.

To Motohiko Kogo, Keibo Oiwa and Taka Tsuji for their outstanding work in protecting the mangroves of Ecuador and for introducing me to Peter Berg, with whom I began the Eco city work. To Peter (†), the father of world bioregionalism, who, I am sad to say, has just left us. He signed his book *Envisioning Sustainability* to me, "*Patricio, with such great rewards from our friendship of 10 years, I look forward with wide-eyed anticipation at what will evolve over the rest of our lives*". I hope I can fulfill his and our dream. To Judy, his life companion, for letting us have Peter here in Bahía for such long periods of time.

I would like to thank Carlos Ortega Maldonado, Albert Eyde (†), Leyla Solano, Amos Bien, Ernesto Barrera and many more university presidents, deans, professors and student friends that formed much of my academic and professional life during my studies at the Florida Institute of Technology; the Universidad de Especialidades Espiritu Santo of Guayaquil, Ecuador; the Universidad de Cooperacion Internacional of San Jose, Costa Rica and the University of Buenos Aires in Argentina.

I would also like to thank Henning Nielsen and Napoleon Martinez for believing in the Ruta del Spondylus (the sacred Red Spiny Oyster). The tour operators Alfonso

Tandazo, Willi Duennenberger, Carmita Santander, Raul Garcia, and many others. The team that worked with me for the Ruta del Spondylus project; Cristina Borja, Pedro Saad, Cristina Castro, Hector Bohorquez, Cristian Mera, Luis Flores, Ricardo Zambrano, Jairo Intriago, Carlos Chica, Marcelo Luque and Renato Dillon.

I appreciate all the work and advice given by the diving teams that included Bill Seliger Jr., Bill Seliger Sr., Haig Jacobs, Joel Ruth, Gary Clohan, Gustavo Ortega, Eduardo Espinoza, Sonia Basantes, Denise Cucurny, Santiago Ferreyros, Oscar Cornejo, and Ernesto Rodriguez. Thanks to the Ecuadorian Navy. Gratitude to Javier Veliz Alvarado, with his help we proved there was once land where now you just see ocean, (thanks to Spanish Armada maps he researched). To Robert Marx, world famous treasure diver for his invaluable advice and to Jacob Santos, my operations manager and good friend, whose historical perspective was the key to many of our successes.

I would like to express my gratitude to Patricia and Ron Farmer, to Tess and Mike Neuroth, to Mike Peru, for their commentaries on the draft chapters. I would like to thank Natalie Pyrooz, for her work in the Dry Tropical Forest of Bahía and Graciela Moreno for sending me an essay on Bahía. My thanks also to Torsten Loeffler for sending me an important document and photos. To Leslie Flaman for her valuable information on Expats in the Bahía area. To all my friends and surf buddies that did not see me in the water for long periods of time, thank you for your patience.

To my staff at Casa Grande and Chirije, especially Mariquita Cabal, Mercedes and Jesus Parrales, Francisco Paladines, Juan Jose Rodriguez (alias el Chino), Pablo Gonzalez, and Tammy Cedeńo for pitching in extra time to cover for me, and for accompanying me every step of the way. As I say in the book, they are all part of my family, and they have my deepest gratitude.

My recognition to the President of Ecuador, Rafael Correa for his hard work with the National Plan of Good Living and for giving Rights to Nature in our Constitution. For keeping the Oil in the Soil with the Yasuni Initiative; for presenting a good investment incentive plan with the Code of Production and for ensuring the infrastructure and connectivity present here on the Pacific Coast. This will enable us to start sharing the best-kept Secret of Paradise.

See the President's praise of Chirije on the internet:
http://www.youtube.com/watch?feature=player_embedded&v=8UbLu5iWyiM.

Creating a global tourism initiative for one's country comes with sacrifice, passion, and teamwork.

Patricio Tamariz

FOREWORD BY BO RINALDI

The Secret of Paradise presents the deep and profound truth that we as human beings can live together in harmony with nature and each other. These secrets are most evident in the rich culture, beauty, and history of Bahía de Caráquez, Ecuador, which is the central area of the country, where Patricio Tamariz lives, works and has found the inspiration to create this work. *The Secret of Paradise* focuses on the Pacific Coast of this rich and colorful nation, and as soon as I met Patricio and his family in 2011, I knew he held the secrets of the past and the keys to our future and that we needed to share these with everyone. Being a best-selling and widely published author and entrepreneur, I immediately knew we had a message that the entire world needs to know. You have now found the keys to this secret, and we believe that by knowing these, your life will be forever changed as well.

Patricio is an ambassador for peace, a living example of being in harmony with nature and all the people of the world. He and his family own Casa Grande, a beautiful retreat right on the tip of Bahía. They also own the spectacular and historically breathtaking Eco-resort known as Chirije, an amazing archaeological site, which as you will discover from reading this book, also holds many of the secrets. Patricio has helped start the first Surf Association in Ecuador, created the Spondylus Trail project, was the First Executive Director of Tourism Promotion for Ecuador, and now develops the coastal properties of the area, using sustainable and thoughtful means. He is a sought after consultant for anyone interested in sustainable agriculture and aquaculture, tourism, community and businesses of all kinds as he truly lives his passion. You see, in 1998 when El Niño hit Bahía, he and his family, with the help of hundreds of friends and dozens of key agencies, had to set out to rebuild their area, they rose above that devastation together, and created the movement for one of the world's first and most incredible Bioregional cities, Bahía de Caráquez, Ecuador. It is one of the most beautiful places on our planet, and the center of interest for our work together in revealing these Secrets of Paradise.

Why is this true? Well, the answer is as diverse as this book. You will learn here about the discovery of chocolate, the ancient history of medicinal herbs, the amazing ivory nut, the historic quests of the Conquistadors, and who really discovered the Americas. You will learn about the first ancient civilization in the West, the Valdivians, who themselves lived in harmony with nature and each other, creating pottery with the first female figurines of the Americas and other cultures that might have created images of strange flying objects. In addition, you will learn about the strange and unidentified lights that seem to rise out of the beautiful Pacific Ocean of Bahía even today, and then how they disappear at seemingly unimaginable speeds. You will learn about Patricio's ancestors who fought against Napoleon, helped in the consolidation of the Galapagos Islands for Ecuador, and helped to create entire industries around the natural wonders of Ecuador.

One of the secrets you will learn is how we can work together to create sustainable communities and a peaceful future together. You will feel the heart of a culture that lives today and is so inspiring you will quickly see that *The Secret of Paradise* is that we can still create this together on our Planet Earth today. I am eternally grateful and fortunate to work with Patricio and our team of editors and artists to present this work for you. It is a book you are a part of. As a team, we are members of many organizations and groups, including the Pachamama Alliance, Ecotrust, the Rainforest Action Network, and the Planet Drum Foundation. However, there is truly no group, no movement and no ideology as powerful as the human spirit and what we can create together. It is our hope that by reading and enjoying our book that you will be inspired to help bring to life *The Secret of Paradise* wherever you live. Moreover, that you are so moved to be a part of the lasting experience that is present today on the Pacific Coast of Ecuador. We invite you to time travel with us to a land of true peace and harmony as you enjoy this book, to learn all about the rich culture and history around Bahía, Ecuador and to come visit us to see just how beautiful this Paradise on Earth truly is.

The Secret of Paradise

Mysteries of the Pacific Coast of Ecuador

TABLE OF CONTENTS

CHAPTER ONE

The Surfer Who Found Chirije

I was born in Bahía de Caráquez. My parents and I left Ecuador when I was 2 years old. I lived in the United States for 13 years – from 1963 to 1974 – during a time when Bahía had gone into an economic slump. I later returned to the United States for four more years of college and had many wonderful experiences. I give my family thanks for making incredible sacrifices so that I could pursue my education.

Our trip to the United States began with 20 USD in our pockets. Our yearning for the land of opportunity in that great nation was similar to many people at that time. My mother remembers that we left Ecuador at the beginning of the same year when John F. Kennedy was assassinated (1963). Our family arrived on a propeller aircraft and landed first in Miami, then on to New York. Because of lack of space on our Miami to New York flight, we were upgraded to first class. Nice welcome!

My mother has many memories… some that are good and some that are bad. For example when we first got to New York, we were sleeping at the apartment of a family friend in Manhattan, which was quite nice, but there was a shortage of beds. Due to the number of men working day and night shifts, we were able to take turns sleeping in the beds. Our stay (which we appreciated) was just for a couple of weeks and that included sleeping in a foreclosed building, until my father was able to get a job, and we were able to move toward Newark, New Jersey.

My parents were happy to have their own rented place to live, but it was not the best. We were in a dark basement with our own entrance, but Mom remembers the rats (the size of rabbits) that ran through it. The owners that lived up above never made friends with us, nor did they inspect or properly maintain the house. Another memory of this place was the abuse we had from the kids of the neighborhood. One day, during the snowy winter we spent there, the kids locked us in. From here, we moved back to New York and lived in Astoria - right next to the electric generator buildings. Mom said we were sick many times because of the toxic smoke from the generators.

I have a funny anecdote. When I was about 4 years old, mom took us to the sidewalk outside of the multi-complex building we lived in to wait for my dad because he was bringing home dinner. I saw him coming with this funny thin white cardboard box. The closer he came towards us, the more a nasty smell was coming thru this box - a smell I had never had before. The smell was nauseating to me.

Dad said "dinner" and I start crying – especially when he opened the box and I saw this round, flat, weird food. He said "Hey, its Pizza!", I cried so hard. I did not want to taste it, but finally, once I saw everyone eating, I took a bite and said *"que rico!"*. I loved it! So much so, it is now one of my favorite foods in all the world… "New York Pizza".

Position of Ecuador on South American Map

My dad and I and friends coming out of the soccer stadium in NY
1968 - BARCELONA OF ECUADOR vs. DEPORTIVO CALI FROM COLOMBIA

En la composición gráfica observamos a este grupo de bahieños residentes en los Estados Unidos de Norteamérica en 1975: Sr.Patricio Tamariz Mejía, su hijo Patricio Tamariz Dueñas, Sr. Guillermo León Rodríguez, Sr.Pepe Vaca Bernal, Sr.Pablo García Barberán, Sr.Alfredo Parra Pazmiño y Sr.Bosco Farías Viera, a la salida del Estadio Randall Island de New York, luego del partido que Barcelona de Ecuador sostuviera con el Deportivo Cali de Colombia. Este inolvidable encuentro se celebró en la residencia de uno de ellos, en donde se recordaron tantas anécdotas vividas en su lugar natal. Lindos tiempos estos. Difícilmente se reunirán nuevamente; dos de ellos, Patricio Tamariz Mejía y Pepe Vaca Bernal, ya se adelantaron, rindiendo tributo a la vida. Hoy se los recuerda con añoranza.

Diario El Globo of Bahia
(100 yr old newspaper company)

We moved again to a better house that we rented close to Belmont Park in Long Island. I remember my impressions of things. I remember the first night there… the only night that we truly did not have anything to eat (we were very hungry). My mom put us to bed and we said our prayers…and as we were about to doze off, Dad came home with a carton of milk and some bread. I remember starting to go to Public School, and I found some friends. I remember a good friend named Alberto Serpenti from Albania. Alberto used to invite me to pick berries out of the tall bushes that he had in his backyard. In my backyard I had only apple trees, so it was a super-forest compared to where I had lived previously. I stayed there until I was 8 years old (1969), when our family moved to Florida.

We rented a small house in Hialeah, Florida. I started playing a lot of sports then – baseball, football and basketball. It was fun! My parents liked the climate. I remember the day my mom received a call and learned that her dad had died. (My grandfather, who was a tall and distinctive man, owned the Coaque Hacienda, where the first measurements on the equator were completed to study the arc of the Meridian to figure out the real shape of the Earth. This study was conducted by the Royal Academy of Sciences of Paris led by Charles Marie de la Condamine.) Afterwards I learned that he had left an inheritance to my mother, which my parents used to buy our first house. The price of it was 3,000 USD in 1969. One day I took my mom to Miami to revisit the old places where we had once lived. I took her by that house and we spoke with the owners and saw that the house still looked the same. About 6 years earlier, the new owners had paid 150,000 USD.

My dad's jobs got better and better, and he was able to work at the famous Doral Hotel on Miami Beach. From here they were able to buy a beautiful house in Homestead. I joined the Civil Air Patrol out of Homestead Air Force Base.

One thing I know for sure is that I had an excellent education in my schools in New York and Florida. In Homestead Junior High I was put in the Strive level with a great group of students, due to my advances in academics. My life was set to be in the United States until my father fell ill. He was in Jackson Memorial Hospital for about 6 months. Then he was flown out (at no cost to us) to the Bethesda National Institute of Health in Maryland where he spent around 2 years...without diagnosis. He was only given a couple of years to live, (this was in 1973), but luckily he stayed with us until 1997, when he died of cancer.

Due to my father's sickness, we returned to Ecuador when I was 14, but I kept my English skills because I attended Senior High School at the American School of Guayaquil in the International Program. I was an all around athlete and captain of my school basketball team. What a great time I had there, and what great friends I made. Overall, I have had more than 12 years of University and Postgraduate education.

My father brought the idea of shrimp farming to the Manabi province and was able to leave my mother with a small lot. She became the first woman in Latin America to cultivate shrimp... and later the first woman in the world to work with organic shrimp.

My mother worked very hard, but in other aspects, it was not the hard life that I saw my parents and friends have in the United States. The values of pride and effort I learned in the US helped me dearly in all I have done. My passion and vision for seeing things is probably because of being bicultural with a great education. Ecuador to me was a great new world I was discovering. My passion with Ecuador starts with its history.

I had not known of my country's past and especially the pre-Hispanic history of the incredible legacy that had flourished on our coast. The history of the Americas to me was based only on what I had learned in the United States. This was limited to Columbus, the pilgrims, the Revolutionary War, the Civil War, and so on.

Never had I thought of ancient civilizations, especially in Ecuador. My mother had purchased a small finca, or farm, called Mundo Novo (*New World*) long before we arrived from the United States. It was close to Bahía de Caráquez (about 25 miles) up into the watershed. I remember when I was a kid my mom would make us save up so we could send money to Ecuador to buy a cow for the small farm.

One day, when I had just arrived in Ecuador and visited Mundo Novo, I was surprised to see archaeological pieces there, which I brought back to my high school. My teacher saw an opportunity for a field trip and we left with my schoolmates to explore this land. This became my first contact with the ancient cultures of Ecuador.

In 1978, after graduating, I got hooked on surfing our beautiful beaches. This was fantastic! To be part of that first crowd of young surfers

Flor Maria holding organically grown shrimp from her farm

discovering secret spots (especially in the Manabí province) who spent beautiful days, seemingly without a care in the world, was amazing. On one of these days, a friend invited me to surf some point breaks off the beaten path. After we had left the water he said to me, "I want to show you something". As I left my last footprint on the sand and stepped onto the dry land of the tropical forest, I was amazed to see archaeological pieces everywhere (the difference with what I saw at Mundo Novo was the quality of the pottery shards). I picked up a couple of pieces and my friend said, "These are from your ancestors". I asked, "How old do you think they are?" He answered, "probably a couple of thousand years old." I was impressed.

This place was a double river valley with a beautiful forest that came out to a central platform on the beach. I remember when I went still further in and saw mounds with white slab rocks on them, I assumed they had been there for a long time and were probably burial sites. As time went on, I forgot about the unique experience I had that sunny day, surfing the waves.

Surfing Chirije

Patricio Spraying Some Water

President of Ecuador, Rafael Correa, surfing Chirije secret spot with Patricio Tamaríz

In 1994, Sixto Duran Ballen, the President of Ecuador at that time, who was also an ex-mayor of Quito and a good friend to our family, visited us. His vacation home was in Bahía de Caráquez. He told us that he was going to choose the first Ministry of Tourism of Ecuador. He also wanted to create an international airport in San Vicente across the bay. He accomplished the first goal of creating the first Ministry of Tourism. He was also able to expand the airport, but not to the international level (due to much opposition). He came over to our house to have coffee and "pan de yucca", and said to us that we should invest in tourism, because it was going to be one of the main areas of development and production for the future of Ecuador. My mother and I listened attentively to him.

Those were good times for shrimp farming. Mother had been the first woman in Latin America to grow farmed shrimp, and the first woman in the world to get an organic certification for shrimp production. Sixto would be the one to get us into the tourism business.

Three weeks later, my mother came to me saying that there was a piece of land for sale on the beach and that maybe we could put some bungalows on it and get our feet wet in the tourism business. We left for the spot, about 15 minutes away on the beach south from Bahía. I recalled making this trip with my dad when I was around 14 years old. Someone told me that this was the old highway from Bahía to Manta in the first part of the last century. It used to take 40 minutes to reach Manta.

View in Front of CasaGrande
Digital Print Image by James Petersen

Long before the time of Manta, there were no houses or anything else on the beach (around 7 km north of San Clemente). During the whole ride to the site, there was nothing in the distance. When we finally arrived to Chirije, the first thing I saw was a bearded man on a hammock reading a paperback in English. Funny thing, all the way out here, where we had not seen a soul and here we meet this person, the owner of this place, who went by the name of Eduardo Veliz (who later became a Member of Parliament, representing the province of Galapagos). He told us the name of the place and showed us around. Once I stepped onto the land, I started seeing pottery shards all around me. Then, I recalled this was the very place where I had seen archaeological remains, some 16 years earlier, on that cool surfing trip to the secret spot. Of course, I immediately told mother to buy it. I was 34 years old then. I had just been to Machu Picchu in Peru and really was blown away by the combination of tourism and archaeology.

Once we bought this archaeological site (240 hectares or close to 600 acres), I gathered up a bagful of ancient ceramic artifacts and send it to my dad in Guayaquil, asking, "Dad, please take these to the Central Bank of Ecuador Anthropological museum, and find out what cultures we have present in Chirije. Please do not say they are from Chirije because they might expropriate the land, due to it being an archaeological site." He told me that the next day, after handing over the pieces; the archaeologists were very interested in them and wanted to talk to me about it.

I am sure my father at least told them that they were from the Bahía area, or possibly even Chirije. Once he had told me that in the Chirije area he used to spend the weekends camping and netting lobsters on the reef, so he knew this area well.

When I called up the Museum, I was not prepared for what they were going to tell me. "*Ahhh, Mr. Tamariz, I will pass you on to Felipe Cruz our ceramic analyst*" said Olaf Holm, director of the museum. Olaf, born in 1915 in Denmark (he came to Ecuador in 1940), was the founder of this museum (which had the largest collection of archaeological artifacts in the country) and contributed through his studies to the deepening knowledge of our national identity. I was able to meet with him a couple times, however he passed away at the age of 81, two years after I met him.

Felipe Cruz, an expert in Ecuadorian coastal pottery (who also passed away a couple of years ago), started to tell me that the pieces of Chirije were very interesting, that Emilio Estrada the famous archaeologist of Guayaquil had discovered Chirije back in 1960, and had written a book titled, *Archaeology of Central Manabí*, which mentioned Chirije. My eyes were opening more and more. In his book, on the opening page of the Introduction, out of all the archaeological sites mentioned, the only one in capital letters and in bold was Chirije. This was an important site to him and he had investigated and actually named a new culture called Chirije. That was it – I couldn't open my eyes any wider. I could not believe it.

Then why didn't Emilio Estrada (and Julio Viteri Gamboa) keep on investigating the site? The book *Arqueologia de Manabí Central* (where Chirije plays a significant role) was published by the Victor Emilio Estrada Museum in October of 1963. His last message in the book was in November of 1961, and just a few days later, he died of a heart attack at the age of 45. That is why the site had a hiatus of investigation up until 1995 (we bought the land in 1994).

In his chapter on Chirije, Estrada notes that the bases of their houses were made of long cylindrical stones (24 inches long and from 6 to 10 inches wide) with holes through the middle from top to bottom, about 1½ to 2½ inches in diameter with sticks through them. This was the only site – out of all the archaeological sites of Ecuador -- that these stones were being used as foundations. The stones were laid in a vertical position, side by side, with sticks up into the air, where they were interlaced with other wood sticks, tied down and then adobe or clay with straw sculpted and shaped as walls. These were in rows; making squares about 15 x 15 meters wide (so this would be about the size of the houses, around 2421 square feet).

Estrada also discovered a new culture named Chirije that dates approximately from 500 A.D to 1110 A.D., (though on the site we have the Valdivia, Machalilla, and Bahía and Manteño cultures). An additional important discovery he made is that the name "Chirije is certainly the aboriginal name of the site because it appears in the Condamine Map in 1751." The Mission of the Condamine of the Royal Academy of Sciences of Paris' mission was to measure the arc of the meridian and ultimately find the true shape of the earth.

They had passed in front of the beach of Chirije in 1736. Estrada says:

"Another strange element in the Chirije culture is the hand grinding stone, constructed of cooked clay, finished at the top with a curved point, like a bird's beak, or with an anthropomorphic figure. Only in the Tairona cultures of Colombia and in the Mayan city of Chichen Itza can we find this element typical of the Chirije and Jama-Coaque II. The relationship is strange, vague, and does not clarify the origin of Chirije. These hand-crushing stones were used to grind some sort of food paste; aji (chili)-like was suggested for the region of Mexico. We believe that here these were used to grind incense in religious ceremonies."

One day I hope to translate all of Estrada's work on this region.

Felipe Cruz, curator of the museum of Emilio Estrada, helped me make contact with the Austrian born archaeologist John Staller (who went to live at a young age in the United States). He had come to Ecuador to investigate the ancient cultures back in 1984 and was investigating the Valdivia culture in southern Ecuador. John was a great friend of Felipe and participated in many of the scientific adventures on the coast. The day John visited me at Chirije I was so excited to see this team of archaeologists (Felipe came also). I felt like I was living my dream.

By the time I finished high school, the archaeology bug had already bitten me via one of my teachers. I was seriously thinking about studying archaeology – I loved history – and what would be better than studying the pre-Hispanic history of my own people? It didn't work out that way though. Since my mother worked on the shrimp farm by herself, I decided to study Aquaculture. Later, I became the first exporter of Blue Crab in Ecuador and was doing well with the seafood business until the President of Ecuador visited me, at which time I got into tourism.

So at 33 years of age, I was living my dream. John's visit to Chirije opened a brand new chapter for me. I tapped into my "Indiana Jones" or "National Geographic" explorer mode. Here is what happened.

The Chirije site, especially the area by the beach, had been cultivated by fishermen forever, they were there with the ex-owner renting the place. So we cleaned the place up, the main platform was barren of all vegetation. All of the sudden John Staller said, "I want to show you something, please follow me."

So I followed him on the Indian trail we have that goes up the hills of Chirije and past various water reservoirs that the Indians had left. In Spanish they are called Albarradas, and were particularly useful in the dry season from May to November. Many of the old timers that lived in the region say that after the rains, during our green season (December to April); the people would have enough water through the dry season until the next rains came. I once flew in a helicopter over the whole province of Manabí and saw hundreds of these albarradas (some 10 meters wide and some 10 times larger) they looked like small ponds. I could pick them out because it was about May, and the sun had helped reproduce the algae in them. The information I learned from them was incredible.

A good friend of mine, the Ecuadorian archaeologist Jorge Marcos (one of the most respected archaeologists of the Americas), told me about a project he did on these albarradas with NASA. From the NASA article:

Tree-Ring Study Reveals Long History of El Niño (2002):

"One record kept by archaeologist Jorge Marcos, Polytechnic School of the Littoral, Guayaquil, Ecuador, mentions "albarradas" (archaeological and small historical dams) built by the people of Ecuador and copied by the European conquerors, said D'Antoni (scientist at NASA Ames Research Center in California's Silicon Valley).

Albarradas turned the damaging effect of runoff during ENSO [El Niño Southern Oscillation] episodes into a way of replenishing the groundwater table and aiding agriculture on the dry coast of Ecuador, according to D'Antoni.

The older albarradas are 2,270 years old, according to radiocarbon dating. These dams were in extensive use 1,000 years ago, and some albarradas are still being used.

D'Antoni stressed that records such as those of Marcos provide "circumstantial" evidence of the historical ENSOs. "Our reconstruction suggests that there were many ENSOs, some very intense ones, in the last 750 years," D'Antoni said. "All of these experiences amount to a stronger support for prediction of future changes, which is one of NASA's goals."

Dr. Marcos calls the albarradas "artificial water reservoirs" and cites the book *History of the Discovery and Conquest of Peru,* written by Agustin Zarate in 1555, where he writes:

"The land is very dry, even when it rains often, it is of few fresh waters that flow, the majority of the water comes from wells or it is trapped by small dams that the natives call Jagueyes (now the term commonly used is albarradas)."

Dr. Marcos continues and states:

"Putting to value the observations registered through Zarate we can say that the Ecuadorian Dry Tropical Forest is a zone that is to be occupied and to be intensively taken advantage of; it required an accumulation of environmental knowledge and of a laborious social organization to carry out efficient and numerous works to maintain settlements that every time they were more extensive and complex" (Marcos, J. 2000).

Emilio Estrada, in his book, says the following on the albarradas of Chirije:

"The wells of 3 to 4 meters of depth, which we appreciate in figure 28, could have served as water deposits, the usual albarradas of our littoral, the Jagueyes, which were named like this long ago in Manabí. Well no. 5, on the eastern side has a path of stone. Could this have been a sacred pool for the Manteño priests in the époque of gold of Chirije?"

As we walked up the hill, the archaeologist John Staller said, "Look over there... see those oval-shaped spots on the ground? Those are burials. As you walk down there on level ground you cannot see them, but from up here you can. The dark spots of these ovals (the inside of the perimeter), tell us that dirt has been redeposited due to a person being buried there millennia ago. It has convexed inward with time, and you can only see that from up here". Many Huaqueros, when they are searching for burial sites with good archaeological artifacts as offerings, go up to see the view from an aerial position to find areas like this.

Curiosity kills the cat, or makes him the Tiger! After John and Felipe left, I donned my national geographic explorer clothes, my African safari hat, went out and bought trowels, buckets, and brushes and returned to Chirije. To do what? You guessed it, go and poke in one of those holes. I shouldn't even be writing this, but I have to tell exactly how things happened.

I shoveled out the first couple of feet of hard dirt (clay) from the top of the hole until I reached white volcanic ash. Could this have been for better conservation? Maybe. But as I continued downwards, I made a hole a good 4-foot wide and about 3 feet down, I found my first evidence; it was a square, white, horizontal stone about a foot and a half long. Then a couple of feet lower I found another one, pointing in another direction. Both of them were lying flat and by the looks of it, were placed this way. While I was troweling away at one of the sides of the hole, the trowel hit something and it made a "clink" sound. I saw a piece of pottery, which I thought was another shard (up to now all that I had seen were tons of broken shards on the surface). I took my brush and start brushing away the ash around it when the piece that I had discovered started getting bigger and bigger. Oh my, I remember telling myself that it seems like a whole vase.

I was able to clean enough around it that I finally popped it out of its place. What I found was marvelous. It was a shiny green/black globular vase that had a lovely bird sculpted into it on the top rim on one side. On the other side, there must have been another bird, but I didn't find it. It was just amazing. I remember I brought it home to show my mother and she could not believe it. She said the person that had created it was trying to show something very tender or affectionate. She was surprised – as anyone would have been -- that I had found this piece.

Getting back to my dig, I figured if I found that piece I could find more, so after I retrieved the vase and put it on one side of the entrance to the dig, I kept on troweling away. All of a sudden I heard a "crunch" instead of the clink. I looked very closely at the small piece I had just hit, and I finally realized it was human bone. Oooooooops!

Right then and there I said to myself that my digging days are over, I should not be doing this. Later on I read that the Huaqueros and amateur archaeologists just destroyed everything if they did not know how to record it. In their process of looking for the best pieces, they actually destroy incredible amounts of information. Someone once told me it was like putting fire to a library, you would lose all the information that maybe someone now or in the future can take advantage of for furthering our knowledge of our ancient past.

I called Felipe Cruz and told him that we were willing to help finance a modern investigation here in Chirije. He made contact with the archaeologist Javier Veliz (now one of my best friends) that in turn made contact with MSC, Cesar Veintimilla. Javier, now one of my best friends, has an incredible history of investigation behind him. He was curator at the Nahim Isaias Museum, investigator at the Anthropological Museum of the Central Bank, and director of the Julio Viteri Gamboa Museum (all in Guayaquil). He was also a member of the Historical Maritime Institute with many investigations under his belt and was one of the first archaeologists to work with us in Chirije.

Cesar Veintimilla specialized in Paleobotanical research and was the head of the team of archaeologists that came from the Center of Archaeological and Anthropological Studies of the Escuela Superior Politecnica de Guayaquil. I would like to thank the team comprised of Carlos Gonzalez Butragueño, Angelo Constantine, Brandt Rubio, and Fernando Mejia. This was the beginning of the first investigation post Estrada (45 years later).

During the prospecting and excavation they discovered various primary and secondary burials. Primary burials are where the natives bury the corpse as is, with all the rituals pertaining to the culture. In secondary burials, the bones are taken out and in some cultures the bodies are left to rot on wooden platforms in the forest then the bones are gathered to form a packet and are buried. Remember when I found the beautiful vase with the bird on it and the bones that I hit? Afterwards, the Polytechnic team dug this area out and a secondary burial was found. The bones were actually in a square package with the skull on top.

The Polytechnic team also found remains of construction, deposits of cooked clay, clay stoves, very abundant shell and ceramic materials, fossil animals, huge Megalodon Shark teeth, Mother of Pearl adornments, bone and copper needles, and Spondylus beads and ritual figurines from the Bahía, Jama, and Manteño cultures.

When my father was working in NY as vice counsel for the Ecuadorian Gov., unfortunately he had a heart attack. My dad was taken to Washington D.C. where he was treated and where my Uncle Teddy was an important doctor. While I was in Washington D.C. during my father's recuperation, I was able to visit the Smithsonian Institution and talk with Betty Meggers, American Archaeologist and South Americanist, which was one of the highlights of my life. I asked her for her help. She said Emilio Estrada had come to see her in the 50's in almost in the very same circumstances. What a fine and interesting scientist, I thought, and was very impressed upon seeing her efforts in still trying to prove that there was transpacific contact and that this had an influence on the first culture that worked with ceramic arts (Valdivia) in Ecuador. In a chapter I have written for this book, *"Who Discovered Paradise?"*, I inserted an article from Time Magazine (Jan. 6, 1961) where Estrada states the archaeological artifacts that most closely resemble the Asian cultural manifestations were the ones found in Bahía de Caráquez. Up until the day of his death he believed in transpacific contact.

On this same trip, I was able to contact Dr. Douglas Ubelaker, curator of the Department of Anthropology of the National Museum of Natural History, consultant to the FBI (since 1978-present), and President of the American Board of Forensic Anthropology. One of the most important physical anthropologists of the world, (author of *Bones: A Forensic Detective's Casebook*) he also has helped established modern procedures of forensic anthropology and has been an investigator in many archaeological sites, including those in Ecuador. I invited him to come down to Chirije to help the Polytechnic School with their investigation.

It was very interesting to hear him explain the process of dental age determination that, with his book, (charts that included pictures of teeth at different ages) has helped archaeologists and anthropologists around the world. The carbon dating method and other dating techniques reveal which era the human being studied lived in, but the age of death is a totally different and a relevant matter in analyzing human skeletal remains. For Chirije, Ubelaker wrote *"The Analysis of Human Remains in Chirije, Ecuador inside a Historical Perspective"*.

During his visit I picked up a tooth with a cavity right next to a plant in the Dry Tropical Forest. He told me that nomadic hunter-gatherers' teeth were exceptionally healthier compared to the natives of the time of contact with the Spanish. When agriculture and sedentism set in, the sugars of the maize (corn), which was the common food and drink, increased tooth decay (sugars turn into acids that eat away the enamel). Seafood was good (I think there is a good source of fluoride there) in general before they started maize agriculture.

A year after the investigations, Javier Veliz helped me in constructing the on-site museum in Chirije. This was done over an archaeological excavation on one side of a hill. I had built a beautiful and rustic museum for the peoples of our country and of the world to see. We had close to 1000 visitors in 1996-97. We also made bungalows with solar energy for the travelers to stay in if they wanted to. I added on a restaurant, and with the beach right in front, it was a great place to stay.

After all this effort trying to promote the cultures of the Pacific Coast of Ecuador, something really irresponsible happened. A Ministry of Tourism brochure was printed in seven languages, with the provinces of the coast as the highlights. That was not irresponsible; the problem was that when it came to the segment where our province is named Manabí, there was a large historical and geographical error. It said "*Manabí, the center of the Maya Culture*". I could not believe it. I said, "*Who the heck is in charge of promoting my country?!*"

This was something that changed my life, because in the year 2000, I accepted the offer to become the Province Director for the Ministry of Tourism of Ecuador. Later on, I was named director for the Pacific Coast, then the first Executive Director for Ecuador's Tourism Promotion Fund. Both were great experiences that filled me with much pride. I met many good people and others that were not the best.

Returning to our story with Chirije, the El Niño event of 97-98, (with major rainfall in the area) and the earthquake (7.1 on the Richter scale) left us with less than 1% of visitors for the next couple of years. What a setback that was. Luckily it is over now.

In 2003, the archaeologist Dr. Jean Francois Bouchard from the Centre National de la Recherché Scientifique of France, also pre-Columbian art professor of the Musee de Louvre of Paris, investigated the site. He and his team found many things, for example, an interrelation between various cultures within the Chirije site, which possibly occurred through maritime exchange (due to the mixture of archaeological pieces of different cultures found there). They also found that the amount of seafood that was present there exceeded the local necessity, and probably through a simple system of goods exchange, the foods were traded towards the interior, perhaps through an even more complex economic system. One of the most beautiful pieces he found was a round seal (see picture at end of this chapter) depicting a row of people holding hands.

One important subject that I talked with him about was all the archaeological groups (Estrada and Viteri, ESPOL, and CNRS) that had been excavating there found ancient "fogones" or clay/fiber ovens all over the site. These are horseshoe-type open ovens, about a half-meter wide to a meter in length.

The point is, maybe another institution would have taken up investigating this area just because of the sheer quantities of ovens present. I had talked to Dr. Bouchard about that once. I had seen a passage in one of the accounts of the Spanish Conquistadors explaining that when the ships would go by the valleys of our region they would see these valleys lit up very brightly. Could these ovens just have been used for lighting up the paths between the houses and temples inside the villages?

We were able to put up a museum on site; the pieces in it have four sources of origin. The first is from Chino's dad, who had dug the pieces up from Chirije long ago, hoping to one day write a book on the archaeology of Bahía. Luckily he did not sell them and now they form part of the listed and registered artifacts in the National Institute of Heritage (Instituto Nacional de Patrimonio Cultural). The second source is from the archaeological investigations, and includes some really beautiful pieces. The third source is from travelers who find things on the beach or by mistake, just walking in the dry riverbeds during the summer. The largest source has been from our gardener and keeper of Chirije, Francisco Paladines, who has been with us a while.
Thanks to him we have been able to keep the gardens in their prime state. With the rains, Francisco finds incredible pieces, which show up right on the surface of the land. It is a small and rustic museum built right over an excavation, and many people like it.

My quest for more information and more answers has led me to ask Universities to come and form a field school here. Imagine beautiful cabins for their students, right on the beach and very close to the Eco city of Bahía.

I remember while we were walking the site with Dr. Douglas Ubelaker from the Smithsonian Institution, I asked him how intense of a site this was, and he said, "there is enough here for an archaeologist to last a lifetime". This is the letter I have been sending out, and if any of you, even a graduate student or a student who wants a project for their Masters or PHD would like to come, Chirije welcomes you. The letter follows.

Dear Dr. Xxxx,

My name is Patricio Tamariz, ex Director for the Tourism Promotion Board of Ecuador (2004-2007), ex Manager for the coast for the Ministry of Tourism (2000-2003) and proud owner of the archaeological Site of Chirije on the Pacific Coast of Ecuador. I am the creator of the project Spondylus Trail (bi-national plan for tourism development for Ecuador and Peru). This is inside Ecuador's Sustainable Tourism Plan 2020. The Spondylus trail (the tourism development plan was born due to having Chirije since 1994), where we have sustainable tourism and archaeological sites, is part of an important movement of national identity for Ecuador and for the world. (I will attach a small executive summary of the Spondylus Route).

The main objective of this letter is to attract more investigators or even to form a field school at this site.

My family bought the site in 1994. Once we knew that Emilio Estrada investigated the site back in the 50's and published "Archaeology of Manabí Central", one of his masterpieces, with Chirije in all capitals and in bold in the Introduction of this book, we knew that we had to coordinate further investigations on the site.

Emilio Estrada, along with Betty Meggers and Clifford Evans from the Smithsonian back in the 50's discovered the Valdivia Culture (6000 BP), which at that time was the earliest known culture in the Americas to work in ceramics. He later discovered Chirije, which he says with certainty is the aboriginal name of the site because it appears in the Condamine (mission of the Royal Academy of Science who came to measure the shape of the Earth) map of 1751 (they passed through this point in 1736) as Punta de Chirije.

This site was investigated later by:

In 1995 by Centro de Estudios Arqueológicos y Antropológicos de la Escuela Politécnica de Guayaquil, Ecuador.

In 1995 by Dr. Douglas Ubelaker, Physical Anthropologist of the National Museum of Natural History of the Smithsonian.

In 2003, Dr. Jean Francois Bouchard, team leader of the CNRS France and pre-Columbian art professor of the Louvre Museum of Paris excavated and studied the site. (I am attaching his publication, the seal that is on the cover was found here in Chirije).

Interesting points to further study here are:

❖ *The fossils used as the base of houses (Estrada found them in-situ, but did not discover that they actually are fossils. This is the only site in Ecuador where there is this type of fossil use, we found them on the sea facing cliffs, which was once marine sea floor. We have also found ancient fish fossils, Megalodon teeth and many other things).*

❖ *Estrada notes that Chirije is a new culture for the chronological order for Ecuador. Many of the scientists who discuss this claim it is only a phase. The majority of archaeological sites investigated are much more south of Chirije, mostly at the Machalilla National Park (and even farther south). Only Estrada, Bouchard, and Zeidler lead studies on the central or northern coast. Dr. Jorge Marcos, our most prominent coastal archaeologist also states that there is definitely a Chirije manifestation.*

❖ *On almost all the units excavated, many (straw and clay) ovens have been found with no residues of food or metal neither on nor in them. According to the Spanish accounts, when ships passed the Manabí (our province) valleys, they would see these valleys lit up very brightly. I wonder if these ovens (fogones) were used simply to light up the area at night. As I have said, they are all over the place.*

❖ *Ceramics litter the place on the surface and all the way down to 6 meters in depth.*

❖ *Chirije is on an oceanfront platform (we actually own 238 hectares or 588 acres) with two valleys making a central platform between two dry riverbeds. The archaeological site now consists of almost 40 hectares or close to 100 acres and is bordered by a Dry Tropical forest (in great condition) to the east and the Pacific Ocean to the west. Due to marine transgression, we know that this site was huge at one point and now has been eroded away by the ocean. The Condamine in 1736 state on their map Punta de Chirije (or Chirije point) does not exist anymore. There is still a large quantity of shards on the beach today. Since 1994 we have seen how the ocean has eroded the site 1meter per year. We have protected it with large boulders, but there are plenty of platforms still needing to be protected.*

❖ *Estrada (up until his death 1961) and Meggers still believe in some sort of transpacific contact with the Valdivia Culture. We have some ceramic figurines on this subject that may interest you (we have an onsite museum for travelers visiting the destination).*

❖ *The Instituto Nacional de Patrimonio Cultural (National Heritage Institute) came to do an inventory of the museum and found one of the pieces to be a Valdivia piece. The gardener found it randomly during his work. (Now we have an Eco lodge with beautiful cabins here).*

❖ *There are many skeletal remains in the site, including a deformed cranium typical of the Bahía Culture.*

❖ *Lots of metal can be found here (gold copper earrings, copper nose rings, hooks, needles) and lots of shell work, from mother of pearl and also the Spondylus shell.*

I can say many other things about the site, but I know time is limited.

I thank you for your time. I am gladly available for further contact. I am attaching some publications so if you are interested, I can send you this. The site is a beautiful one; with cabins on the beach, it would be great for an international field school. Plus, here in Bahía de Caráquez where I live and have my offices, we have one of the most important archaeological museums of the coast. We also have laboratory facilities here in this museum, which can be used for posterior analysis after the digs. It is dry here from May through November, so there is ample time available for excavations. You have a great connection here with me (I am attaching my CVitae). I have friends in the National Heritage Institute that will surely notify you on the permits to get, and as I said please feel free to contact me at any time.

Please view www.chirije.com.

Sincerely, Patricio

If this happens, I will be a happier man than I already am. We just had a Valdivia piece confirmed by the Heritage Institute. This means Chirije could go back past 6,000 years of continuous human occupation. I have a beautiful Eco lodge at the site, so people from Ecuador and around the world can come and visit. You can explore the many artifacts all over the grounds and on the beach, hunt for the Megalodon Mega Shark teeth, hike the trails in pursuit of rare birds, and view all the evidence of the native's technology concerning water catchment. You can learn to surf, walk on wide long beaches with no crowds at all, or just relax in hammocks and enjoy the native local cuisine, mainly based on seafood.

My quest for new news and investigations to reconstruct the life of our ancient peoples cannot be satisfied, so I wish for the American and National field schools to be present on this beautiful site to aid me. I would like to share the everyday work of these scientists with you. I am sure they would want volunteers to do specific work with them. When the first archaeological teams were there excavating, I joined as often as I could and I promise you, every day was an explorer's fantasy.

Would this not be fantastic!? What new mysteries would Chirije have us embark on?

The experience for the traveler on our Pacific Coast should be unique. The person should understand that the archaeological sites of Ecuador are *Sacred Sites in Sacred Landscapes*. This is what we came up with while working on the Ruta del Spondylus (Ministry of Tourism program for the Spondylus Route) with my friend, the archaeologist Richard Lunniss. Our goal is to present images and experiences that evoke the past and help the traveler go beyond the present to explore visions of the pre-Columbian world through its archaeological sites and artifacts.

So it is true for Chirije.

Ray Bowman, a friend and frequent guest
at CasaGrande found a whale bone
on the beach of Chirije

Chirije Rare Artifacts

Bahia Giants
displayed at
Museum of Bahia de Caráquez

Some of the largest pre-Columbian clay figurines of the Americas ~
averaging between 1 ½ to 3 feet tall.

Archaeology Dig at Chirije

Dr. Douglas Ubelaker, Physical Anthropologist of the Smithsonian Institution,
Investigating ancient human remains in Chirije 1995

Apart from being an intense Archaeological site,

this is also a paleontology site with many ancient fossils found.

Many Megalodon (Megashark) teeth have been

found by the archaeologist on the land site and

many travelers on Chirije's beach.

CHAPTER TWO

Bahía of the Pacific

I returned to Ecuador in 1983 after spending the first part of my life in the United States. I was born in Bahía de Caráquez and probably will be buried here. This is where I have always wanted to live. Fate, you might say, has preserved Bahía as a city of unique beauty. For years, Lloyds of London wouldn't insure the ships coming into the bay because they would run aground on the sand bars. The then-president of Ecuador asked the authorities and peoples of the main port cities what would be the best way to expand the ports. In Manta and Esmeraldas asked for Oceanside piers and docks, but the people of Bahía due to the beauty and practicality of having the cruise and merchant ships inside the bay decided to ask for a dredge, which was a bad decision for progressing into a larger port due to receiving a faulty dredge, which did not deepen the entrance. Bahía was the second largest port of Ecuador for many centuries but losing its status as a shipping destination helped preserve the beauty of the city we have now.

I have a grand quality of life here, with many of my good friends (natives and gringos alike) around, a pretty apartment looking over the ocean, work in tourism promoting my city and country, and two other interesting jobs, coordinating and helping people look for new lives and homes, and working as a national tourism consultant. I have been rewarded with many accomplishments, both for my country and myself. I was the first director of the promotion board of Ecuador, advisor to the Mayor in Tourism and Environmental issues, worked as an aquaculture technician, have been involved in archaeological themes with my archaeological site, I surf when I want to, and play tennis for sport. I feel like I spread love all day and night. I am the proud dad of two lovely kids, Pat and Melissa (7 and 10 yrs. old) and am fortunate to be married to my beautiful and loving wife, Juliana. What more could I want? Life has definitely blessed me.

Living in a quaint beach city with a rich history and model movement towards an Eco city is a dream. Though Bahía is one of the places I enjoy living in, Santiago de Guayaquil has also been my second home. It is the largest city in Ecuador and the economic center of the country. I have spent many years living and working there. How can I describe the city and its people? It is a very tropical place, filled with palm trees, beautiful buildings, has great climate, (it gets warm in our summer) and is right on the large Guayas River. The people are great, warm and very proud of their heritage. You might have heard of the saying, "Don't mess with Texas"…here you say, "Guayaquileños Madera de Guerrero (or natural disposition of warrior)".

Aerial View of Bahía de Caráquez

When I attended University in Florida back in the 80's, I visited a bookstore and I was flipping through a World Almanac (I love to see statistics) and I saw one section titled, "*Dirtiest cities of the world*".

Here I was surprised to see Guayaquil-Ecuador in the number 1 spot for the tonnage of garbage left out in the streets. Guayaquil is a large city and also has a slum area, but recently has undergone major changes. The mayors of the four last terms, Leon Febres-Cordero and Jaime Nebot, have reconstructed the city on all levels. The United Nations Development Program has distinguished it, recognizing it as a model city. Many mayors around the world visit to learn how Guayaquil was raised from the ashes to become what it is now, a *Model of Urban Regeneration*.

I also lived in Quito while I was the director for the tourism promotion board (2004-2007). Quito has the largest and best-preserved colonial center of Latin America, and was the first one to be recognized by the UNESCO as a World Heritage Site. It has fantastic landscapes and incredible places to visit; for example, just south of the city, you have San Agustin de Callo, a Hacienda that once was an Inca fortress. It has an incredible view of one of the highest volcanoes of the world, the Cotopaxi. You can only imagine the impressive scenery with the snowcapped giant converting this part of the

Andes. Cuenca is also a pretty city with a spectacular colonial sector to it. This is where one line of my family comes from (Tamariz).

This chapter is on Bahía de Caráquez, but I wanted to mention these cities, as the proud Ecuadorian I am. The **four worlds** of Ecuador (**Pacific Coast, Andes, Amazon** and **the Galapagos Islands**) are all truly great to visit; they are just a half hour apart, except for the Galapagos, which is 1 hour 35 minutes from Guayaquil. So visiting the Pacific Coast is a lovely way to finish your trip to the four worlds. Bahía has the perfect location; it is in a pretty setting with the bay (Chone River Estuary) on one side and the Pacific Ocean on the other side of the peninsula.

I remember my dad, Patricio Tamariz Mejia, as a loving, intelligent and generous man. He was adored by all and had friends everywhere. He occupied the position of Vice-Consul for the Ecuadorian Consulate in New York. Right behind his desk was a panoramic photo of Bahía taken from one of the highest hills (now there is the panoramic point of the Cross there). I did not understand why he loved Bahía so much until I got older. Dad has since passed away, and is buried here.

Why are people so interested in living here? Perhaps it is the fantastic geographical features and the nice climate year round. Another important element is the small and close-knit community here. Friends here are friends for life. This city is also an historical and ecological one.

Historically, we know that the Amerindians occupied this area for many millennia. We still don't know exactly when inhabitants came to the Bahía area, but the archaeologists James Zeidler and Deborah Pearsall did find terminal Valdivia culture in San Isidro, (which is part of Sucre, the county which Bahía is the administrative center of) where cultural occupation is dated around 1700 to 1550 B.C. However, Karen Stothert's work, another archaeologist, dates the beginning of the Las Vegas culture to around 10,800 years ago; could they have been in this area as well? Is the evidence of their occupation in our area now underwater due to marine transgression?

Bahía of Cara

The first written account regarding relations with Cara is from Bartholomew Ruiz (Francisco Pizarro's main expeditionary ship captain). He reported how the natives (that were captured on the first native sailing vessel called the Balsa) described this area, a part of the Salangome chiefdom.

The word "Cara Lobes" is on the list of the towns/peoples recorded from the interpretation of the native guides. This was on Pizarro's second expedition in 1526-1527 (while Pizarro was adventuring on the mangrove coast of Colombia, he sent Ruiz to scout ahead). Many believe that this name, Cara Lobes, has a direct relation with the people of Cara, who were living around the Bay of Caráquez.

According to Miguel Estete's account, (see the chapter titled "*Magic of the Red Spiny Oyster*") the bay where the city now stands was first named Bahía de Caraque (without the z) by the Conquistador Francisco Pizarro in 1531. Francisco Pizarro was named Governor of New Castile from 1528 to 1541; this included the territories from the border of modern Colombia and Ecuador all the way to Chile. I inserted it again due to the importance for this chapter:

"*From the village of Pasao [where this expeditionary force found the shrunken human heads-Tzantzas and mummies], moving forward on the coast [towards the south], the governor departed with his people and arrived at a branch of salt water that was one league in width and named Bahía [bay] de Caraque; because this is the name of the province of where it comes out*".

The term "province" used in this account actually relates to this quote from Estete's writings back in 1531, which means "including the territory and its inhabitants". (Dueñas de Anhalzer, Carmen1986 quoting Moreno Yánez, 1981 in his book *Contribuciones a la Etnohistoria*),

Then we know about the Friar Tomas de Berlanga, who left Panama to arbitrate a problem that the Spanish Crown noticed the partners of the conquest, Francisco Pizarro and Diego Almagro, were having. After accidentally discovering the Galapagos Islands, his first point of entry to the mainland was the Bay of Caráquez on April 9, 1535. In his letter to King Charles I, he described the bay as being, "one of the most beautiful ports of the world that can be". He also wrote about the destruction left behind by Pedro de Alvarado.

We know that Alvarado and other conquistadors wiped out the population in this area. According to my aunt, the anthropologist and historian, Carmen Dueñas de Anhalzer, in her book, *Historia Económica y Social de Manabí*, "*Alvarado's expedition lasts 3 months in Manabí and it brought devastating effects over the native population*".

The Founding of the City

Juan de Velasco, a Jesuit priest, stated in his book, *History of the Kingdom of Quito in Southern America (1789)*, that the local tribes of the Bahía area were conquered by a foreign nation from the west (coming from the land where the sun sets) and they had arrived in balsas (sailing craft).

"*It is renowned that this nation seized the coast and because of this it was called Cara. The head of this nation or the sovereign was called Scyri [Shee-ree], which in their language meant, the "Lord of all". They constructed over the bay and that is why it is called Caraques [first written account of the naming of the bay, is from Pizarro, and it is Caraque, from the account of Miguel de Estete 1531, so it correlates to what the natives stated in their oral tradition]. The city is also called Cara, but most call it Cora. Over the very ancient remains of this city, all of cut stone, the Spaniards founded theirs with the same name.*" Please read more in the chapter on *Who Discovered Paradise*.

The first founding of the city of Cara (Bahía de Caráquez) by the Spanish was by Captain Francisco de Ribas in 1562, according to Giandomenico Coleti's historic and geographic dictionary, *Dizionario Storico-Geografico Dell' America Meridionali (1771)*. This can also be found in Antonio Alcedo's *Diccionario geográfico-histórico de las Indias Occidentales ó América: es á saber: de los reynos del Perú, Nueva España, Tierra Firme, Chile, y Nuevo reyno de Granada (1786)*.

What can throw all the historians and locals in Bahía into debate is a passage I found a few years back when I was researching the history of Bahía de Caráquez. It mentions Francisco de Ribas, the first founder of the city in 1562 and it mentions the location of the city. In Emilio Estrada's book, *Arqueología de Manabí Central*, he says that the French Geodesic Mission (who came to investigate the arc of the Meridian-shape of the Earth back in 1736) situated the city on the northern side of the bay (where San Vicente is now) in the map of the Condamine (published in 1751). Coleti's dictionary also backs this up, saying it is located on the north side. In 1811, a map (can be seen in Estrada's work) was constructed that situated Bahía in its actual spot (south side). The modern city is on the south side of the Bay at the mouth of the Chone River.

Juan de Velasco, Ecuador's first historian, states:

"Ribas could not have many followers and he was hardly subdued by the way of arms, but made alliances with those tribes that were not warlike and inhabited the shores of the sea. He founded that same year with few Spanish people and with some Indians, the small city of Cara, over the remains of the ancient one".

Velasco also states that there were not many troops, certainly not enough to combat and subdue the tribes in the forests, which had the source of rich minerals so there was no progress for the Spaniards in that area. In 1589, a plague arrived in South America and decimated the population of Cara, which officially ended as a city in 1590.

According to a conversation I had with my Aunt Carmen, there were two official foundings. The first one with Ribas in 1562 was a failure due to the reasons explained above. The second was by the merchant Martin de Fiuca and the priest Diego de Velasco in 1619. They called it San Antonio de Caráquez in honor of Antonio de Morga, the President of the Real Audiencia of Quito, which was the direct governing body of the territories under royal control with Viceroyalties overseeing them. The Real Audiencia of Quito belonged to the Viceroyalty of Peru, it had rule over what is now southern Colombia, all of Ecuador, north of Peru and parts of the Amazon basin (1563-1822).

Martin de Fiuca and Diego de Velasco wanted to open a road from Bahía to Quito. The bay had a nice climate and health conditions had improved after the plague. The Friar Diego de Velasco in 1617 said,

"The bay, big and deep enough for anchorage for all kinds of ships, is sheltered of all winds, we can populate her and have subsistence in labor, cattle, fishing, hunting and salt mining in the region".

According to Carmen Dueñas de Anhalzer in her book, *Economic and Social History of Northern Manabí*, Diego de Velasco and Martin de Fiuca were supposed to donate money to help found the city and also open the road. In return, they would receive ample economic benefits and political positions. This contract was made in 1617 with the President Antonio de Morga.

There is a letter from the King (probably Phillip III), to Antonio de Morga stating:

"I appreciate the good resolution that you have come to that was proposed by Don Diego de Velasco about the discovery of the port of Caracas [Caráquez], the new road, and the population it offers to Canzacoto [Santo Domingo located just a little southwest of Quito], without any cost to my "real hacienda" [which meant the grand and efficient apparatus that was put in place to collect all the taxes in the New World]. All is happening as it was proposed and I believe it will be carried out, this will be a convenient business not only for this province, but also for the rest of Peru and the Tierra-Firme and the areas of navigations." [Tierra-Firme means continent, but officially the Spaniards included this term to signify the lands of New Andalusia and Golden Castille]

I found it interesting enough to include here, especially for the citizens of Bahía and the new ones arriving, that I have translated the following letter's main points into English. A letter from the King Phillip IV in 1628 to the Viceroy of Peru, Diego Fernández de Córdoba, from the book *The Letters by the Kings, Our Lords, Popes, Viceroys and other Ministers of the Real Audiencia to the Council of Quito 1589-1714*, found at the following site of Gobierno de Caráquez on Wikipedia: http://es.wikipedia.org/wiki/Gobierno_de_Car%C3%A1quez.

"To The King, Our Lord.

Marquis of Guadalcázar, my relative, my Viceroy, Governor and Captain General of the Provinces of Pirú, or to the person or persons who would be in charge of its government.

On behalf of José de Larazábal, resident of the city of San Francisco of the province of Quito, I have been told that Martin de Fiuca, also a resident of this city, has taken a contract with Doctor Antonio de Morga, President of my Audiencia Real in which this city is located (resides), obligating it to open a road to the Southern Sea and Bahía de Caraques. The aforementioned Bay is a calm and enclosed port, is only six days travel to the city of Panama, and is very close to the above-mentioned province of Quito. Using this bay, ships can avoid the ocean and other rivers to reach the Southern Sea through the Port of Guayaquil and Puna Island [Island at the mouth of the Gulf of Guayaquil]. The poorly constructed road already there goes from the descent of the Tambo [resting place w/supplies, lodgings or settlement], which they call Pucara [Indian fortress in Quechua] all the way to the quay [or wharf] on the river, where you navigate to the port of Guayaquil. There are other inconveniences along the river, the water comes over the banks and floods much of the flat lands of quay [or wharf]; all of these issues will cease with a road to the bay. One could arrive straight from land to the sea

[Quito is almost straight west of Bahía, just a half degree south at the most] and it would be capable of providing shelter for big ships coming in of high tonnage and for the ones already there. Since there is a narrow and enclosed entrance, its shores defend against the enemies that would want to invade.

When the agreement was made with Martin de Fiuca, giving it to him as its guarantor, as he was in the process of opening the road when [supposedly] Indians of peace killed him and another companion. They wanted to prevent this road from opening. Upon this tragedy, the President sent Jose de Larazábal to carry out of what Fiuca was obligated to. He sent a good quantity of Spaniards to open the road, with commissions and other collected funds that were given by the President. They hired the necessary Indians to cut all the vegetation [I am using -cut the vegetation- to translate desmontando], spending more than 19,500 pesos.

Finally the road has been opened and there are many Spaniards with horses and mules, carrying out salt and fish. It is expected that these comings and goings will continue with cloths and merchandise of these and other Kingdoms, and the exportation of fruits of the province which are; wheat, flour, dried meat, cheeses, chickpeas, lentils and other seeds that are produced there. This will be of much benefit for its inhabitants and of Tierra Firme; the provision of rope, gunpowder, sandals and other military equipment for its defense, to bring my silver and gold, and other merchandise that comes down from the Kingdom of Tierra Firme. Textiles can be transported to the city to the city of the Kings, as well as wines and other merchandise.

Fruit will be obtained in converting a great quantity of unloyal and barbaric Indians to the holy catholic faith and another grand quantity of mulatos that secluded themselves in the province of Coaque close by. They perform heathen rituals, even though many of them are baptized. Satisfying the agreement, there has to be a city founded, giving them land where they can plant wheat and corn (maize) and other seeds of these kingdoms, like grand fields of cacao trees. This can sustain and bring wealth to the inhabitants that will settle there, and my real hacienda will increase. Many ships and galleons can be made and built there, as it has plenty and very good wood for these purposes and sites for shipyards.

I ask for title of Founder/Settler and Governor of that province with the preeminences and favors that are given to the conquistadors and founders of new provinces and kingdoms. I desire to continue my service that I have done until now on the road. The President now has enough power and faculty to do this and adopt the contract. My Council of the Indies has been begging me to give attention to this, that the requests made by Martin de Fiuca over the discovery and the opening of the road be honored. In the conservation of the Indians and of all the land it would be favorable to order adhere to the agreements, giving title of Governor of the Province, in accordance to the boundaries, demarcations and expressed conditions in a petition that I present before the President.

I ask this favor on Martin de Fiuca's behalf, to carry out with the obligation that he had. I put forward Licenciado Juan Pardo de Arenillas, my attorney in the council, because I want to know if Martin de Fiuca carried out with the agreement that he made on the opening and discovery of the new road, or did he die before it was finished; and if Jose *de Larazábal, as his guarantor, finished it and if the expenses that were made in the process, were accurate. I wonder if it is good to take a new contract over the new populations in Bahía de Caráques. I order you to send me your opinion and an account of everything, so that my Council can provide me with what would be advisable.*

Done in El Pardo [Royal Palace near Madrid], on the twentieth of January of One Thousand and Six Hundred and twenty and eight years. I, the King. By order of the King, our lord.

Antonio Gonzales de Legarda.

Señalado del Consejo."

(End of the letter from King Phillip IV)

The opening of the road was key to settling in Bahía de Caráquez and for the increase of the shipping in the area. It is said that to reach Quito from Bahía it took 18 days on horseback.

Velasco (1789) wrote, "*In the primitive days of the conquest the bay was the best of all, so secure due to the rivers Tosagua [Carrizal] and Chone that it had space for the anchoring of a whole squadron of warships. However after the arrival of the Spanish, the bay was unutilized due to the many sand shoals that were present*".

Since the writing of Velasco's historical book, there has been sand and clay erosion, especially from the mountains, enlarging the sand bars in the middle of the bay. This still happens today. In those times, the Spaniards saw infinite resources in our forests that surround the bay. They took down many forests so as to use the fine dry tropical forest wood that is one of the best of the world (please see the chapter, What is a Dry Tropical Forest?). As stated before, we know that that many fine woods, especially from the Cordillera of Balsamo, (the forest that starts in Bahía and goes all the way to San Clemente) were used for building ships and houses in the other territories of the Viceroyalties of the Spanish Crown.

From Guillermo Arosemena's article on the Exchange of products between Guayaquil and Lima, "*Estructura y actores del comercio exterior colonial entre Guayaquil y Lima*" (2009) he states, "Adam Szadsi and Dora Leon Borja assert that commerce with Lima started at the beginning of the 5th decade in the 16th century. They affirm that in 1547 a ship carried with wood left Puna Island (at the mouth of the Gulf of Guayaquil) for the construction of the house of Gonzalo Pizarro in Lima. Szadi and Leon Borja cite Cristobal de Molina (An Incan fable) in 1552:

"There are mountains that are called mangroves, to the ocean-land full of inlets [salt and brackish water creeks] and wetlands- and very tall trees and very straight, which are named mangrove, the wood is incorruptible, and so hard that the axes fall to pieces when they cut with them. The inhabitants of this town, because the wood is highly

esteemed on the coast and in this city of Lima, send their Indians, which have encomendados [people responsible over the native] so they can cut of this wood".

This was pertaining to the mangroves from the estuaries, which the territories of Ecuador had many of. Arosemena's article further reveals that the Spaniards were using the tree called Guachapeli (also from the Dry Tropical Forest) for the construction of the ship structures, the mangrove for the masts, and balsa for light ships that could navigate in small creeks and rivers. Most of the wood came out of the Guayaquil area but the (Chone River Estuary as it is called now) bay of Caráquez also served this purpose.

There are many things that happened during the 17th and 18th century. We know that there were hardships involved, experiences to be had and told. Many a ship and crew and new settlers and pioneers arrived and left the port.

According to my friend Graciela Moreno, local Bahía historian, in an article she wrote on the history of the area, *"in 1864, the straw hat (erroneously named Panama hat), was the main economic generator for the province of Manabí, although in that year new products like rubber and vegetable ivory nut came into demand".*

According to (Dueñas de Anhalzer, C. 1986), up until 1867:

"Bahía was comprised of just few houses and one or two commercial establishments. Sporadically ships came in to pick up the cacao of the valley of Chone. In 1871, the population duplicated due to having a nucleus of businessmen centering their activities here, also hacienda owners form Chone, Rocafuerte and Canuto also settled here.

Around 1882, Bahía had 3 neighborhoods delimited by its 3 streets, the neighborhood of the "orilla" [riverbank] where you found the commercial establishments and houses of the wealthier population, the neighborhood of the "calle segunda" [second street], and the neighborhood of the "calle tercera' [third street].

There was a crisis in the straw [toquilla straw] hat industry and the unemployed rural people of Montecristi and Charapoto were drawn to Bahía's economic prosperity. They helped in the preparation, embarking and disembarking of the products of exportation".

United States Consular Agency in Bahía

"This economic prosperity helped, so that in 1883 a Consular agency of the United States of America was created here in Bahía, following after the consular agencies of Colombia, Uruguay and Chile that were formed. In 1884, the consular agent of United States, Paul Goddard, an English commercial trader living in Bahía [was agent for 10 years], described the population in the following terms: its temperature is 72°F, it is the main port of the province [Manabí] and would be as much as Guayaquil, if there was a railroad constructed Bahía-Quito. Apart from the climate, its advantages over Guayaquil come from its position on the sea, its bay, its ease for disembarkation and its proximity to the capital, it is only 50 leagues away, as Guayaquil is 80 leagues".

In the same report, made to attract North American investors, he manifests that:

"I am surprised that no American firms have thought of establishing a depot at this port for American goods and manufactures. I am convinced that in this province of growing importance there exists splendid opportunities for American enterprise and Industry (Consular correspondence, June 30, 1884). [Dueñas de Anhalzer, C. 1986]

In 1884 a contract was signed between the government of President Caamano and a group of local engineers and promoters residing in Bahía for the construction of the railroad Bahía-Quito. They were Gualberto Perez, Julio Santos, Pablo Rockwell and Ignacio Palau. This never got underway due to the revolution.

Then Bahía entered the revolution, where one of the most famous Presidents of Ecuador, General Eloy Alfaro (B.1842), the leader of the liberal movement, paid much attention to this area, having many supporters against President Garcia Moreno's government.

Paul Goddard, the consular agent of the United States, describes the situation:

"The province is in a state of revolution, government troops are burning the towns down, ... Charapoto was burnt down on the 28th ... Alfaro arrived the 21st and left the 24th to restore some kind of order." (Consular correspondence, November 1884) [Dueñas de Anhalzer, C. 1986]

The revolution failed and Alfaro went into exile. Armament was found below the Casa Santos house, one of the main commercial establishments of the province. There were reprisals taken to some of the supporters of Alfaro in Bahía. One of the main ruffians, General Reynaldo Flores, captured two of Antonio Santos's sons (he was the owner of the Hacienda "El Napo" near Briceño—where Punta Napo is now, it is a beautiful piece of land). There was an order to shoot one of them, but for 30,000 pesos, General Flores would drop the order. The family refused to pay the ransom. The prisoners were taken to Montecristi and there was an intervention by the American Consul of Guayaquil. Most of the sons of the wealthy of Bahía and Manabí had been educated in the United States and England. The two sons were charged with complicity with the revolution. What the government didn't know was that both of them had American Citizenship.

"The intervention of the American Consul brought about the presence of a North American war frigate on the coasts of Manabí. The commander of the Frigate was able to come ashore in Montecristi to verify the status of the prisoners. They were finally freed and transported on a passenger ship to New York". (Consular correspondence. National Archive in Washington) [Dueñas de Anhalzer, C. 1986]

This episode did not stop there. In fact, it grew to such magnitude that it was called the "Santos Incident" in North American newspapers. On December 8, 1885, President Grover Cleveland in his first term (22nd and 24th President of the United States; 1885 -1889 and 1893 - 1897) on his first annual message to Congress, stated:

"The arrest and imprisonment of Julio R. Santos, a citizen of the United States, by the authorities of Ecuador gave rise to a contention with that Government, in which his right to be released or to have a speedy and impartial trial on announced charges and with all guaranties of defense stipulated by treaty was insisted upon by us. After an elaborate correspondence and repeated and earnest representations on our part Mr. Santos was, after an alleged trial and conviction, eventually included in a general decree of amnesty and pardoned by the Ecuadorian Executive and released, leaving the question of his American citizenship denied by the Ecuadorian Government, but insisted upon by our own."

The following is a clipping Aunt Carmen found that is still in the hands of the Santos family:

"In this recent message to Congress, President Cleveland announced the conclusion of a treaty with Ecuador to settle by arbitration the claim made by the United States against Ecuador on behalf of Mr. Julio Santos. The British Legation will represent the United States in the arbitration and the Spanish envoy will represent Ecuador...the claim is for several hundred thousand dollars. It grew out of an affair which took place ten or twelve years ago".

General Eloy Alfaro was President of Ecuador in 1895. He served two terms, 1895-1901 and 1906-1911. As one of Ecuador's heroes, he was the founder of the Liberal Revolution and completed one of the greatest infrastructure feats in the history of Ecuador, the railroad from Guayaquil to Quito, uniting the Pacific Coast and the Andes. He was brutally assassinated in 1912. Parts of his remains are now at Ciudad Alfaro, in Montecristi.

Christmas Eve, the year after the turmoil of World War II
Peace on all fronts, especially Bahía
Velasco Viteri Family Photo Archives

TIMELINE OF BAHÍA

Tatiana Hidrovo, a historian of Manabí, wrote an essay for the Ecuadorian History Magazine titled, *"Manta a Port City in the 19th Century (2006)"*.

❖ 1826. The senate of Colombia granted on March 16, to authorize Bahía de Caráquez as a port of Quito. It can import and export and only pay half the import rights that the other ports pay.

❖ 1830. The port of Bahía de Caráquez remains closed by order of the government of Colombia. [1830, the Republic of Ecuador is formed]

❖ 1860-1865. The port is navigated by national ships.

❖ 1861. There is commercial movement in Bahía de Caráquez but all the processes and paperwork are done in Manta.

❖ 1867. On Oct.15, 1867 Bahía de Caráquez and Esmeraldas become Major Ports.

❖ 1869. The President of Ecuador decrees that the Major Port of Bahía de Caráquez be lifted as such and only authorized for exportation of products not for the importation.

❖ 1883. On April 24, the National Assembly elevates Bahía de Caráquez as a Major Port. (Hidrovo, T. 2006)

In 1895, the American Consulate agent stated that the population of Bahía was comprised of whites and mestizos. In 1891, the population of Bahía had 800 inhabitants, and in 1898 it reached 1,200 inhabitants.

In 1909, Bahía was the second largest port behind Guayaquil. This was due to the grand quantities of Cacao (cocoa) being produced in the northern part of the province of Manabí starting from the decade of the seventies of the 19th Century".

"In 1909, because of the Cacao boom (Bahía being the exporting port), the centers of production of Calceta and Chone were connected via a railroad constructed by a French company called "Autofer de'Equateur", with a distance of 79 kilometers. [What I heard was that this railroad could have gone all the way to Quito, but that the French company had to leave due to World War I]. The government then took over its operation up until the decade of the 40's. In 1910, Bahía became a very distinguished city, the streets were paved and public and private buildings became very clean and elegant. It then had 3,000 inhabitants". (Dueñas de Anhalzer, C. 1986).

Here is an interesting collection from various works, one from a newspaper of Bahía (El Globo), which was included in Carmen Dueñas de Anhalzer's book (1986):

❖ *In 1916, the first automobile was introduced to Bahía. It is said with much enthusiasm from the local newspaper, "it took only an hour and a half by the beach to get to Charapoto and by horse it takes many hours". [The old highway to get to Charapoto or Manta was always by the beach, when you go to Chirije to my archaeological site you can experience this, and see the old seawall at the Punta Gorda. Now it takes 20 minutes, so from an hour and a half, the "horse power" has definitely augmented].*

❖ *In 1918, there was the premier of the operas "Carmen" and "Barber of Seville".*

❖ *In 1923, while in the rural populations they were dancing "el moño" and singing the "amor fino" (native ballad), the society in Bahía was dancing the Camel Walk, The Toddle and Washington Johnny.*

1930s: One of the last decades of prosperity [remembering that cacao hit a low in the late 20's due to disease], there was only a slight bonanza due to coffee and bananas in the 1940's. During the period of Bahía's economic prosperity, local entrepreneurs established many exporting houses.

1940s: Foreign capital also flowed in, from sources such as the German Casa Tagua filial of Tagua Handellschaft, which exported until 1940. The war definitely had effect on Bahía's demand and commerce.

1950s: Larger ships started entering the bay, I remember reading that Lloyds of London stopped insuring them because a large ship had run aground a shoal in the inside of the bay. The last exporting house in Bahía was "la Casa Velasco Santos", and that stopped in 1960. (Dueñas de Anhalzer, C. 1986).

1960s: From what I heard from my father, in the early 60's there were no job opportunities in the area. This is why in 1963 he took us to the United States. I am glad this happened, it was good to have been immersed in two cultures, like most of my grandparents and great uncles and aunts. I remember seeing a picture of my grandfather with baseball uniform on a team in Brooklyn, back in the early 1900's.

1980s: Shrimp farming got big in the 80's here in Bahía, and in the 90's condominiums for the vacationers from Quito were built. Now we have an incredible amount of real estate tourism coming in from the baby boomer market of the United States and Canada. Ecuador has been elected for the third time in a row as the number one place to retire in the world by International Living. Here at our hotel in Casa Grande, we are receiving more and more guests that come for beachfront property tours. This area is quite nice with a very good climate all year round. Quality of life is a priority for many who come down to Bahía and want out of the pointless pursuit of working to the bone in hopes to retire with dignity.

There are now many projects happening around the rural beaches of Bahía to create self-sustaining villages for North Americans. Some are really nice with an eco-perspective, which fits in nicely with our "Love Life" country brand. Other new comers are moving into the many new condos that are sprouting up.

I like a saying that one of my friends from the United States, Frank Tripp Martin, who now lives here and I consider a good Bahieño, told me once:

"I met Maye at the Club Nautica in Cartagena, Colombia and we sailed together down to Bahía. As soon as I got here and I was walking along the streets alongside the water, I felt the good karma of this place immediately. This is the place I wanted to stay. Here you know everyone. The climate is great and it is safe. If there were one way to describe this place, I would say it is Mayberry USA. My mother visiting said it was like Geneva, Alabama in the 1940s. I just walked with you on the boardwalk and in 5 minutes we had 4 or 5 places to eat a good ceviche. Watching the sunset over the Pacific ocean like this with this breeze, doesn't get any better than this."

Tripp is the co-owner; along with another good friend, Rodrigo Velez, of the marina "Puerto Amistad", where sailors and cruisers from around the world come in to dock their boats. It has a beautiful bay view and an open-air restaurant where the locals and the Expats meet. Since his arrival, Tripp married Maye, and has a little beautiful blond Bahieña called Francesca.

I don't know if there is some type of magnetism or spiritual vortex that anchors you in (we are almost right on the equator), I know it did for the Spanish Kings and their fleets, for pirates, the cocoa traders, the steam lines, and the revolution. The locals have a saying, *"Bahía no tiene Copia!* (Bahía has no Copy!). Everyone who is from here is very proud of being a Bahieño. There is a Bahía in Brazil, very famous worldwide, and there is a Bahía in the Pacific. Our Bahía has not yet gotten that incredible branding of the Brazilian counterpart, but we might just become the Bahía of the World.

In 2012, Climate Week, Britain's biggest climate change campaign (on the Yale Center for Environmental Policy and Law website) there is news naming Ecuador as one of the world's top 5 green destinations: "Ecuador - Ecuador currently has an EPI of 60.55 and is listed just behind Brazil. Being home to many national parks, rainforests and the wildlife rich Galapagos Islands, the environment is now being treated as a national priority in Ecuador and its city of Bahía de Caráquez has been named as one of the most sustainable in the world. After suffering damage from natural disasters, the government decided to rebuild the city to become more sustainable and it was declared an ecological city in 1999. The people of the city have even begun composting organic waste from public markets and households to support organic agriculture. Ecuador has also developed new programs to protect biodiversity and regenerate wildlife areas and is becoming a big eco-tourism destination."

Thanks Dad, I do understand why you loved Bahía so much. I do too.

Rich Beauty and Pacific Harmony of Ecuador

Chirije
Photo by Patricio Tamariz

Hacienda Palo Alto
Photo by Torsten Loeffler

Beauty and Peace of Chirije Sunset

Photos of Beach by Torsten Loeffler

CHAPTER THREE

Bahía the Eco City ~ A Tribute to Peter Berg

*"We didn't play it for the Big Time. We didn't play it for the Small Time.
We played it for the Real Time."*– Peter Berg 7/24/11

"Hermano, good to see you again", was our most common phrase of greeting in the last years with Peter. Sometimes this was the only phrase we would to say to each other on a yearly basis, especially on his last few visits. This was partially due to my being busy with the government or on a special project consulting for the Ministry of Tourism and not having enough time to sit with Peter here in Bahía . I always was saying to myself "next time he visits I will meet with him like I used to".

Peter would travel many times a year to work in Bahía for the Planet Drum Foundation. His work centered on Bahía, its people, and surrounding natural systems, so that one-day we could have a Model of Urban Sustainability, our Eco city. This was something I asked of him since the first time he came to our quaint beach city in 1999, still battered by the natural disasters of 1998. My only wish is for you to understand my relations with this man, who was so ahead of our times and truly part of my family.

It was November 26 of 1997. I was sitting out on the Malecon (promenade) waiting for a pizza at Donatello's place, [*close to where Puerto Amistad is now and long before we even thought of building the new bridge that is the longest in Ecuador, spanning out to San Vicente*], when it started raining, the first rains of the El Niño of 1997 - 1998. I remember the date well because the next day I had an expedition with some professional diving friends to a site I wanted to explore 5 km out in the ocean, where I had found walls underwater almost 20 years earlier. If you are interested in seeing one of my projects, a team of divers from a local university created a nice video on the expeditions (in Spanish): http://www.youtube.com/watch?v=VP9a9GhW4FU.

Ecuador's Pacific coast does not experience hurricanes or tornados, which is one of the reasons many sailing vessels from the Caribbean and Central America come to our beautiful port and stay for months on end. Their instruments suffer from all the electrical storms in those areas, of course magnified with all the humidity. With our green season and dry season, and with the influence of the warm Panama and cooler Humboldt Current, we have perfect weather all year long. We did experience what was earlier known as the Phenomena of El Niño, now called an *event* due to scientists figuring out that this actually has occurred with some periodicity through time.
The 1997 and 1998 events were the most extreme in recorded history.

This fantastic story starts with my meeting a group of Japanese friends from ACTMANG, (Action for Mangrove Reforestation) an NGO that had come to Ecuador offering technical and financial support for the preservation and reforestation done by local residents of mangrove areas, and the research, study and promotion of those activities. In Ecuador, in addition to their main objective was a specific one of protecting and investigating the tallest mangroves (*Rhizophora mangle*) of the world, which are on our coasts north of Bahía (Majagual). These grow up over 60 meters (180ft) tall. ACTMANG has also worked on many projects in Myanmar and Vietnam.

I was already doing voluntary work with this NGO here in Bahía, helping and coordinating mangrove reforestation and studies. I started a great friendship with Takayuki Tsuji, (better known as Taka) who was then a junior officer (now a world expert, working in Brazil) of this organization that had come to Chirije www.chirije.com, where we met for the first time. He thought the bungalows there were great and wanted to build something similar in Olmedo for a group of Afro-Ecuadorian women who were looking to start a tourism operation for the conservation of the majestic Majagual forest.

Taka led me to know a good number of the honorable members of ACTMANG including its Chairman, the famous Japanese explorer, Motohiko Kogo. Many personalities were brought together for this worthy cause and it was a prodigious honor to be in his NGO. It was out of great respect and admiration that I became friends with Kogo San. This interesting personality was one of the first climbers, with a team from the Mountaineering Association of Japan, to ascend to the second tallest peak of the Himalayas, K2, and almost was the first to conquer the tallest peak of Antarctica but came in second behind another team. I already knew of some of the feats achieved by Motohiko in the environmental area; in the Arabian Peninsula a royal family member had asked him to bring back the forests in the sea, so he re-established mangroves back and like magic, fish and shellfish returned to this site. Due to this great deed, he was awarded the Rolex Award for Enterprise and was a primary advisor for mangroves for the United Nations. A couple of years ago, I heard the Worldwatch Institute had stated that Motohiko Kogo was one of top ten reasons for the world turning tides towards sustainability because of the work he had done in Vietnam (much of the mangrove was destroyed there, from the use of Agent Orange during the war to the building of shrimp farms), Myanmar and Ecuador.

One of his honorable members that I have had the gratitude of meeting and becoming good friends with is Keibo Oiwa, one of Japan's leading cultural anthropologists and environmentalists. He wrote a book with David Suzuki (who hosted the program "*The Nature of Things*", which was a television series that aired in over 50 countries) that was titled *The Japan That We Never Knew: A Journey of Discovery*. He is also the founder of the Sloth Club, Japan's leading Slow Life environmental club. I am also member of the Sloth Club, number 007. Though Keibo knows how active

I am jumping on many projects, he says that although I am member of the Sloth Club, I am from the Monkey Division.

Last time I saw Keibo was in 2008 on CNN International being interviewed about the Slow Life movement. I was so happy to see him there as the authority he is. Further on in this account I will explain how his intervention was very important in my meeting Peter.

Our most difficult rainstorms are called "Nortes (Nor-Tes)", coming from the north and from the sea. They usually come in from the sea and drench everything for about half an hour, sometimes accompanied by thunder; it is wild to see the dark clouds just fly right by. This first storm in the 1997-1998 rainy season (green season really) was oddly a Norte. Oddly I say, because the Nortes usually come in later in the season. Another unusual thing was that this storm, instead of lasting around 30 minutes, lasted for almost 4 hours with very strong winds.

Just a few months before (during the Northern Hemisphere summer), I was in the United States at a good friends house when the catalyst for my worries (which were not much at that time) were the news channels and TV documentaries/programs advising that there was going to be a very strong El Niño during the upcoming winter. It was the first time I started to follow the graphs shown on TV illustrating a long tongue of red fire jutting from our Ecuadorian coast into the Pacific and following the equator towards the west. These were the SST graphs (Sea Surface Temperature) that showed the anomalies of the oceans' surface temperatures in real time.

We are just a half of a degree south of the Equator, surrounded by mountains on a beautiful peninsula with the bay (Rio Chone Estuary) on the northeastern side and the Pacific Ocean on the southwestern side. I have noticed here when we start having rain it is about when the ocean sea surface temperature reaches 26°C or (78.8°F).

So on this November evening in 1997 when the rain stopped and there was no more sign of El Norte, the bayside streets were flooded. What a premonition of what was to come.

The National Oceanic and Atmospheric Administration of the United States Department of Commerce (NOAA) states the following:

"The Earth's climate is dynamic and naturally varies on seasonal, decadal, centennial, and longer timescales. Each "up and down" fluctuation can lead to conditions, which are warmer or colder, wetter or drier, more stormy or quiescent. Analyses of decadal and longer climate records and studies based on climate models suggest that many changes in recent decades can be attributed to human actions; these decadal trends are referred to as climate change. The effects of climate variability and change ripple throughout the environment and society – indeed touching nearly all aspects of the human endeavor and the environment. Perhaps the most well understood occurrence of climate variability is the naturally occurring phenomenon known as the

El Niño-Southern Oscillation (ENSO), an interaction between the ocean and the atmosphere over the tropical Pacific Ocean that has important consequences for weather around the globe. The ENSO cycle is characterized by coherent and strong variations in sea-surface temperatures, rainfall, air pressure, and atmospheric circulation across the equatorial Pacific. El Niño refers to the warm phase of the cycle, in which above-average sea-surface temperatures develop across the east-central tropical Pacific. La Niña is the cold phase of the ENSO cycle."

Source: ENSO Cycle: Recent Evolution, Current Status and Predictions
Update prepared by Climate Prediction Center / NCEP 1 August 2011

The event of the 1997-1998 El Niño was the strongest in recorded history. The damage in our country was calculated in 2.8 Billion dollars, 4 times more than the event of 1982-1983. It was reported that seven million people in Ecuador had their lives altered in some aspect or another due to this extensive oceanic and atmospheric event. The province of Manabí (where Bahía is located) was the most affected and due to the specifics of currents and atmospheric chance, Bahía de Caráquez was the worst hit city on the whole coast of Ecuador. I believe it was one of the most impacted by the El Niño on the eastern Pacific shoreline of the Americas. The words *"We have nothing, we have lost our house, our land to cultivate and a family member"* were commonly heard.

The roads were so interrupted that in some places there was about 21 feet of mud over the highways, leaving no chance to travel out of the city for up to 3 months. The supplies, food, etc. were being brought in by the ferry that crossed from Bahía to San Vicente, which was now used because of the emergency from Manta (about 1 and half hours away on a good road). In Bahía around the seaside promenade there were tent camps set up for the homeless.

Mud was the everyday scene and with only a few machines that were working to clear it up but for another rain at nightfall, just left the panorama the same (we did not have as many companies as we have now constructing highways, these now have many land moving machines, tractors, retro excavators, etc.). Our actual President, Rafael Correa has made an impressive administration and management on the topic of new infrastructure.

Right before the winter of '98, I remember distinctively my mother, Flor Maria, having a meeting below the house of Samuel Zambrano, our shrimp farm administrator. He lived with the first floor open on all sides (where hammocks were hung for lazy afternoons) and the main living quarters were on the second floor where his family lived. This was very typical of the Manabí countryside constructions. His wife (now passed away with cancer) and his two sons were of great help to us. All four lived on the second floor.

This meeting's main subject was to prepare for the upcoming El Niño.
I remember that mom burst into tears due to her preoccupation with this event's impact

on her hard worked business and on the people she might not be able to sustain if something of a disaster hit again. The 1982-83 El Nino event was still fresh in her mind. This was the second largest event in recorded world history. She had braved that by herself because I was studying in the United States at that time. Again, another premonition arose at that meeting. In that very same place, months later during the heavy rains of March 1998, a flash flood came up and covered the house and the water came in through the second story window. I imagine it was at least 15 feet high and caught everyone by surprise. Samuel jumped out of the opposite window with his wife and two kids hanging from his back towards the tree situated on one side of the house. The family was able to survive because Samuel was able to stay clinging on that tree. More than 50% of the shrimp farm was destroyed.

Event after event in Bahía de Caráquez catalyzed an uneasiness of the local community that grew into indignation and frustration of why nobody from the central government had ordered a National Disaster declaration for the area. All of this happened in waves of succession, up to when there was a large landslide and 12 people died in the upper area of Bahía. I had one good friend, a hotel receptionist, who died there. At this time, a group from the community that was coordinating help for Bahía including Flor Maria, had invited a Minister to come to Bahía (by plane and/or helicopter) so that he could see the disaster firsthand. When he arrived he was detained, so he couldn't leave Bahía. This was finally when attention started to be paid to the disaster.

The rains that usually last into April, because of the abnormality of the sea surface temperatures, lasted into almost late June. The land was saturated with water. Anything that fell from the sky made the dirt, clay and trees move down the slopes. Then the rains stopped.

I remember I felt like a king when I was able to cross Bahía's outer rural area (about 3 km in 40 minutes). Just to go 20 km you had to make 6 different transfers on different vehicles. With coordination being done by the municipality, central government, the Stuarium Foundation and Civic Action groups in Bahía, help was little, but surely trickling in. It was sad to see a medium sized tent city with a homeless population of about 300 families that were relocated into a barren mud flat called Fanca.

Friends living elsewhere in Ecuador did not truly grasp what had happened in Bahía and jokingly they would say, "Is that true all the mud we see there?" Sometimes I would get angry with this, and I would answer that what they saw was only the foot or so of mud that the TV cameras and reporters took when they followed the national authorities through some of the lesser-affected areas. This was the truth. Only our local radio and newspaper reporters knew what was really going on.

The sadness of our story does not stop here. On August 4, 1998, just about over a month after the rains had stopped, at about 12pm, Bahía was shook by 2 earthquakes. My part of the story goes like this:

We were in Guayaquil with my mom and sister, when all of a sudden I got a telephone call from my secretary, Patricia Borja. I noticed a frightened tone in her voice as she said that there was a big shake and that plaster and cement had fallen on the computers at the office (Bahía Dolphin Tours) and that the mayor's wife had come down the stairs crying (Dos Hemisferios condo where we had our office). During the time I had lived in Bahía the maximum shake had been a 4.0 on the Richter scale. This one was larger (5.4). Just a week before, we had heard about the earthquake and tsunami that hit Papua New Guinea and that had killed thousands. Due to this, Civil Defense was at that moment patrolling Bahía with loudspeakers saying that there could be a tsunami and that everyone should look for higher ground.

Patricia went on and told me about the earlier event, and then she started screaming "Oh no, it's happening again!" She and her family were in an open-air park and were pretty safe there, but she was very alarmed as she told me how she couldn't stand up. Then she screamed, "a building is falling; all the air is filled with dust and debris!" About a minute later, the city of Guayaquil where I was started rocking hard. That is when I told myself, the epicenter is in Bahía. Within about 15 minutes all the news channels started to communicate that effectively the epicenter was just off Bahía in the ocean.

So it came to be that after such a devastation of El Nino we were hit by a 7.2 earthquake epicentered off of Bahía and Canoa at 1:59pm on August 4, 1998.

The United States Geological Survey states:

"Three people killed and forty injured in the Bahía de Caráquez- Canoa area. Approximately sixty percent of the buildings at Canoa severely damaged. Electricity, telephone and water services disrupted and most buildings with three or more stories damaged at Bahía de Caráquez. Considerable damage in many other parts of western Manabí Province. Landslides blocked a road between Bahía de Caráquez and Canoa. Felt strongly at Guayaquil and Quito. Felt in much of Ecuador and also at Cali, Colombia. Two large events occurring about 3 and 7 seconds after small onset."

How was it an earthquake of this magnitude occurred and so few were dead? We thank Universal Energy for the first shake that was a 5.4 on the Richter scale at 12:35 pm (exactly one hour and 24 minutes before the big earthquake of 7.2). This first one made everyone alert for a possible tsunami and aftershocks and so the majority of the citizens were out of their houses and buildings. How many times do you get a warning like this?

The television views from the helicopters over Bahía were appalling; we could not believe the destruction. All the buildings looked like Swiss cheese. What a beautiful city we had. My grandmother always said to me that about 50 years ago a strong earthquake had happened in Ecuador. Many of the local citizens say that about every 50 years it shakes hard around here.

Many of the Ecuadorians around the country asked themselves why this happened to this beautiful and quaint area. The worst hit city in the west coast of the Americas from El Niño, and a 7.2 Richter scale Earthquake concentrated in such a short time span. Jamil Mahuad, Ecuador's President at that time, said on National TV, *"We will start the reconstruction of the Coast first from Bahía de Caráquez."* This never happened.

Around a week or two after this last natural disaster, my friends from ACTMANG arrived in Ecuador. Motohiko Kogo, Keibo Oiwa and Taka were part of this group that came immediately to Bahía de Caráquez. As I was taking them around and showing them all the disaster areas there was something that always will remain deep in me, and this was the meaningful and brotherly feeling of these friends from Japan. I was appalled by the quake impact in Bahía and thought their attention would be on that too, but I was surprised when they stated that more than the earthquake damage they were amazed what destruction the El Niño had done.

Eco City concept born

We had finished a long day of seeing the destruction; meeting with people and checking out the projects ACTMANG had started in the area. During dinner at a local hotel, Kogo, Keibo, Taka, the rest of the important team (and forgive me for not remembering all the names) and myself were discussing the next steps. I remember the energy was high (in a good sense) and formal at this meeting.

I began a new conversation stating that if I could capture the essence of El Niño and of the Earthquake in manifestations or expressions that our sensory organs could assimilate most easily, it would be the following:

❖ If *Visual* for the El Niño, it would be a big poster with a boot covered in fresh mud.

❖ If *Auditory* for the Earthquake, it would be the Toc-Toc of all the hammers hitting nails throughout all of Bahía (even towards nighttime) with everyone reconstructing.

I felt sad as I said this to my Japanese friends who had just seen the after effects and destruction of my very beautiful city. Looking at Keibo Oiwa, I said, *"But you know, we are strong people and we will be able to reconstruct the city and get it as beautiful as it was before!"*

Keibo returned my expressions in the way I will never forget. As the wise man as he is, I captured the essence of his following statement:

"Patricio, this city might have been beautiful, but only on the outside, but on the inside and in its bases it is not. It has a long way to go for it to become truly beautiful. Its citizens and the infrastructure of this city need to strive to synchronize for a perfect balance with the natural systems surrounding and hosting it."

I listened carefully and asked Keibo, "You mean like an Eco city?" He replied, "Yes, like an Eco city". This is when the term Eco city was born for Bahía de Caráquez. He then said, "I know the man who can make this happen, his name is Peter Berg!" *"Can you bring him here?"* They replied, *"Yes we will invite him."*

From here ACTMANG's role was of most importance, especially on helping us transmit the idea to the mayor and to the main Foundation by the name of Stuarium, which was proactive in the necessities and reconstruction of the city. We had a great meeting with the Fundacion Stuarium with all their members present and they accepted the proposal to move towards a Model of Urban Sustainability, as I put it in more formal terms the concept of Eco city.

We had great support from Dario Proaño and Nicola Mears (who is originally from New Zealand) who have worked as pioneers in ecological tours and have a beautiful example of sustainable land management through permaculture design at Rio Muchacho. As soon as ACTMANG and I explained the concept at the round table they understood and pushed for it. So with the Fundacion onboard, now we needed to reach the mayor, who at that time was Fernando Cassis. As he was a friend, I contacted him and started to move the idea towards city hall.

The city of Bahía and its city council at this moment was bombarded with all the effects of the disaster to attend to, so it really gives them merit that they actually listened during the lowest level of hope Bahía ever was at. Calamity gave way to opportunity.

Our shrimp farm in its majority was destroyed, and the economic network of Bahía was inexistent. We had no revenue for the family and all I had was a small factory exporting blue crabs to the United States. I was the pioneer of the first blue crab exporting company here in Ecuador. It was a tough job and had a weak money return for all the work I put into it. Later on, I understood it was an extracting industry, which I finally put a stop to. I wish I had been able to cherish the final moments of the political linking my mother so beautifully made (between the Fundacion Stuarium and City Hall), but our economic survival took precedence.

With no money coming in for the family, I had to leave to Guayaquil and start an operation that was on standstill there. I left my mother in charge of dealing with city hall for the Eco city movement. I can describe my mother, Flor Maria (Flower Maria) as a strong, hard working woman and also as a delicate loving human. This, combined with a powerful personality, makes her a tough act for many men to follow. She has had a successful life in many areas and was awarded best citizen of Bahía in 1994.

Her mother, who had few economic resources, brought up Flor Maria. When she was 13, my Grandfather, Alfredo Dueñas, brought her in to the Hacienda Coaque where she became the right-hand-man handling the only outpost of goods from San Vicente to Esmeraldas (a pretty good stretch of coast). This Hacienda was where originally Francisco Pizarro set up one of his first Spanish Conquistador camps in 1531, found the gold he needed to buy the ships, and pay the soldiers needed for the capture of the Inca Atahualpa. Then 205 years later, in 1736, it was where the French mission of the Royal Academy of Science of Paris set the first equatorial marker. They came for measuring and to discover the shape of the earth by studying the arcs of the meridians. Of course this also helped give name to our country (Ecuador).

My grandfather was educated in the United States. Many people from Bahía were educated in the major cities of the world. Bahía de Caráquez was the second largest port of Ecuador and for many passenger lines it was a primary destination. With the education Flor Maria received from her father, she was formed for a different world. When my grandfather died in an accident, her inheritance allowed her to buy a small, inexpensive house in Miami where we lived. Once we came back from the United States with my dad's grave illness, she had to start from zero, but became the first woman in Latin America to grow shrimp by aquaculture and was the first woman in the world to get an organic certification for this process. Our shrimp farm, the Eco-Poseidon, is the only one in the world to have more than 15,000 mangroves planted inside the ponds. With the proceeds from this, I was able to get educated in the United States and we were able to start our beautiful projects at the archaeological site of Chirije (www.chirije.com) and Casa Grande in Bahía (www.casagrandebahia.com).

Returning to Flor Maria's intervention for Bahía de Caráquez Eco city, I told her to take my place in the movement, trying to assure that the City Council and the Mayor would help us achieve the declaration. She did a great job and was the one honored to unveil the plaque at City Hall on Feb 23, 1999.

My mother, Flor Maria, unveiling the Eco City plaque on
February 23, 1999.

Mayor Fernando Cassis on the left.

Meeting Peter Berg

I have inserted San Francisco Chronicle staff writer Robert Hurwitt's obituary of Peter, which appeared in the Sunday (8/14/11) edition and online:

"Bioregionalism, which Mr. Berg is credited with developing, relies on natural systems, such as watersheds, as the basis from which to develop sustainable societies.

Born in the Jamaica section of Queens, N.Y., Mr. Berg grew up in Florida, where his mother moved when he was 6. He attended the University of Florida at Gainesville and served in the Army. After spending some time in New York and participating in civil rights activities, he hitchhiked across the country and settled in San Francisco in 1964.

He joined the Mime Troupe, writing and acting in a half dozen plays, and directing. It is also where he met Judy Goldhaft, who would become his life partner.

About the same time, Mr. Berg helped found the Artists Liberation Front and the Diggers, which ran daily free-food programs, a free store and other projects in the Haight-Ashbury.

He was the primary writer for the Diggers, penning terse, scathingly funny ant capitalist position papers and exhorting the city to prepare for the coming mass arrival of young hippies now known as the Summer of Love. An autodidact and voracious reader, he is often cited for his skill in synthesizing new concepts.

Mr. Berg's interest in environmental issues began in his childhood. It happened, Goldhaft said, when "he and his mother were driving through a swamp in a heavy mist. Then the mist opened up and there was a Native American fishing in a flat-bottomed boat. But by the time he could say, 'Oh look,' the mist had closed in again. It was a revelation to him."

Mr. Berg developed the concept of bioregionalism and founded Planet Drum after attending the 1972 United Nations Conference on the Environment in Stockholm.

Along with its many publications, some of Planet Drum's major projects have included education programs and Green City projects, such as native plant gardens. In 1999, Mr. Berg began a project with the coastal city of Bahía de Caráquez in Ecuador, which had been ravaged by floods and an earthquake.

Though Mr. Berg had been battling lung cancer, he remained active, holding ecology workshops in Heron's Head Park in Bayview-Hunters Point and in the Tenderloin this year and participating in the urban sustainability project in Ecuador. He died of pneumonia, Goldhaft said.

Besides Goldhaft, his daughter, Ocean; stepson, Aaron Rosenberg; sister, Elizabeth Arnold; and two granddaughters survive Mr. Berg. "From Peter Bergs book *Envisioning Sustainability* (2009):

"Planet Drum Foundation (PDF) was begun in 1973 after my return from the UN conference on the Environment. A slow house-truck trip back to San Francisco from the East Coast made it clear that the traditional environmental conservation approach was

inadequate to stop assaults on nature. There was new evidence of fresh damage along the route I'd covered just a year before. Planet Drum's goal was to develop a place-located ecological philosophy and movement to restore bioregions that could eventually replace the disinhibitory view of industrialism. Using as a logo the image from Sweden of a Sami shaman playing an oracular drum, PDF began corresponding with the network of committed groups, new settlers and activists who had been contacted during the caravan (I referred to them as the "planetariat") to begin evolving this new perspective.

Our most important area of concern is identified as local-planet rather than nation-world, and cities are given responsibility for developing appropriate ecologically sustainable policies in the regions where they exist."

Once Peter arrived in Ecuador, I was able to partake in long sessions with him and duly arrived at the conclusion that I was with an illuminated and intelligent man for our times. He made me hope that one day we could achieve the Eco city status. Although it was clear that most of the work had to be done by the locals and ourselves, our first chore was understand the bioregionalism concepts and believe in them.

As Peter told me, Bioregionalism was a term that he and Raymond Dasmann, a conservation biologist, coined during the early seventies. I knew that Peter had been one of the first activists that had given a statement at the first United Nations Conference on the Environment in Stockholm, Sweden in 1972.

On Peter's arrival to Bahía de Caráquez, I knew immediately that Bioregionalism was much more than environmentalism and that it depended not on geopolitical boundaries, but on geographical boundaries that made so much more sense. The water sheds, so important for all types of life human/animal, plants, trees and more, led way to important natural systems that held their own ecosystems. From there on, I made the deductions that human history from one water shed (or bioregion) to another evolved in harmony with the own specifics of each region, different but complementary to each other.

A genius in life, Peter was a maestro for someone who was searching for more and wanted Bahía to excel in leading Ecuador to become a sustainable paradise. He came in, set up his foundation and was able to keep the dreams of an Eco city alive here in Bahía.

On his first trip here in February of 1999 and into the first rainy season after the 1997 - 1998 El Niño, guess what happened? It was still raining! Peter was a great writer, and wrote his Ecuador dispatches from the start of his stay here in Bahía. Please view at: www.planetdrum.org http://www.planetdrum.org/ecuador_1999_feb.htm#report.

I have many favorites but this one so eloquently captured just a small taste of what we Bahieños (Ba-Ye-Nyos, as we call ourselves from Bahía) lived during the

El Niño. Here is a quote from his dispatch from Ecuador titled "*Two and a half Doses of Reality*" from February 16, 1999:

"*A comparatively half-size reality appeared in the form of a new creek across the path when Patricio Tamariz and I were returning on an already mud-rutted road from a visit to the coast at Canoa. Ominous sheer clay cliffs rise a hundred feet high at 80-degree angles alongside the road at several points. Edges of rain-broken clay hang on their faces like draped theater curtains, waiting for enough additional soaking to ooze down across the road on the way to the beach. Only a few trucks had stopped for the water crossing the road when we arrived but the rain suddenly switched its volume upwards almost as though a faucet had been opened to full.*

By the time it was our turn the creek was beginning to flow at the level of the door bottoms. Fast-moving, brown, gravel-spitting water was verging on impassable when Patricio began to charge through and it became untraversable just as we entered the lowest point. Stuck with water rising quickly, Patricio asked me to take the wheel while he jumped out to slog in the current examining the situation with searching eyes and half-started gestures. If the water continued to rise, the truck would be carried across the embankment on the other side of the road. He threw a fairly wide log across the creek where it bordered the road, causing water to gush in both directions around the truck and fill underneath with gravel. Several local people and other drivers frantically dug out the front and rear wheels but the truck couldn't budge forward. Everyone came to the front and pushed to get some movement in reverse, then, they rushed like a team to the rear yelling and gesturing to heave the truck forward. It rose up onto the underwater gravel with uncertain slowness until a final heave carried it forward like a boat dragging bottom. I yelled to Patricio that I wouldn't stop until the truck was down the road well beyond the point where it became dry. We had already seen the water rise by a foot while we were in it. The storm continued on the way back to Bahía and through the night. The road in that section might easily be a river canyon by now."

As we started to work together, I was invited by the national government to become Provincial Director of Tourism for the Ministry of Tourism in the year 2000. I was then appointed Pacific Coast Manager for the same entity, and became founder of the Tourism School for the new Community College of Guayaquil called Eco Tec. In the latter part of 2004, I was appointed Executive Director for Ecuador's First Tourism Promotion fund. www.ecuador.travel.

My government work ended in 2010. I was able to see and meet with Peter more than other years. I was blessed to be part of his bioregional effort. I have proposed to both city and national governments to have a new plan for sustainable tourism and to develop a strategy that associates human progress in all fields, even agriculture. This would include the baseline matrix for planning to be the Bioregions.

One of the beautiful projects that sprang out and caused a great effect not only in Bahía but also in other cities of Ecuador such as Guayaquil, was the Eco-Kids Clubs that Flor Maria founded. This was part of an undertaking that is praiseworthy to mention. She took in 150 kids from the homeless families and brought them together for afterschool environmental and family values education. She later was appointed as International promoter for the Latin America Eco Club network.

I have to thank Clay Plager-Unger, the manager of the Planet Drum Foundation in Ecuador. His hard work and sacrifice has surpassed my expectations and he still needs a lot of help, especially in funding. They have done an incredible job in revegetating the dangerous, high-risk hills for future El Niños.

The environmental cause is still strong here; in my lifetime there is so much to be grateful for, but I do not think there are words that could describe my gratitude to the Japanese ACTMANG team, as they introduced me to Peter. I have to thank the Stuarium Foundation and also the ex-Mayor Fernando Cassis, who with his city council helped in the declaration of Bahía de Caráquez going forth as an Eco city. I also have deep gratitude for my mother, who was able to create the Eco Bahía Environmental Learning Center and keep it functioning during dire times. Thanks to the members of that foundation like Jacob Santos, who like me, along with the citizens of my birthplace, Bahía de Caráquez, were in for the trip of a lifetime.

As I said, on a local level we have a good group of people concerned with sustainability. This includes Nicola and Dario, who work at the Rio Muchacho Organic farm, along with many other women groups who make beautiful Eco-Papel out of recycled paper. Marcelo Luque is another stand out; he works for the conservation of Bahía's forest Cordillera del Balsamo and has Cerro Seco, which is a true example of conservation of the Dry Tropical Forest.

More good news is that the President of Ecuador has elected Bahía de Caráquez to become the pilot city for creating a total recycling program. I hope the city government has enough push to keep this program going. I always tell the Mayor I can help and he says "but Ad-Honorem", which means "for the honor of", not seeking any material reward. It is commonly used in institutions for some unpaid positions and I always say to the mayor, "You bet".

Dr. Carlos Mendoza, the actual mayor of Bahía has had many milestones in his lifetime, including pushing the building of the longest bridge of Ecuador that unites Bahía with San Vicente. He has worked with the ex-President Sixto Duran Ballen, whose holiday home was in Bahía at which time the city had an important growth. Papio, (Pa-pee-oo) as I call Sixto, which is an affectionate phrase used by his children and grandchildren was a great president in his time (1992-1996). Papio actually brought in my wife to his family when she had just graduated high school and helped her through her schooling when her dad died. Juliana had a grand political experience being with Sixto through the campaign and his 4-year presidential term. She was great to talk with and get opinions from when I had my almost 10 years active experience in the government.

My cousin Carlos is a good guy with a good heart and good intentions, but there are many fires to put out on a daily basis with him and he needs all the help he can receive. As I now have come back from public life (national government positions) to private, one of my challenges is to get the Eco city committee working again. He was very sad to hear about Peter. In the last Eco city day he knew Peter wasn't doing well and in a formal council meeting proposed that Peter be given an award. I have just talked with the mayor in these days and he has made a plaque and will name the new Recycling Plant in Peter's name.

Here is an email that I received from Judy once I sent my condolences. I felt guilty that just 3 weeks before his death, I was in San Francisco for one evening, contracted by the national government to do a presentation based on "*Ecuador a Sustainable Tourism Destination*", and was too busy to meet with him.

From Judy Goldhaft:

"Dearest Patricio,

Don't be sad that you weren't able to see Peter during your visit to SF. He understood the difficulties of scheduling during a business trip. Peter had lots of love and respect for you...after all you were the one who invited him to work in Bahía. Thank you for your kind words and for also sending the news to Ron Mader so that he could post it too.

I guess he didn't make the 50/50 chance to go to Bahía again...we had planned to come again in November and would have I'm sure, except for the surprise pneumonia complication. Peter loved the projects in Bahía and loved describing them to everyone.

Ocean [his daughter] has suggested that we make a trip to Bahía together in a few months.....maybe after the New Year. I'll let you know if/when we have plans.

Love, Judy"

Peter gave me as a gift his book *Envisioning Sustainability* on November 20, 2009. He autographed it with the following words:

"Patricio,

With such great rewards from our friendship for 10 years, I look with wide-eyed anticipation at what will evolve for the rest of our lives.

Yr 'mano, Peter"

So as I close this chapter I wish these words that I have written will be printed so I can fulfill a desire from Peter to have the Eco-Mandato shown to others. I am attaching the page in English and Spanish. Let his work go on, let us work and play hard, let us survive in a world where Peter's and our main message was of Intergenerational Solidarity for the peoples of the *Third Planet from the Sun.*

ECO-MANDATO 2008
Bahía de Caráquez, Ecuador
March 13, 2008

Eco-Mandato 2008 aims at changes in four fundamental areas that require urgent attention. There could be a much longer list of environmental problems, of course, but these have been persistent difficulties and involve local bioregional realities that are experienced by everyone: water, food, soil, and development of ecological economic activities. Since the city government also administers the territory of the whole county there is a stronger emphasis on agriculture and resources than might otherwise be found.

Water is a primary concern considering this region's long dry season. Reliable water isn't easily available to the overwhelming majority of people so piped sources need to be made available. Rooftop rainwater collection systems are under-utilized and could be facilitated with city government assistance. Conservation and re-use through diversion of wastewater to gardens or toilets should be taught and encouraged.

Food production by organic permaculture methods including growing native fruit trees needs to be demonstrated to both rural agricultural producers and city gardeners. The public should be informed about health and ecological benefits to stimulate demand for farm products grown in this manner.

Soil enrichment through production of compost should be encouraged by education and assistance with equipment. Organic wastes for this purpose must be successfully collected from households, markets and restaurants. The present massive burning of brush as a means to obtain whatever minimal nutrients are provided is ruinous in terms of soil health, erosion, river siltation, and pollution.

Develop **new ecological businesses** by providing resources such as education, training, marketing, and use of public lands. Teach manufacturing of commercial products from recycled materials including metal, glass, plastic, and paper.

ECO-MANDATO 2008
PARA HACER BAHÍA DE CARÁQUEZ UNA ECO-CIUDAD
El 13 de marzo, 2008

La Fundación Planet Drum y Los Amigos de la Eco-Ciudad de Bahía de Caráquez, Cantón Sucre exhortamos acción inmediata en las siguientes áreas básicas públicas para lograr un equilibrio con el medio ambiente y ganar el reconocimiento como una verdadera eco-ciudad.

Estas acciones deben ser asumidas por todos los miembros de la ciudadanía en general, empresas privadas y el gobierno. Para lograr ser una eco-ciudad las agencias públicas y oficiales tendrán interés genuino en estas acciones. Además formarán parte de plataformas de campañas de candidatos políticos futuros para responder al impulso de la población.

AGUA - Desarrollar las fuentes necesarias para la disponibilidad de suficiente de agua segura para todos. A la misma vez, promover la conservación y reutilización de agua, por ejemplo: recolección de agua de lluvia, dirigir aguas servidas a jardines y uso de llaves de flujo reducido, entre otros. Repartir la información y recursos necesarios para realizar estas metas a todos los usuarios públicos y privados.

AGRICULTURA SUSTENTABLE - Proveer educación para la producción de alimentos con prácticas de permacultura bioregional para cultivar cosechas orgánicas que sean más saludables y conserven el suelo y agua. Pro-mover información e instrucciones sobre agro silvicultura para que agricultores y jardineros aumenten el uso de árboles nativos de frutas comerciables y la alimentación de ganado.

MEJORA DEL SUELO - Enseñar técnicas de separación de desechos orgánicos e inorgánicos y la producción de abono a gran escala e individual a todos los agricultores para reemplazar las prácticas de corte y quema, con métodos de limpieza y fertilización orgánicos de los terrenos.

EMPRESAS ECOLÓGICAS Y TRABAJO - Ayudar el crecimiento de nuevas empresas y organizaciones ecológicas con recursos como educación, capacitación, marketing y terrenos de uso público. Enseñar la fabricación de productos comerciales de materiales reciclados incluyendo residuos de metales, vidrios, plásticos, y papeles. (Peter Berg)

Miss you hermano.

February 23, 2009
10th Anniversary Ecociudad
Parade all around Bahía

Peter Berg, behind my son Patricio Jr. (on the bicycle);
Mayor Dr. Carlos Mendoza (second from left), Patricio on the right

CHAPTER FOUR

Lost Treasures of the Pacific

When I was Ecuador's first tourism promotion director (2004-2007), one of my responsibilities was to execute the International and National Marketing Plan. Within this plan there was a program to target the press. One of the actions was to invite journalists on 1-2 week trips to discover the impressive sites and activities in all the 4 worlds (Pacific Coast, Andes, Amazon and Galapagos) in a country the approximate size of the state of Colorado. With an investment of around $500,000, during the 3 years that I was Executive Director of the promotion board, we were able to produce more than $150 million in free press in the form of newspaper and magazine articles, TV shows, documentaries, etc. This is the amount in PR value we saved the Ecuadorian Government and the private sector, if they ever had to contract advertising spaces in the media. This is a very effective and efficient way of promoting the destination – *"Advertising is what you pay for and PR is what you pray for"*. Nathalie Pilovetzky said this back in 2003, when I coordinated a conference on tourism marketing at EcoTec Tecnológico, (back then a community college, now a University). I was the tourism school founder and director at that institution. Nathalie was the President of Latitude PR for many years, which promoted Ecuador as a destination to the United States and Canada.

On one of these trips funded by the Fondo Mixto de Promoción Turística, we invited Ivo Goetz, a travel writer for the *Frankfurter Allgemeine*, a well-known newspaper in Germany. He wanted to take a good diving trip, so I had him meet with my close friend, William Seliger, who is an experienced diver and treasure hunter. They went diving and Ivo found a coin on the ocean floor. What more could you want on a trip? You can imagine the nice article we got as a result.

The story does not end there. Just a couple of weeks later I was flying to Europe, specifically to Berlin, to one of the biggest travel fairs of the world named ITB Berlin (more than 10,000 exhibitors, 100,000 trade visitors and 7,000 visitors) and guess who sat right next to me on the plane? Ivo Goetz! Incredible coincidence, or was it? Of course, he showed me a photo of the coin and started to tell me about his experiences on his dive accompanying the main team of divers at the Santa Maria de la Consolación shipwreck. He told me he had a great trip and that finding the coin topped everything off with a cherry.

I was able to meet with a good many treasure hunters and excellent divers that came through my hometown of Bahía and I was absolutely blown away by all the detail they put into searching for sunken ships.

Having many of these divers here on the coast actually catalyzed the forming of underwater archaeologists in the Instituto Nacional de Patrimonio Cultural (Heritage Institute). I have made many good friends over the years that have interesting stories.

William Gene Seliger, Bill to me, is one of them. He is one of the best divers I have ever been in the water with. I am not an expert diver, I free-dive mostly and that is how I found the underwater walls 5 km off of Bahía de Caráquez. I met Bill through Javier Veliz Alvarado, an expert in maritime archaeology. The team that Bill was with were expert treasure hunters and also good friends of mine. Haig Jacobs was one of them, a great, fun guy with an incredible spirit. To me, he was the reincarnation of a good English Pirate. Haig is a skilled diver and great cameraman.

One of the team's main consultants was Robert Marx, one of the world's foremost treasure hunters. He told me that he had found ten times more treasure than any other treasure hunter and/or government in the world. I researched him later and found out he was not only one of the most important treasure hunters in the world, but also one of the pioneer American scuba divers and had written many books. He told me that he had just been asked for advice for the movie "*Pirates of the Caribbean*", and was responsible for rediscovering Port Royal in Jamaica, the sunken city of 1692 due to an earthquake and tidal wave. I know he is one of the most important researchers having investigated the old archives in Spain, England, the Vatican and in Vienna.

He was enticed to come to Ecuador by Joel Ruth, who led the dive at the El Matal site (45 minutes north of Bahía) for the *Nuestra Señora de la Magdalena, (Our Lady of Magdalene)* which sank about a mile off the Jama River in 1612. This ship was armed with 56 bronze cannons according to EXDELMAR (Exploracion Del Mar Del Sur S.A); Joel is the founder and general manager of the company.

Joel had brought Haig Jacobs, a grand treasure diver, along with Bill Seliger and his dad, William K. Seliger, an expert in metal detection instruments. I was told this ship had many tons of silver. Richard Marx (according to EXDELMAR report) had stated from his research that this ship was carrying 7 million pesos. Apart from silver bricks (some of them were 70 lbs.) they would carry pie shaped wedges in barrels. The silver has two values: its worth on the street and its historical significance, which is more important.

Bill Seliger was diving off of Guayaquil but would go to Jama once in a while to help out. This was when he would stop in Bahía and I would talk to him and find out the progress.

Later on, I remember being in Guayaquil at the team's headquarters when they showed told me something I will never forget. It was on the *Magdalena (sank in 1612)* and the *Derrotero*. It seemed like the man with all the information was Robert Marx, scoping out clues from old manuscripts, ship logs and the Derrotero, he had spent many years investigating everything that pertained to shipwrecks.

"X marks the spot"

I knew they had spent 3 months using the metal detector back and forth along the Jama River mouth area and showed me on a laptop the finished scan they had done. I could see the Jama River from this sophisticated navigational map and how the coast turned on the right side like a large cove towards the point (looking at the laptop screen display and the map, towards the top lay the beach and land and towards the bottom, the ocean) and to the left on the top, I saw how the river finished its meander and flowed out into the ocean. To the right and towards the middle of the laptop screen I could see the point, which is actually a beautiful hilly point that is just now being visited by many beachfront property seekers.

Almost right in front of the river, there was a huge clayish red oval, of course, where metal was detected.

They then flung out a thin sheet of acetate and on it, in great detail, were almost the exact same geographical features that were on the navigational map on the laptop. The transparent sheet had a map drawn on it too and in the middle of it I saw an X that had been drawn. When we flipped it onto the laptop map to make it match, in unison everyone said… *"X marks the spot"*. The X drawn on the transparency laid right on top of the red oval stain on the laptop screen like it was meant to be.

At that point, I asked, "where did you get that drawing with the X on it?". Then I was told about the *"Derrotero"*.

On July 29, 1681, an infamous pirate called Bartholomew Sharp (B.1650) captured a vessel called Nuestra Señora del Rosario off the coast of Ecuador in front of Cabo Pasado (just about 20 Km north of Bahía de Caráquez). It was on its way to Panama from Callao. A special team of Spanish officials were on board, carrying the book *Derrotero del Mar del Zur,* made in Panama in 1669. This book carried over 149 chart maps and detailed the routes/sailing directions from the tip of South America (Magellan Straits) all the way to California. It also had many maps that were drawn to scale of where some of the Spanish ships were lost. This was a lucky strike for the buccaneer Sharp. This information came directly from the crew of the downed ship. They drew the exact site where the ship went down… where it still lies!

At the time of the capture of the Derrotero, England and Spain were not at war. The stealing of the Derrotero document an became an international incident because they had signed the Treaty of Madrid, (July 1670) which stated England was to keep possession of Jamaica and would respect Spain's trading monopoly in America. It was a great business for Spain; bringing back treasures of the New World and bringing much needed goods to the colonial settlers.

I am sure Spain wanted Bartholomew Sharp executed for this and England almost did it for them, but the importance of the book overshadowed this desire when it arrived in England for King Charles II, as many secrets were discovered. He pardoned Sharp and ordered copies made, not from printing press but drafted by hand. I am sure many of the pirates working for England must have received copies of it. Robert Marx had seen the Derrotero and had a copy. I confirmed with him that it was a copy of the Charles II original translation into English.

The pirates of the Caribbean were definitely more famous, but the Pirates off the Pacific Coast of Ecuador were also important, even though most people do not know about them. The treasures that were found by Roberto Aguirre in the Gulf of Guayaquil on the Santa Maria de la Consolacion were substantial. I believe this is where Bill found close to 50,000 silver coins.

I had always thought Spanish coins had a round shape until I started to see the actual results of these salvage operations. Of course some were rounded, but the majority of the silver coins that were salvaged were called silver cobs. These were broken or chiseled off a silver sheet or bar. No two were the same and all were irregularly shaped. They were then reheated and hand stamped by hammer, shaping the face of the coin to put in the denomination. The weight was important for each coin denomination. So if you are looking for treasure washed ashore on a beach in Ecuador, remind yourself - don't only look for round coins.

I remember traveling to Bahía with one of the divers and we stopped to poke around in a small rural antiquities shop (really almost out on the yard) on the side of the road. We were surprised to find one of these coins just lying there on a shelf. I forget the denomination of the piece, but remember that it cost my friend 10 USD and he said that back home (USA) it was worth 100 USD at least. It was an original coin. I asked the owner of the shop about it and was again surprised by their detailed answer; "this coin was picked up by a native diver off the coast, probably around the areas where organized teams were bringing up the booty". On the piece I could see the word *PLVS VLTRA* (Plus Ultra using the V's for U's), which meant "*More Beyond*". It was produced far off in the foreign possessions of Spain. Bill told me once that More Beyond referred to when they realized the world wasn't flat after all and that there was actually more beyond the Pillars of Hercules.

In the second half of the 16th century when the production of silver from the mines exceeded local necessity, the silver became important. This is when the fleets started carrying tremendous cargos. The Magdalena should have carried 300 tons of silver.

This silver is produced in large quantities from the hill at Potosi in Bolivia. It is truly a wonder of nature. The peak is at 4,824m (15,827 ft.) above sea level. The amount of silver exceeded everyone's expectations. It was discovered in 1545 and has been mined for more than 467 years! An archaeologist once told me that there is now a mountain next to the original one with all the leftovers from mining operations since then. I am not sure if it is true or not, but I do know the death and the suffering from this mine was tremendous. Death came from all the hardship, the closed in tunnels, the use of mercury, the exposure of the fumes of this element, and the transporting of the silver. From various sources I have heard of almost 8 million natives dying for over a Billion Reals and much more that the Spanish minted.

Apart from coins, especially at the beginning, much melted gold and silver was poured out into ingots and pies. According to the Spaniards, the large caravans of mules and slaves that had to cross the mountains to reach the ports of Arica and Callao and then the transfer across the Isthmus of Panama were well worth this sacrifice, for all the value that these metals brought to Spain.

The Spaniards had taken gold out on their fleets since 1531 (Pizarro's first plunder at Coaque) up until 1599, when it diminished and the silver from the mines of Potosi, Bolivia took over and became the main metallic product shipped out. Paoletti states "The standard was gold and silver as regular currency, up until the mines of the continent started to put Silver out as a main actor and gradually pushed gold to one side".

Robert Marx told me that the last fleets of the Armada del Mar del Sur were in 1776. Imagine the amount of gold and silver that passed by the coastline of what we know now as the territories of Ecuador. There were many shipwrecks and incredible stories of the Pirates of the Pacific. The city of Guayaquil was looted numerous times. This is a beautiful city next to a river that flows out to the largest estuary of the west coast of South America (Gulf of Guayaquil). Drake, Dampier, Le Picard and many other pirates raided and had battles with the Spanish off the coasts of colonial Ecuador.

There is an interesting story of the Santa Maria de la Consolacion, a more than 400-ton ship carrying 100,000 pieces of 8 (Reals). In 1681, the ship was part of the Spanish "*South Seas Fleet*" that was supposed to leave Callao in April of the same year. Somehow the cargo for that ship was delayed (it was coming from the silver mine of Potosi), and the ship left after the rest of the fleet, (against the wishes of her captain) so it became interesting prey for the pirates. On the exterior of the Gulf of Guayaquil, there is an island called Santa Clara (named Isla del Muerto-or dead person, Javier Veliz told me that the original name is El Amortajado or Man wrapped in shroud. The island actually looks like a man lying on his back, when seen from afar). The pirate leading the raid was Bartholomew Sharpe. When the Spanish ship carrying treasures and goods were sure to be taken by the pirates, the crew was ordered to set it on fire and sink it. They did this and the pirates, seeing it was on a dangerous reef, could not salvage it. The pirates were furious and killed all the Spanish that had swam or row boated to the shore of the Island. It is said that 350 people were decapitated.
The legend is that the Island is haunted because later on a Spanish sailor also had a fateful ending when he was stranded there, thus the nickname.

Many other shipwrecks are still lying on Ecuador's ocean floor. Some of them have been quite important. Robert Marx told me "the biggest find was done by various people on the Concepcion, lost in 1654 on Chanduy Reef [on the outside of the northern perimeter of the Gulf of Guayaquil]. The majority of the finds were smuggled out of the country. At least ten million US dollars was the value of these finds".

Javier Veliz Alvarado, one of the first archaeologist friends that I made here in Ecuador, is a man with great knowledge of the old colonial manuscripts where he gets most the information for his writings. He helped me on the Chirije archaeological site and also in the search for the settlement on the Baja Santa Martha reef in the Bahía de Caráquez areas. He told me that he had researched documents and believes they prove the find of the Consolacion was actually from the vessel *Nuestra Señora de Sucuñaga* of Basque origin. He was going through documents at the National Archives of Quito and found a trial in which there were claims to boxes of coins that were from the sale of textiles to Peru. In the trajectory, the covers of the boxes from Callao (pieces of 8) were changed with the covers of boxes that were used for smaller denominations in Paita. On the ship there was a total of 100,000 coins in all these boxes. This is an item of discussion between the experts.

Javier Veliz is one of those serious investigators that base all their sources on primary information, including the earliest documents and onsite visual inspection. He told me that he was the one who pinpointed the Magdalena off the Jama River. The diving team (he was the national archaeologist and advisor) was anguished at the results they found. He said the first find was a newer ship that was on top, with electric saw markings on the wood and in the hold there was Tagua (Vegetable Ivory Nut, which was widely exported from the ports of Ecuador in the 19th and 20th century). According to Veliz, the Spanish silver laden ship was found further down, at 8-9 meters deep. Looking at it logically, he said that this find was done more with his geographical knowledge and less with ambition.

It was interesting to look at the map of the Derrotero and the GPS navigational map that was used as the baseline for the magnetometer scan of the cove in comparison to the acetate transparency with the "X" I was shown in my experience with Joel Ruth's team. The only real difference I noticed on the navigational chart and the Derrotero (chart of where the Magdalena sank) was the Jama river mouth pointing in one direction, and on the Derrotero chart drawn by the Spaniard that saw the ship sink, it was pointing the other way. Over the hundreds of years since this case in 1612, (400 years to this present year) many El Niño events have occurred (there have been 19 since 1951). Through the dynamics of water transport due to the torrential rains of these events, the river is now flowing out in another direction in this modern era. I found this pretty interesting.

At the beginning of the discovery they found in a single excavation; broken olive jars, large timbers, bundles of black coral handled silver knives, bone gambling dice, bronze sewing pins, silver spools of pure gold metallic thread and the gilded remains of the vestments of an Arch Bishop (according to JR EXDELMAR SA update report) well preserved and stuck in the mud off the Jama River. Modern gadgets on their ship like the R/V Nautilus with twin 36-inch blowers and modern up to date magnetometers helped to find many other targets in the area. They also found many harquebuses, (predecessor to the musket, a firearm that was lighter) which denoted that the ship was well armed and must have carried great treasures.

It was probably impossible to salvage the cargo of this vessel due to it sinking fast and being heavy in the muck a mile from the river mouth. In most of the ships that went down, the Spaniards would salvage as much as possible.

A colleague and good friend of mine, Jacob Santos, director of the Central Bank Archaeological Museum of Bahía de Caráquez, was in custody of most of these items and particularly enthusiastic over the knives and harquebuses. If the salvaging had continued, I am sure we would have had many pieces for our museum.

Bill Seliger sent me a letter after I had already retired from the government asking me to express how important underwater archaeological discoveries were. He wanted me to talk about the items these finds brought up and that should be conserved so that Ecuadorians could learn from them and not allow treasures to deteriorate underwater.

Let me explain why I am saying that salvaging isn't going on. In 1997 there was a law passed that gave companies with private funds limited permits to search and recuperate artifacts from colonial galleons in the territorial waters of Ecuador. This led to the discovery of various shipwrecks. A good number of artifacts were recuperated and conserved and were divided between the salvagers and the Institute of National Heritage (I heard was that the government got their pick of the unique objects they saw fit as samples of spectacular cultural heritage). Many of these artifacts were put on exhibition and some of these can be seen in the Maritime Museum of Salinas (Javier has directed the work there). The rest is inside a Central Bank vault.

In July of 2008, when the new constitution of Ecuador was being drawn up, the government, under pressure of the UNESCO, signed a new decree that put an end to all the archaeology discovered and rescued with private funds. This decree followed the principles of the UNESCO and it was decided the new stand for Ecuador was to leave the entire marine cultural heritage, which included shipwrecks, untouched in the water.

In the letter Bill sent to me, he quoted Robert Marx, saying that "there are 2 million shipwrecks that have still not been found and are lying in situ on the ocean beds, and there are only 250 professional underwater archaeologists and less than a dozen on full time projects".

Can you believe that Spain is still filing claims that the ships, which sunk centuries ago, are under Spanish flag and the country has ownership of the cargo in their hulls, which is strewn about on the ocean floor? The ones that should be claiming the wrecks are the countries of Ecuador, Peru, Chile and other Latin American countries that have had their prized heritage melted into ingots, coins and more.

Even though I agree with Bill that these sites need archaeological investigation and the funds and the scientists to do it, we should also hold them very sacred in the memory of all those who drowned on these ships and also of all the indigenous populations decimated producing these treasures.

Spanish Silver Treasure Coins
Found off the Pacific Coast of Ecuador

8 REALES

1 REAL

Treasure Coin Photos by Bill Seliger

CHAPTER FIVE

Who Discovered Paradise?

"Who discovered paradise?" This question is an enigma to some, although not to all. I will tell you all the facts I have on my plate. From data collected by archaeologists, anthropologists, and historians, and from my personal investigations, I think it is a little more complicated to answer the question: "who settled the Pacific Coast of Ecuador"? I present my personal views for your interpretation.

Did Christopher Columbus discover America in 1492? I believe not. The first humans crossing the Bering Strait Iceland Bridge must have. There are also accounts of the Vikings being the first Europeans to land here. In addition, there is the theory of the Chinese circumnavigating the world as early as the 15th century.

My opinion is that crossing the Ocean during pre-Columbian times was feasible. The Ocean is finite, it is not the Universe or infinite. If we look at communication via the ocean, it totally depended on the technology available at that time; ship construction, navigation savvy, survival skills, ample rain and food, the goals set out for and of course, good luck. I think it was very possible that humans were crossing the oceans via seaworthy craft during the last thousand years, and definitely before Columbus's time.

We know that the Minoans of Crete were using celestial navigation, along with many other civilizations, especially those that were heavily involved in overseas trade. Stars were the known reference for pinpointing positions, particularly once you lost sight of land.

For example, the Jomon culture of Japan was navigating thousands of years before Columbus discovered America. Other groups had probably crossed the land bridge of the Bering Straits, even sailing from bay to bay and island hopping, they could have crossed and landed in the now known areas of Alaska and territories to the south. It seems like with modern investigations we could find proof of earlier navigational efforts towards the Americas.

I do not want to lessen any of the exceptional efforts the explorer Columbus made in trying to find a path to Asia and in helping Spain beat out other nations in the spice trade. His name is hallowed for discovering America, but we also have to consider the variety of evidence that surrounds the many peoples who made a transoceanic exploration and colonization before his time. We need this information to justify the settling of the Pacific coast of Ecuador as well.

Map of the Coast of Equador

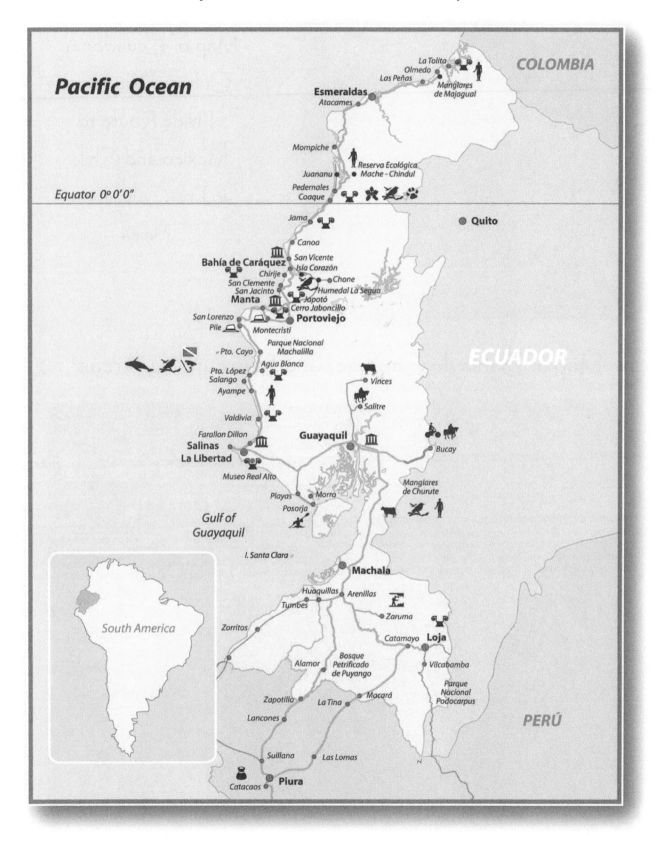

Map of Ecuadorian Cultures Maritime Trade Route to Mexico and Chile in Pre-Columbian Times

Map of Bahía de Caráquez and Surrounding Areas

Changing Landscapes

Questions we have to answer, first, was the sea level lower than it is today? This has been proven. The level fluctuated up to more than minus 100 meters (300 feet) when we had our first known culture, Las Vegas, on our coast. I was told by Johan Reinhard, explorer in residence and archaeologist of the National Geographic Society of which I highly respect, that about 40,000 yrs. ago the sea level was more than 63 meters below the actual level. This means that our coastline was probably 20 miles or more out towards the west than it is now. I have seen figures in charts saying that it could have been more than 50 miles out.

I can also prove this from the almost 18 years that we have had our beachfront archaeological site of Chirije, and witnessing the amount of wave erosion at the base of the cliffs. We could say that over this span of time the land has drawn back about 15 meters or more, or let's say approximately 1 meter (3 ft.) per year. Of course global warming now accelerates this - ice packs melting, etc. Roughly 6,000 years ago when the Valdivia culture was flourishing here, our archaeological site in Chirije could have been 6 kilometers or more out towards the ocean. In other words, there has been a loss of dry land due to sea-level rise and wave erosion. At this moment, we can see a rocky-based point out in front of Chirije, which must have had land on it in the past. I can also justify this because Emilio Estrada, who discovered the pre-Columbian site of Chirije, says that with all security the aboriginal name of this site is Chirije, due to it being listed as such on the map of the Condamine, which was published in 1751. The map has Punta de Chirije (Chirije Point) drawn on it, exactly the same spot where it is now (the point has long since eroded away) and where you can still see the foundation of the point at low tide. This mission of the Royal Academy of Sciences of Paris led by Charles Marie de la Condamine came to the lands of Ecuador in 1736 to measure the arc of the meridians that would finally mathematically describe the shape of the Earth. Nobody knew back then if the Earth was round or flat at the poles, etc. They needed to pinpoint the stars on the Equator and at sea level before they went up to the Andes for further measurements.

Now what I see in front of Chirije is the base of that point, which is a good rock shelf (where native oyster fishermen come to harvest). Land must have existed here and about 300 yards out over the beach. In Estrada's map of Chirije of the 1960s, there is a much smaller point there that now does not exist.

Photo by Betti Sachs

On Foot Across Land

Second question, do I believe there was human migration through the ice bridge at the Bering Straits? Yes, there is too much information that coincides with this.

There is a 2007 research article based on DNA sampling, titled *"Genetic Variation and Population Structure in Native Americans"*, which states:

"...Much of Native American genetic ancestry may derive from a single wave of migration from Siberia."

Third, did these groups come down the coastline of the eastern Pacific and all the way south through South America? Undeniably yes. Again I quote the information from the same research paper:

"The pattern of genetic diversity across populations suggests that coastal routes might have been important during ancient migrations of Native American populations. Detectable Siberian similarity is visible to a greater extent in Mesoamerican and Andean populations [this would include the populations in the territories of Ecuador] than in the populations from eastern South America. In addition, recent geological evidence indicates that ice-free areas west of the Cordilleran ice sheet may have existed as early 14,000 years ago, suggesting the possibility of an early coastal migration. Within South America, the coastal colonization model suggests an early southward migration along the western side of the Andes and is consistent with an interpretation that modern speakers of Andean languages may represent descendants of the first occupiers of the region."

I am sure that these first groups chased and hunted the Mega fauna all the way down. For example, just a couple years ago, crossing the bay of Caráquez in the San Vicente area, a skeleton of a Mastodon was found. I believe these were the first groups of nomadic hunter-gatherers that arrived, originating on the tip of Northern America, reaching Tierra del Fuego, and passing through the area of Bahía de Caráquez, journeying through miles of land now underwater. Logistically, it was easier to travel down coastal routes than inland routes. The first settled or sedentary groups that we have here on our coast were the Las Vegas Culture dating back 10,000 years BP (before present).

From my answers above, we can see through marine transgression there for sure is loss of many ancient archaeological sites that were once oceanfront. Evidence of this is the quantity of pottery shards on the sand that I have seen in many sites on the coast, especially in the Bahía de Caráquez (Chirije) area.

Sea Voyagers

Lastly, did they also come via other means? Yes, I believe so. There is much evidence that the Polynesians were expert navigators, and also the Ecuadorian coastal cultures could have been the "Phoenicians of the Americas", due to their maritime abilities dating back thousands of years ago.

In the territories of the Pacific Coast, pertaining geopolitically to the Republic of Ecuador, it is proven fact that these sailors, notably from the Bahía (Ba-ee-a) culture (500 BC to 500 AD, from the regional development period) and the Manteño

(Man-Ten-yo) Culture (500 AD to 1534 AD, of the Integration Period) navigated on giant balsawood sailing vessels and were trading demanded items (especially the Spondylus princeps or the Red Spiny Oyster) along the coast all the way up to Mexico. Dr. Jorge Marcos, one of the most respected Ecuadorian Archaeologists, states there is a known Manteño site on the west coast of Mexico.

Javier Veliz A., a good friend of mine, archaeologist and historian, states in his article "*The Balsa*," published in the National Institute of Maritime History of Ecuador that the first representations of aquatic vessels in clay were done at about 3300 BC. We know of the first contact of the Spaniards in 1525 with a group of natives aboard a very large balsawood sailing vessel being well documented through drawings and descriptions in the Samano account. We will talk about this account in the chapter on the Conquistadors. It is a 5 page document that describes the most important events of Pizarro's first and second journey to the south, discovering the riches of South America, and especially of the encounter off the now known territorial waters of Ecuador.

Up until the decade of the 60s, it was widely read in our country that the cultures of the region of Mexico had landed in the regions of what is now known as Ecuador. For example, in some of the historical accounts of Bahía de Caráquez, especially in the festivities of our Canton, they repeat every year that the Mayans arrived in 800 AD. This we cannot prove, since we were not there to write this history. What we can prove is that they did have contact via maritime trade. Ceramics from our coast date back earlier than the earliest known ceramics of Mexico and of other areas in South America. Valdivia dates back more than 6,000 years before present (BP).

Javier Veliz Alvarado states that an archaeologist by the name of Julio Viteri Gamboa (who had worked with Estrada in Chirije) cited an archaeologist from Mexico, Jose Corona Nunez in 1963, who says *"once the populations settled in northern and southern Ecuador, they settled in Colombia and Peru, and afterwards while in balsa traveling to the north, along the Pacific coastline, they established settlements in adequate lands"*. Viteri was the first one to proclaim this in Ecuador. Veliz follows and states that there are accounts of traveling all the way to Mexico and also to Chile. In Antofagasta, they have found models of balsas according to the Ecuadorian archaeologist, Presley Norton, citing Nunez [1979].

So the coastal cultures on the coast of what is now known as Ecuador were expert navigators, as confirmed with the data I have collected for you. As we see, there was communication via the ocean, but this is intraregional, how about long distance communication?

My feeling on this is the following; I do believe we had contact from across the Pacific Ocean during pre-Columbian times, whether it was from the Chinese, or Polynesians or others. Also, I believe our coastal groups did the same, or vice versa, and traveled to their lands. There is an incredible amount of information, primarily of our first Ecuadorian historian Padre Juan de Velasco [1727-1792], a Jesuit priest, who compiled much data from the conquistadors and other priests/scribes that lived during the southern America Pacific Coast Spanish conquest period. This is translated in fine detail for you later on in this chapter. It embodies one of the most important facts for history regarding our Bahía de Caráquez area and for the entire Pacific Coast regarding transpacific contact.

What I am trying to say again is that first, the ocean is finite, if you had good maritime and survival skills, a good ship, with shelter especially from the sun, I think without any doubt that you could reach the innumerable islands and other continents. Of course, this was proven by Thor Heyerdahl, who in 1947 (his boat the Kon-tiki was made with Ecuadorian balsa tree logs) navigated from Peru to the Tuomatu islands (4700 miles) in 101 days. Also Vital Alsar, who traveled on the balsa sailing vessel in 1970 from Ecuador to the port of Moololaba, Australia (8,565 miles) in 161 days. The Spaniard said that he definitely thought that the ancient mariners knew the way. Alsar repeated the feat three years later. This journey consisted of three rafts with 4 people on each one. The rafts were launched from Guayaquil, Ecuador and reached the coast of Ballina, Australia after 179 days at sea. Alsar proved that a fleet of small ships/rafts could have been responsible for colonization of many islands and lands in the Pacific.

Ancient sailors and their ships

I went on a mission coordinating a diving mission with Dr. Johan Reinhard, one of the Explorers in Residence of the National Geographic Society to the lake "Laguna Culebrilla" up in the Ecuadorian Andes at 4000 meters in altitude. The object of the mission was the search of offerings to prove that this lake was sacred as was always stated by the Cañari people of southern Andean Ecuador. We were able to find the sacred Spondylus Shell (red spiny oyster) from the Pacific Ocean up in this cold fresh water lake that in the past the Cañari or the Incas had used as an offering. He showed us (the diving team also with the National Institute of Cultural Heritage – INPC of Ecuador) a beautiful presentation on some of the most relevant dives he had done in his lifetime. He had been the pioneer in diving the Lake Titicaca site and also in many wrecks in oceans around the world. He is also famous for the discovery of the Ice Maiden mummy discovered in the high altitude of Mount Ampato in Peru and the Child Mummies discovered in Mount Llullaillaco in Argentina.

One of the slides he showed us was the comparable size of the ships at the time of Columbus's landing in the Americas. He showed us the size of the Pinta, Niña and the Santa Maria and compared it to the Chinese Junks. These Asian ships looked like the size of aircraft carriers alongside the Spanish caravels. You see the mission of the Chinese Junks belonging to the 1421 fleet, which I will get into in a moment here, brings up another mystery.

I have to say "Columbus landing" because I also have my views on who discovered America for the Europeans. First, the indigenous groups that came over the

Bering Strait land bridge were the first, seems there is no doubt about that. We know that other groups visited, like the Vikings, who have confirmed sites in North America before Columbus visited. One site in New Foundland dates to 1000 AD.

Many investigators believe in other theories as well. My view is that Easter Island (which pertains to Chile now) was populated by the peoples of Oceania, (experts say from 700-1100 AD) maybe at the same time Hawaii was populated. The Austronesian peoples who originated in Southeast Asia also in turn populated the early people of Oceania. My question is, did they just go further east from Easter Island (2,180 miles more) and land on the South American continent? It may seem so.

Gavin Menzies, the famous author of the book, *1421: The Year China Discovered America*, states that there was a Chinese Emperor named Zhu Dhi who built an enormous fleet of leviathan ships that were sent around the world for various purposes. Some of these were to proclaim the advances of the Chinese civilization, impress the foreign rulers, colonize, tax the new lands, and also bring back treasures. The investigation also came up with these leviathan ships or treasure ships that were 480 feet in length and 180 feet across. The rudders were as long as the flagship La Niña that later Columbus sailed on. Without making landfall, these ships could travel a distance of 4,500 miles or three months in open seas.

Curious details have been discovered regarding one of the most important European maps of the time. Early navigators like Columbus could have based their travels on a map that was drawn by the navigators of Admiral Zheng He's fleets. What is important about Gavin Menzies is that he was a submarine commander for the British Navy, had traveled the world for many years and was an expert on celestial navigation. This basic information helped him to understand these maps. In one point of the book he states there was a detailed map that showed the Pacific coast of America predating the conquistador Hernando de Alarcon in 1540. This is the Waldseemuller World Map made in 1507 and is the first to detail latitude and longitude with precision. He says, "The Pacific Coast of America is strikingly drawn on the Waldseemuller chart and the latitudes correspond to those of Vancouver Island in Canada right down to Ecuador in the south".

Archaeology's evidence

In the summer of 2011, while I was away on a mission presenting Ecuador as a travel destination for the Ecuadorian government, my mother called me to tell me that she had just seen a documentary on History Channel where there were wheels with holes in them just like the ones I had my team videotape underwater on a site I discovered on a reef 5 kms off of Bahía de Caráquez years ago. In the documentary they believed these were Chinese anchors. This was a program based on the Gavin Menzies book *1421: The Year China Discovered America*. I made contact with Gavin Menzies and sent him and his team all the information I had recovered from my site and also sent pictures of archaeological pieces from the archaeological site of Chirije, which we own and administer.

The Bajo de Santa Martha site, a rock reef west off Bahía is where I found interesting underwater structures, this is a place where I had just started to surf back in 1978 with a group of friends. I was actually the first surfer in the water there and my boat captain Rodolfo Saltos, who was a lobster fisherman on the site, had told me that they had seen geometric shapes under the water. So I started to uncover the history of a site pertaining to a legend.

My great uncle Gonzalo Dueñas had said that in the 1950s a Jesuit priest by the name of the Bishop Silvio Haro [1904-1983] had documents of Padre Juan de Velasco, of a city lost by a cataclysm. He had shown me the picture of him and the priest on the beach ready to go out on an expedition. I have this on a video. In addition, my great aunt Bertha Santos de Dueñas states in her book, (Estampas de la historia de la Bahia de los Caras) "the fishermen in the beginning of the last century would see evidence of construction on the biggest moon tides at the low tides". So I dove in the water and found a double lined wall (looked like an aqueduct) that was about 70 yards in length. In 1997, a couple of my friends that were on the team I made for that year's expedition, filmed even intersections that the walls came up to and also other objects that looked like parts of perfectly curved and rounded walls. All the expeditions since then never saw the same objects we saw in that expedition due to the visibility of the water.

The archaeologist Javier Veliz investigated and came up with maps of the Spanish Armada from 1680 and 1730 of Bahía de Caráquez and where there is land drawn as Islands that were once connected to the other side of the point of the bay at Punta Napo (across in San Vicente). These are exactly the areas, sand and rock reefs that we went diving in, which at the lowest tide of the full moon or new moon are no more than 4 feet deep. Like I said before, we have lost much land to the rising of sea level, the areas that we were diving were once dry land. The ocean has risen 4 feet in 282 years, almost a foot every 70 years. Johan Reinhard,, explorer in residence of the National Geographic Society, (who accompanied me in the last mission) told me that there was possibly human activity on that point. That is all we know now. It would be nice to create a marine reserve there for people who want to see nature at its purest and also help look for evidence of our ancient cultures.

Please see video that my diving team from the Catholic University created on the expeditions: http://www.youtube.com/watch?v=VP9a9GhW4FU.

With these videos, photos, Emilio Estrada's evidence, and the writings of Padre Juan de Velasco I wrote to Gavin Menzies.

His reply email states:

"Thank you for your most interesting email on June 28, which I have studied with care. I have watched the 3 videos and printed out the 3 attachments. I am particularly interested in the bead necklace and the axe head next to it for the reasons that follow. My General Interest in Ecuador in 1969 is of a Captain of a British Submarine H.M.S. Rorqual. The submarine was circumnavigating the world. The penultimate leg was from New Zealand to South America thence through the Panama Canal to Cartagena and Santa Marta (Colombia) and then home. Our landfall was Bahía de Caráquez, which we photographed before embarking Ecuadorian and Colombian Naval Officers. For 2 weeks Rorqual became the Flagship of Admiral Magin Ortega Saccamente. From that day on I have considered Ecuador and Colombia exceptionally beautiful and fascinating countries. Voyages from long ago to Peru, Ecuador and Colombia in 2003 my book '1421 – The Year China Discovered the World' was published in several editions in 28 different languages. We have had tens of thousands of emails from South American readers of the Spanish version of '1421' of these 99 percent accept the Chinese did sail and map the whole world between 1415 and 1424. However, many of these readers believed the Chinese were not the first. Other civilizations had been sailing the world for thousands of years before the Chinese."

Christopher Higham from Menzies team in another email states:

"Dear Patricio,

Thank you. This is the best-documented and photographed account of Chinese international discovery we have received, since I started working with Gavin Menzies 10 years ago. With the increasing influence that Latin America is playing in the worldwide economy and interest, we should think carefully about how we develop this new evidence. Please let me know what role we could most successfully play for you.

Best wishes, Christopher."

The account of Padre Juan de Velasco

As we roll back into my views on who settled the Pacific Coast I have to add the following, which is an interesting part of this chapter, due to it being the closest to home of the first accounts of Trans-Pacific Contact. I have done a direct translation (I think done for the first time) that I have put into English from our first Historian, Father Juan de Velasco. He was born in the year 1727, in Riobamba (Ecuador) and died in Faenza, Italy in 1792 at the age of 65. He was a Jesuit priest that lived in Ecuador and wrote his most famous book, *History of the Kingdom of Quito in Southern America* in 1789 [*Historia del Reino de Quito en America Meridional*]. In an order from the Spanish King, all the Jesuits were expelled from the dominions of the Spanish monarchy in 1767. What we know is that Juan de Velasco took all the documents of his investigations hidden very carefully and traveled across the Andes, the seas, and into Italy with him. It is important to state that he is regarded very highly for his genius, talent, and patriotism and for giving the Ecuadorians a very beautiful account of our historical trajectory. Bringing it down to our local level and due to his account you will see always a sign and/or statement saying "Bahía de Caráquez, la puerta de la Nacionalidad Ecuatoriana" (Bahía, the door/gateway to Ecuadorian Nationality).

Most people who know the legends of the histories know the following version. The first Ecuadorian historian Father Juan de Velasco stated that there was a grand nation that came from across the sea called the Caras, from the land where the sun sets, and they founded their city called Cara. Their leader was called the Shyri, which meant in their language "Lord of all".

The book, *The History of the Kingdom of Quito*, was written in 1789, though it was not published until 1844 (they started publishing it in 1841). This book and the volume is referenced as: *Historia del Reino de Quito en la América Meridional 1789. Volume 1, Part 1*. The Natural History, Government Press 1844. From the writings of Padre Juan de Velasco (from his book, the volume of *Historia Natural*).

I translated this from Spanish, and the next few pages therefore are as a direct quote, you will only see some of my clarifying phrases inside of brackets:

"Padre Juan de Velasco states that Bravo Saravia [1512-1577, Spanish conquistador and interim viceroy of Peru and Royal Governor of Chile] was very detailed and after combining a thousand proofs and traditions, he was assured it was unquestionable that the Peruvians and the Caras were ultimately ultramarine [situated in lands beyond the sea], from a long distance across the sea and that they settled in Southern America coming from the land where the sun sets.

Padre Acosta [1540-1600, Spanish Jesuit and anthropologist, arrived in America in 1571] was sure the Indians of this coast were navigating way before the Spanish came to this land and that the Indians of Ica and Arica used to travel to islands very far off into the sunset on stretched seal skins. Acosta had various testimonies and well investigated traditions.

Such ideas were common and circumstances along the coasts of Guayaquil, Manta and Cara, which were examined by the conquistadors, verified these traditions. All Indians believed there were very big lands and numerous islands in all those seas and that their ancestors had come from there. Also, that from their coast, they had gone to these distant lands passing always through one island to another. Always following the signal of El Camino del Sol, [the Path of the Sun], they arrived at the first of these islands at about 100 leagues, where they provisioned themselves with dried meat from Tortoises. With these assertions the Conquistadors were curious to examine what was true.

In effect, navigating under the equator line (which was the Path of the Sun) at around 110 leagues, they found the Galapagos Islands, of which they took possession over and of whose name is maybe due to the infinity of animals that are there [Galapagos tortoises]. They did not find any Indians, but many caves with very antique bonfires. In reality they found innumerable islands that were expanded from 1 degree latitude north to 5 degrees latitude south. Many were from 8 to 10 or more leagues to cross and some less, forming the archipelagos. Some were very high ones, others low ones, some with freshwater rivers and some without, some very sterile and others prolific, some were filled with a delicious fruit called Mamey and with many birds. The most admirable discovery, and one that and enforces this case, is that with the passing of time, much of these islands have been lost and are disappearing, so much so that when the Englishman Dampier [1651-1715, buccaneer, scientific observer and writer, was the first to give a true account of the Galapagos Islands] came to them, he was only able to find 14 of them, according to his long account.

If you add to the referred traditions and the discoveries made by them, the other evidence is there, no doubt about it. Take in your hands the terrestrial sphere or a very outlined planisphere, observe the 4 inhabited parts of the Earth, located in its major part to the North, look at all the oceans loaded to the South Pole, and note in the middle of the immense sea of the South, there seems to be another part equal to the America almost hidden and submerged. What other things can you understand with the discovery of these grand things in the Tropic of Capricorn? That these are not islands? That the number of numerous large, medium and small islands, known by the Europeans, and planted in all that immense sea, from America all the way to the East Indies, especially in the tropics, are not actual islands?

The last discovery of the famous Cook is the identity and religion of New Zealand and the Island of Tahiti, 645 leagues apart. What does this show? Easter Island or Davis, seen and re-seen by many, a little bit more than 27 degrees south latitude, about 100 leagues distant from the coasts of Peru, what does it scream to show and in a perceptible voice? Don't we know already that this island, only 4 leagues wide at its longest side, has 3,000 inhabitants and is filled with countless giant stone statues perfectly cut and standing at 27 feet in height and all identical to the ones found in Manta in the Kingdom of Quito. Don't we know that giants that also left other monuments made these? Don't we know of these statues and others fabricated that are much more amazing and splendid made of live rock, found in Tiahuanaco near Cuzco that were pieces of works and rooms for those same Giants of Manta and Davis?

Gomarra says, "The Peruvians generally believed that their first Inca, founder of the empire, was a foreigner, not an American. They gave him diverse names, calling him Mancocapac, this means Supreme Lord and Legislator. Others called him Zapalla, which means Only Lord, and others Viracocha, this is fat [or foam] of the sea, due to have taken his first people swimming like foam over the same sea. All these collections of traditions, of Indians, of remains, of proof non-mistaken, means not only that in ancient times there was some sort of communication via the ocean, albeit not that easy, not that difficult either? Everything clamors for and shows that there was some great continent between America, Asia and maybe Africa that was mistakenly taken for Atlantis by the ancient ones. And if this wasn't so, who can deny there was at least many more and continuous islands which were stops for short navigations and which gave way to the same language and religion between New Zealand and Tahiti, the same for Davis [Easter Island], in Tiahuanaco and in Manta to which inhabitants would be recruited from one to other parts.

In time this communication has been lost, because the stops on these islands, which I refer to as the Galapagos, have stopped due to the disappearing of many of them, even in modern times. Various other islands and extensive coasts of discovered lands with demarcation done by the Europeans have not been able to be found later according to various traveling accounts. This can only come because of the seas of the south taking the blame of making the residual land rises of the submerged continent disappear.

Who is capable of guessing when the main catastrophe occurred? The knowledgeable and expert Count Carli calculates it at 3000 years before the Christian era, because at that time it was known in China, the use of the Quipus or string writings found later in Peru. [khi-pooh, known as the talking knots, were recording devices used in the Inca Empire and earlier societies in the Andean region. A quipu usually consisted of colored, spun, and plied thread or strings from llama or alpaca hair. It could also be made of cotton cords. The cords contained numeric and other values encoded by knots in a base ten positional system. Quipus might have just a few or up to 2,000 cords.]

Following the sacred chronology according to the version of the 70 [the 70 translators employed by Ptolemy for Greek Scriptures], we find this calculation [3000 B.C] not to be repugnant, but on the contrary in order. Challenge others on this point if they want, but I will always stay with my ruling.

Where was the origin of those who populated Peru and Quito?

What has been told unto here deduces clearly that America was populated by different parts and in different times. Many believe that the first settlers could have come from diverse origins or descendants posterior to Noah. This is a labyrinth of pure speculation, because having such a diversity of original tongues, of religion, of uses and customs, there is not a nation in the world where you cannot find some mistaken and confusing remain between the American nations. Some of these are made by the Jews, in attention to the sandals, the long clothing, the hair of Nazirites, or the exact identical word, or just a little different, that you observe in the Peruvians. Others are made by the Tartars and the Scytas [Macedonians?] for certain types of weapons that they use; others are made by the Egyptians for the pyramids, which they call tolas here. Others are made by the Chinese with the Quipus of the strings; others judge them like Romans for their monasteries of vestal virgins. And finally others do and undo of them, as they like, according to the signs they seem to have found.

For me to go in accordance to the calculation of its age; and not to have any base to go on to change my ruling; and to err less, I raise myself to the highest origin, and I stand by the same opinion that the Indians of Cuba had the first settlers, that they are descendants of Can [possibly Cain]. I judge it so, just in attention to its untidy fortune, because it is true that it just takes to see these unfortunate tribes, to see with one's eyes the curse set upon by [either Noah or our Lord-cannot decipher the words scanned]. Of the nations ruled over by the Kingdom of Quito, the most ancient one was the Quitus, from where it took its name. This is the only one whose origin can be investigated.

It was the Quitus that were conquered by a foreign nation who (in accordance to their oral tradition) arrived in America from the part of the west [where the sun sets], navigating in balsas, not in junks [reeds] as is said that the Giants arrived in, instead in great timbers tied with one another. The truth in it is, this type of single craft, simple and easy, of which on top an entire house constructed on if you wanted, has been used on this coast since time immemorial and is still used up to this day, being secure and capable of steering with sails and paddles.

It is renowned that this nation seized the coast and because of this it was called Cara. The head of this nation or the sovereign was called Scyri [Shee-ree], which in their language meant, the "Lord of all". They constructed over the bay and that is why it is called Caraques [first written account of the naming of the bay, is from Pizarro, and it is

Caraque, from the account of Miguel de Estete 1531, so it correlates to what the natives stated in their oral tradition]. The city is also called Cara, but most call it or Cora. Over the very ancient remains of this city, all of cut stone, the Spaniards founded theirs with the same name.

Why did they intern themselves to conquer the Kingdom of Quito, some Indians say, due to escaping the Giants that lived close to Manta and Santa Elena, which they would kill their women using them.

What is true is that this foreign nation was less barbarous and less uneducated than the primitive one of Quitus. This foreign nation had a political government and it was educated and civil, in comparison with the savage tribes that had established themselves in all places. They did not adore idols, only the Sun and the Moon." (Velasco, J.1789)

So this is the real written version from 1789 of our first Ecuadorian historian, Father Juan de Velasco, with the segment of the chapters that interests us and relates to the transpacific contact and that I have translated into English. I think it is interesting because this is the first written account of our history. The part of the natives provisioning themselves with tortoise meat before they left to other islands is remarkable.

I want to say this, that if we look into modern times, the sailboats that arrive into our bay at Bahía de Caráquez (usually mostly from North America), actually go to the Galapagos first and then they sail afterwards to the Marquesas, which is close to 3000 miles away, and takes from 17-22 days with good wind and up to 30 days when it is not favorable. They do this all the time on these magnificent sailboats. So on Balsas, we could only guess it would be 2 or 3 times as long, but makeable on their journeys towards the South Pacific and beyond.

Padre Juan de Velasco says that before the Spaniards arrived, people arrived on our coast and that our coastal people here also sailed to their lands, following the Path of the Sun, on the latitude of the Equator. So it is, but is it? This is something we still need a lot of investigation on. He writes about many sources giving him the information. Does nobody dare to write about this or to study it? I would love to.

In search of Valdivia

My time with Betty Meggers at the Smithsonian Institution was very interesting. I had reached this prestigious institution in search of Dr. Douglas Ubelaker, who also made sure I went to her office. When I started to introduce myself, I had explained that I was visiting in search of help for the furthering of investigation of my archaeological site of Chirije. That I knew that she had, with her husband Clifford Evans and Emilio Estrada (who discovered Chirije), discovered the Valdivia Culture pottery that at that time (1956) dated as the earliest known evidence of pottery made in the Americas. Now we know there are other smaller sites that have early dates similar to Valdivia in South America, but up to this date the female representation pertaining to the Valdivia culture, known as the Venus of Valdivia, is the earliest known female clay figurine known to have been sculpted from Anchorage Alaska all the way to Tierra del Fuego.

Pottery associated with the Valdivia culture of coastal Ecuador was dated officially from 3600 BC to 1500 BC in 8 different phases (now there are earlier dates, please see the chapter on The Magic of the Red Spiny Oyster). In the Bahía de Caráquez area, specifically Chirije, we have found evidence of the Valdivia culture and in San Isidro across the bay. The archaeologist Zeidler established that the latter phase of Valdivia had flourished there.

The Smithsonian archaeologist Betty Meggers states that the Valdivia period in Ecuador exhibit similarities to pottery crafted in Japan during the Jomon period. This group from Japan were excellent navigators since 10,000 BC. Many Ecuadorian archaeologists dismiss this idea and others say these ideas are not correct. They say this is due to parallel evolution of cultural manifestations in the different lands and of different peoples.

Norman Totten who writes "*Categories of Evidence for Old World Contacts with Ancient America*" in the *Book of Mormon: A Keystone Scripture*, cites Hubert Howe Bancroft, who wrote *The Native Races of the Pacific States of North America,* (San Francisco: Bancroft & Co., 1883), p. 52:

"There have been a great many instances of Japanese junks drifting upon the American coast, many of them after having floated helplessly about for many months. Mr. Brooks [Charles Wolcott Brookes who served as Japanese Consul in San Francisco in the mid-19th Century] gives forty-one particular instances of such wrecks, beginning in 1782, twenty-eight of which date since 1850. Only twelve of the whole number were deserted. The author of the paper assures me that he has records of over one hundred such disasters." (Bancroft referenced the San Francisco Evening Bulletin of March 2, 1875).

Emilio Estrada, up until the day of his death in 1963, believed that there was transpacific contact. There is an interesting note I wanted to include in the article, **Fuel & Flame** that was posted in *Time Magazine* on Jan. 6, 1961 on Emilio Estrada and this controversial subject.

Fuel & Flame (Time Magazine, Jan 6, 1961)
http://www.time.com/time/magazine/article/0,9171,874280,00.html.

"Who or what went which way... the question has long agitated Americanists — the scholars and experts who specialize in the prehistory of the Western Hemisphere and who explore the origin and development of such high civilizations as the Mayans and the Incas.

Almost all Americanists agree that the original South and Central American Indians migrated from Asia. The majority thinks that they brought with them only the rock-

bottom culture of nomadic hunters and thereafter built their own glittering cultures independently, without help from across the Pacific. The contrary view is that Asian cultures kept trickling over the ocean, materially helping the Indians develop their advanced civilizations.

Last week the old argument was again alive—and this time because of findings made by wealthy Emilio Estrada of Guayaquil, Ecuador, who dabbles deeply in archaeology even while running a thriving auto and appliance business. He has interested himself in Ecuador's northern coastal region because of vaguely oriental objects previously found there. In 1956, after learning diggers' techniques from Archaeologists Clifford Evans and Betty Meggers of the U.S.'s Smithsonian Institution, he began concentrating on the coastal town of Bahía de Caráquez where, according to ancient legends, a people called the Caras landed from the sea.

A full-dress excavation last year produced a wealth of pottery objects with an oriental look. There were models of houses with peaked gables that looked as if they might have come from Japan or Indo-China. Headrests looked equally Asian, and so did a drawing on a pottery spindle weight that showed a stylized porter carrying burdens on the ends of a pole, as many Asians do. Many sitting figurines had a vague resemblance to statues of Buddha. Carbon 14 tests showed that the objects were made about 250 B.C.

According to Estrada, no similar oriental-looking objects have been found elsewhere in Central or South America. His theory is that a small group of people from across the Pacific found their way to Ecuador, perhaps were shipwrecked near Bahía and founded a colony there. Some of their imported cultural traits, such as a liking for headrests and peaked gables, persisted for a few generations before dying out.

Around Estrada's recently published discoveries, the old argument is brewing anew. Unconvinced, Anthropologist Matthew Stirling, long with the Smithsonian, says that headrests are worldwide, and people living in similar climates are apt to have similar house designs. As for the Buddha-like figurines: "There are only a few ways," says Stirling, "for a human being to sit down." Harvard Anthropologist Gordon Willey is also skeptical. Says Willey: "The high American civilizations from Mexico to Peru had been rolling for 1,500 to 2,000 years before this possible Asiatic migration."

Concluding thoughts

To my fellow national archaeologists I say, friends; your work is most highly respected. As an "Ecuatoriano", I thank you for letting me better know our roots, the archaeological sites, the beautiful ancient pottery and the interesting manifestations of the cultures that have been discovered. I am lucky to have a beautiful archaeological site (Chirije) close to Bahía de Caráquez, which has made me passionate to study and promote the pre-Columbian cultures that thrived on our Pacific Coast. Let's open a new realm in investigation and think about transpacific contact. I think it is important to see the connection.

I also see my fellow Ecuadorians and I tell them, you know, partially due to our past national situation in some areas of education and economy, lack of funding for investigation and many other elements, we have not put into priority investigation, comprehensiveness and pride to our pre-Columbian cultures, at least for the most part, I think I can dare to say. Important to note, I am excluding non-interest in our roots. However, some of you maybe don't care or are not interested, and I accept everyone's free will in this aspect, I don't agree with it, but accept it. Wouldn't it be interesting to find out more about our past? Did you ever think that in our past we had contact with peoples on the other side of this immense ocean?

Finally I look into your eyes and say, I believe we have something here, something that is authentic and genuine, dating back from indigenous oral tradition to our first Ecuadorian historian and then using just common sense for the answer of the question "who settled the Pacific Coast? We did have peoples from the north migrating and/or traveling south, maybe south traveling north, but from the West? We cannot put this concept away in some file or just hide it from the world for another hundred years. Our ancient civilizations are a subject that have been interlaced on the American continent in a way which we only know the surface of, and with the peoples across the ocean, even less so and that is a different story. Of course our indigenous populations have an incredible story with their maritime expertise and their beautiful story of their synergy with nature in our region. This is the coast less known. Let's come together, and to those with wide-open minds, hope you can visit and we can enjoy a beautiful story together.

Just to finish, the following chart comes from a scientific publication, "Scientific Evidence for Pre-Columbian Transoceanic Voyages to and from the Americas", written by John L. Sorensen and Carl L. Johannessen, that lists 98 plant species that are considered decisive evidence that the organism was present in both Eastern and Western Hemispheres before Columbus' first voyage. The chart that follows has been reduced in number of species to include only the better known plants.

Plants for Which There is Decisive Evidence of Transoceanic Movement

Species	Common Name	Origin	Moved To
Agave angustifolia	Agave	Americas	India
Ageratum conyzoides	Goat weed	Americas	India, Marquesas?
Amaranthus cruentus	Amaranth	Americas	Asia
Anacardium occidentale	Cashew	Americas	India
Ananas comosus	Pineapple	Americas	India, Polynesia
Annona cherimolia	Large annona	Americas	India
Annona reticulata	Custard apple	Americas	India
Arachis hypogaea	Peanut	Americas	China, India
Argemone mexicana	Mexican poppy	Americas	China, India
Asclepias curassavica	Milkweed	Americas	China, India
Bixa orellana	Achiote, Annatto	Americas	Oceania, Asia
Cannabis sativa	Hashish	Eastern Hemisphere	Peru
Capsicum annuum	Chili pepper	Americas	India, Polynesia

Carica papaya	Papaya	Americas	Polynesia
Ceiba pentandra	Kapok, silk cotton tree	Americas	Asia
Cocos nucifera	Coconut	Eastern Hemisphere	Colombia to Mexico
Cucurbita moschata	Butternut squash	Americas	India, China
Cucurbita pepo	Pumpkin	Americas	India, China
Cyperus esculentus	Sedge	Americas	Eurasia
Diospyros ebenaster	Black sapote	Americas	Eurasia
Erythroxylon novagranatense	Coca	Americas	Egypt
Garcinia mangostana	Mangosteen	Eastern Hemisphere	Peru
Gossypium tomentosum	A cotton	Americas	Hawaii
Helianthus annuus	Sunflower	Americas	India
Heliconia bihai	Balisier	Americas	Oceania, Asia
Hibiscus tiliaceus	Linden hibiscus	Americas	Polynesia
Ipomoea batatas	Sweet potato	Americas	Polynesia, China
Lagenaria siceraria	Bottle gourd	Americas	Asia, East Polynesia

Morus sp.	Mulberry tree	Eastern Hemisphere	Middle America
Musa x *paradisiaca*	Banana, plantain	Eastern Hemisphere	Tropical America
Nicotiana tabacum	Tobacco	Americas	South Asia
Ocimum sp.	Basil	Americas	India
Opuntia dillenii	Prickly pear cactus	Americas	India
Phaseolus lunatus	Lima bean	Americas	India
Phaseolus vulgaris	Kidney bean	Americas	India
Psidium guajava	Guava	Americas	China, Polynesia
Salvia coccinea	Scarlet salvia	Americas	Marquesas Islands
Smilax sp.	Sarsparilla	Eastern Hemisphere	Central America
Tagetes erecta	Marigold	Americas	India, China
Zea mays	Corn, maize	Americas	Eurasia, Africa?

Source: Sorenson, John L. and Johannessen, Carl L. (2001)

CHAPTER SIX

The Conquistadors

The Conquistadors (kon-keys-tah-dors) were the explorers and adventurers of the 15th and 16th Centuries that brought the lands of the New World under the control of Spain and Portugal. One of the most famous conquistadors is Francisco Pizarro, who captured the last Inca, Atahualpa, and disrupted one of the most complex and extended empires in the world. The territories that the Incas conquered from the earlier cultures expanded from Argentina to southern Colombia.

I have had a fulfilling life here in Bahía through my adventures that have spun off from projects, especially with my archaeological site Chirije and also my grandfather's land at the Hacienda Coaque. It is fantastic to go back in time and read about the journeys of explorers. I also have the privilege of my mother having grown up in Coaque, where Pizarro made base camp in 1531, where he found the biggest bounty of gold in his journey through Ecuador, and where Charles Marie de la Condamine, 200 years later, (1736) came to measure the arc of the meridians to investigate the real shape of the earth, leaving here on the coast the first marker of the Equator line. My grandfather had his house on this point and would sometimes ask my mother to have his breakfast served in the Northern Hemisphere and dinner served in the south. It will be a pleasure to share my knowledge of scientific findings and the history of Pizarro in this chapter.

Pizarro's passage

The passage of Francisco Pizarro through Peru is widely known; especially from the moment he captured Atahualpa and received a ransom of a room full of gold. How true is this? More than likely, due to the accounts of the first scribes and soldiers, it is true. Pizarro passing through the now known territories of Ecuador (known as part of Peru in the conquistador era) needs to be examined because if it had not been for Pizarro finding Coaque (a village right on the equator line) and the biggest bounty in gold of Ecuador, the name of another conquistador would have gone into the history books. In addition, the first account of headhunters and shrunken heads are written about on a Cape (Pasado) that is just south of Coaque. Mistakenly, many thought that these were found first in the rituals of the Amazon natives. The journey of Pizarro starts in 1523-24 (according to Miguel de Estete, 1531).

Map of Pizarro's Journeys

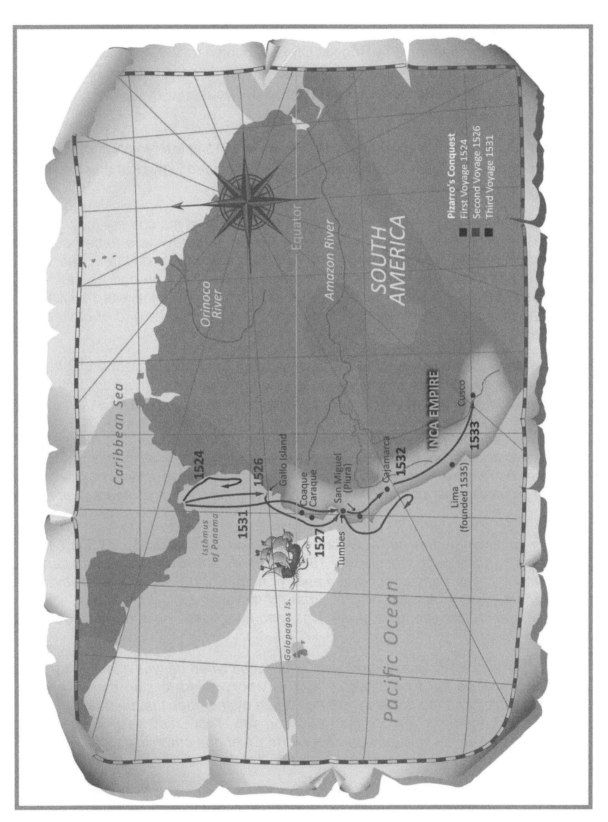

Let me start with the information I have about Vasco Nuñez de Balboa discovering the Pacific Ocean. Many accounts have been written and reiterated in numerous books, I particularly like this one that celebrates the 400 years of Columbus's landing in America, titled *America, Historia de su descubrimiento, desde los tiempos primitivos a los mas modernos* by Rodolfo Cronau, printed in 1892 (translated as: *America, the History of its Discovery, From the Primitive to the Most Modern Times*). I will translate and write the most important entries for your enjoyment. My commentaries are in brackets.

The specific account for this chapter begins in 1511 in the region of the territories now known as Panama, just 19 years after Columbus landed in the Bahamas Archipelago at San Salvador:

"When Balboa went on his trip to study more of the inside of the country [now Panama] he sent Pizarro to see the land of Coyba with 6 men, but they were forced out by the natives. Balboa himself, with 130 men, went forward and captured Careta, the Chief of this land. He then traveled to the province of Comagre where the natives greeted him and his men in a very friendly manner. The conquistadors were excited at what they saw; the house of the Chief was 150 feet long and 80 feet wide, and of course, there were riches inside.

The son of the Chief gave the Spaniards a grand quantity of gold adornments but he was quite amazed that they [the Spaniards] quarreled for the distribution. With this he said; "if this gold is so valuable in your eyes, and for your love of it, you would abandon your country, exposing yourselves to all kinds of danger, I will speak of a nation in where you will completely satisfy your ambition. Behind those mountains that rise to the south there is a vast sea, lined by a people that possess ships with sails and paddles like yourselves, whose king eats in golden dishes and whose nation is crossed with rivers that possess great richness in gold. This metal is so common there, it is like iron is to us."

Powerfully impacted by this news, Balboa set forth on September 1, 1513 in search of this mysterious nation accompanied by 190 Spaniards and 600 Indians that carried all the equipment. He brought a good-sized pack of hounds, knowing that the natives were afraid of these beasts. A most difficult crossing this was, with virgin forest, vines (as wide as an arm and as strong as steel), logs, and very dense bush that made it almost impassable.

His march came to even more extreme circumstances when he was attacked by a large contingent of natives led by Quaraqua, a chief who wanted to stop the advance. He repelled the attack and the natives were frightened by the dogs that tried to shred them. After this attack there were more than 600 corpses. The Chief was killed and many prisoners were taken, including the brother of the Chief and others of lesser importance, who were then condemned to death and given to the dogs.

Finally, on September 25, they reached the foot of the mountain range where the native guide that led the expedition told Balboa the peak above them was the one where he could see the ocean. He only had 67 men with him, due to many getting sick and having to return. He started the difficult climb very early and towards 10 o'clock in the morning he stopped and ordered his troops to stay. There was just one bald peak and he wanted to be the first to salute the Southern Sea.

With his heart beating away the conquistador climbed to the top of the peak and once upon it, seeing the grandeur of the indescribable panorama of this immense ocean at his feet, he was deeply moved and dropped to his knees, crossed his hands in sign of prayer, and thanked heaven for the grand mercy that was conceded to him for making such an important discovery.

At the end of 4 days of marching, he finally reached the Pacific Ocean at the mouth of the "Rio Sabana (river)", which flowed into the Gulf of San Miguel. It is mentioned that they saw the fast flowing foamy waves playing on the coast. Balboa, dressed in white, armed to the tip, with a banner of the Virgin Mary holding Christ the child, walked into the ocean knee-deep, unveiled his sword and took possession in the name of the Spanish Crown. The newly discovered sea, its coasts, its ports, its adjacent islands and nations were all his, and in a combative tone, he challenged anyone who would want to dispute his rights to it.

He spent many days on the coast, and because this ocean was in a counter position of the northern sea that bathed the Isthmus, he named these waters the Southern Sea. He was able to get an abundant number of pearls from the Indians that dove for them in the bays. They had so many that the natives would adorn their canoe paddles with them. On one occasion he was talking to one of the chiefs about the nations to the south and he was surprised to find out about an animal that was a quadruped [4 legged] that carried heavy loads. The chief sculpted him out in clay and to the Spaniard it looked more like a camel. This is the first known account of the Llamas of the Andes. Balboa started his return on November 3 and reached the colony on January 19, 1514, where he sent his message to the King about the discovery of the Southern Sea. [It was Ferdinand Magellan in the last week of November of 1519, who while looking for a more direct route to the spice islands and crossing the southern tip of South America, arrived at an ocean he said was a beautiful, peaceful ocean. Pacific means peaceful, and so it was named the Pacific Ocean. From here it took him 4 months to reach the Philippines, but he achieved one of the most daring feats of any epoch to circumnavigate the globe].

Many of the Spanish conquistadors wreaked havoc and destruction upon the Indian populations during the conquest and even amongst themselves, if one was an obstacle they would get rid of him. Balboa was not an exception. The governor of the Darien, Pedro Arias de Avila, knew that Balboa wanted to go south, be independent and promote himself for being governor there. Pedro Arias de Avila became jealous of his power, captured and decapitated him. Vasco Nunez de Balboa died on January 15, 1519."

I will translate another account from the book *Pizarro and the Conquest of Peru*, by Federick A. Ober. I read here that Balboa was harassed by Avila so much, that he was grounded from exploring any more regions. However, when Avila told Balboa to build brigantine ships on the Caribbean coast and transport them piece by piece to the Pacific, he [Balboa] was alleviated. He needed to get as far away as possible from all the pressure the governor was placing on him. In this account, when Avila was sent to capture Balboa, the one who lead the band of soldiers to capture him was Francisco Pizarro, Balboa's captain/lieutenant and worthy soldier [it is written in other accounts that Pedro Arias de Avila, the governor at that time, was also in with Pizarro in the conquering of the south, but he never received any of the riches, but there could have been between the two a conspiracy against Balboa].

How unfair was Balboa's death! Avila, to further insult Balboa and in an attempt to minimize the great explorer that he was, put his head on a pole and displayed it in the plaza for days. What avarice can do! I want to add what William Prescott wrote in his book of the History of the Conquest of Peru:

"The illustrious discoverer was doomed to fall a victim to that miserable jealousy with which a little spirit regards the achievements of a great one."

It is important to have outlined the history of Vasco Nuñez de Balboa to comprehend the magnitude of the discovery of the Pacific Ocean and to gain awareness of the different Indian nations and their knowledge of the nations of gold to the south. Let's go forward to how contact with the south was done with the translation of Cronau's work. This historical account continues in 1522, to follow up on others who followed Balboa's intention of going south:

"Pascual de Andagoya, the inspector general of the natives of the Darien Isthmus, traveled south of the bay of San Miguel. This is where he met the chief of the region of Chuchama. This chief complained to him that his people suffered from frequent attacks by the inhabitants of Birú, a district located more to the south. With these Indians and reinforcements from Panama, they fought against the Biruvians. They had to turn back though because Andagoya and his people got violently sick. This trip was the reason the district of land all the way to the south of the 18th latitude got its name, Birú [Colombia, Ecuador, Peru and northern Chile]. Later on, it was called Peru. [According to Miguel de Estete in his writings of 1531, the name Peru started to be used in 1524-1525. It is interesting to note that the chief Birú, in his wildest of dreams could have had his name written over such a large area of land, thanks to Andagoya's expedition]. Though Andagoya received a very severe injury showing off a horse to the natives, he was not the man to lead the discoveries to the south, even though he brought many of the riches that lay beyond and of course those of the Incas]. The next adventurer to go south was Juan de Buzurto, a rich plantation owner from Española, but he died while preparing his trip.

Around 1519, three fearsome men got together and started to talk about an enterprise to conquer Birú. The first was Francisco Pizarro, born in Trujillo, Spain [modern day Extremadura] in 1471. He was abandoned by his mother at the door of a church and did not have a formal education. The future Viceroy of Peru did not know how to write but was an audacious soldier.

The second was Diego de Almagro, also of unknown origin, born in 1463 in Almagro, Spain. He was a man of arms and did very well in wars against the Indians. He was more upright and decisive than his comrade Pizarro and less ready to scheme.

[Pizarro and Almagro were almost the first men in the conquest of the "Indies". They participated in the conquest of the large Island of Hispaniola, the second largest island in the Caribbean after Cuba. Now it hosts 2 countries, the Dominican Republic and Haiti. We know Pizarro arrived earlier, in 1502, 10 years after Columbus's landing. Diego de Almagro became the discoverer of what is now known as Chile and was the first European in the territories of what is now known as Bolivia].

The third man was Hernando de Luque [no date for his birth, but, according to sources, was in the mid-15th Century]; he was a master teacher of his cathedral and was a priest in Panama whose character was highly regarded.

Knowing that the Spanish Crown did not give economic resources to facilitate the maritime expeditions, Pizarro and Almagro turned to Luque to find the funds. In the meantime, they would be in charge of recruiting and putting together the troops, crews of the ships and preparing the ships.

First Expedition 1524-1525

In 1524, the energy and the effort of these 3 men were able to set afloat 2 ships, the first one left the port of Panama with 112 men under the command of Francisco Pizarro [Miguel de Estete 1535, wrote that these ships were not the best, due to them being the first ones to travel in the South Sea, also the larger one being the one Balboa built for himself to conquer]. It was convened that Almagro follow him on the second ship after he provisioned himself with food and crews. In between big storms, Pizarro sailed and crossed the Isle of Pearls and unto the continent. Here there were large extensions of coast filled with impenetrable swampy forests and air that was just a cloud of mosquitoes [we know that on the now known territories of Colombia's Pacific Coast many areas are filled with mangrove forests and swamps].

After 70 days of navigation, the ship anchored in a calm bay, 32 men had died due to fevers without reaching any of the objectives that guided this expedition. With this, Pizarro sent the ship back to Panama for provisions under the command of Montenegro, thinking that it would take maximum 12 to 14 days. But it took Montenegro 74 days in the crossing and returning to the bay, calling it the Port of Famine. He found that misery had made such devastation upon the people of Pizarro that there was only 60 persons left in the expedition.

It took all the energy that Pizarro had to control his troops from committing acts of crime from the delirious fever that hunger had produced. They were eating marine animals, snails, lizards, sweet and sour fruits. With the provisions brought in by Montenegro, they were able to somewhat recuperate themselves and keep on the journey to the south.

The first thing they found was a native village on top of a mountain, surrounded by a fence and whose inhabitants escaped when the Spanish approached. In their huts they were able to stock pile great quantities of maiz [dried corn for meal] and cacao [cocoa beans] and also a large number of golden adornments and vases. The troops convinced themselves that the natives were anthropophagus because of the contents of some of the cauldrons that were on their fires [in another account from Herrera in his writings, Historia General, it states that between the flesh in the pots there were hands and feet of men].

Without warning, the Spaniards were brought under attack by a great number of Indians. In the fierce battle that ensued, 5 Spaniards died and 17 were wounded, amongst them was Pizarro. He was so severely hurt that each one of the seven wounds he had could have been considered fatal. Their lives were saved when they were transported back to the ship due to the opportune intervention of Montenegro, who just had returned after some raids. At that moment, there was no need to think about penetrating deeper inside the country, they returned to Panama loaded with many valuable treasures.

Almagro had just left Panama with the second ship to bring to his 60 men and provisions for them. He arrived a little later to the sacked village in which he also had bloody battles with the natives, one in which he had lost an eye. Even though this happened, he did not desist in looking for his comrade in arms. During his travel he assaulted more villages and also discovered the Rio de San Juan at 4° latitude north. Having found no traces of Pizarro he returned to Panama with a bounty that included a real treasure.

Even though they had not made the discovery of the real Peru, it was demonstrated that rich nations to the south really did exist and were abundant in gold. Because of this, on March 10, 1526, with Pizarro completely recuperated; the three allies signed the famous contract that would be the ruin of the powerful kingdom of Peru and the dynasty of the Incas.

Second Expedition 1526-1527

For a second time, Luque agreed to contribute 20,000 pesos in gold [bars] for a new expedition. The other 2 comrades agreed that each one would receive a third of the lands, gold, silver and precious stones that they would discover and conquer. This contract was solemnly sworn with a hand put upon the gospels, and all three having communion with a consecrated host which they broke off in 3 pieces.

The preparations for this second expedition were done rapidly and in the spring of that same year, Pizarro and Almagro, with 2 crewed [manned] ships and 170 Spaniards, left Panama. They sailed in a direct line towards the mouth of the San Juan River. Bartolome [Bartholomew] Ruiz was an excellent pilot and led the expedition [Bartholemeo Ruiz was from Andalucia, from a village called Moguer, which supplied most of the seamen for Columbus's voyages]. Everywhere they went they saw Indians in possession of gold adornments and in a village at the mouth of a river they found an abundant amount of this metal and precious stones. The prisoners the Spaniards took told them that there were many big cities and fertile lands towards the interior of the country. With this information, Pizarro decided to send the ship commanded by Almagro to Panama to look for more reinforcements while he waited at the conquered village. Ruiz, on the contrary was ordered to explore the coast towards the south with another ship.

Both emissaries completed their missions. Ruiz went as far as 2 to 3 degrees latitude south. A little after he passed the Equator [in what now is off the coast of the Republic of Ecuador. He may have been the first European to cross the equator line in this part of the Pacific], he and his people were surprised to see a strange vessel with its unfurled sails that was traveling in their direction [In the Samano-Xerex account, the description is of a vessel that could hold thirty tons].

At first they thought this vessel was European, but as they closed in, they were amazed that the whole crew was Indian and that the ship was a balsa raft constructed with thick logs, pointed at the bow [front of the vessel], with low lateral walls. Over the logs there was a deck made with thinner logs [bamboo canes] in which a small chamber was elevated. To make it sail, they had cotton sails tied down with hemp ropes to very tall masts and for anchors they had heavy rocks. It was understood that it was crewed by traders due to the objects that were in the cargo, like belts, hats, armor, head ornaments, vases, mirrors, a great number of gold and silver jewelry and other things. There were also many scales, big and small, destined to weigh this merchandise [in other accounts they describe these as very similar to Roman scales and scales for weighing gold and silver]. Both the traders that were on board and their women wore very fine wool dresses, on which, in yellow, black, blue, green, carmine [vivid crimson pigment made of cochineal-comes from crushed bodies of the scale insect] and white colors there were many animal figures embroidered. These figures were birds, cats, fish and flowers.

I am finished using the very detailed history written by Rodolfo Cronau, and will now use the account written by Samano-Xerex (a 5 page document), who wrote about Pizarro's first and second journeys. The Peruvian historian Raul Porras Barrenechea believes it was written between November 1527 and July 1528.

Joan de Samano was the secretary of the emperor Carlos V, and wrote about the news he received from Francisco de Xerex [or Jerez, Pizarro's secretary] and others. Samano took the news from the log of Bartolomeo Ruiz [who was Pizarro's lead captain for the first reconnaissance trips south], and also from the scribe Anton Quadrado who was appointed for that trip. This is one of the first written accounts of the conquest of the west coast of South America. This document also details more about the discovery of the Balsawood sailing vessel.

The account states that there was up to 20 men on the craft, 11 of them jumped in the water and the rest were captured, the pilot and others were left on land, but the Spaniards stayed with the last 3 Indians. They brought all these items [as described before to exchange for red and white fish shells (red spiny oyster - *Spondylus princeps* - shell, the white shell, the mother of pearl, *Pinctada mazatlanica*]. These mollusks have been of great sacred value for many of the Pacific Coast Amerindian cultures since the earliest of times.

The remaining 3 Indians that were taken were of great use. They learned the language quickly and helped the Spaniards understand that they were close to an empire of riches to the south. What I have heard is that these 3 natives were poly-lingual and they were valuable to the conquistadors. Their names were Martincillo, Felipillo and Francisquillo. They were even used in the march up to Cajamarca where they captured Atahualpa on his last voyage. These Indians were from Salangome and the account states that they were people of higher quality and manner, of expression and of color. Their women were very white and well decorated and dressed.

Their Chief ruled over almost all the villages and regions on the central and north coast of pre-Columbian Ecuador [The chiefdom of Salangome].

The Samano-Xerex document states the following towns/peoples that these natives reported to be part of this chiefdom;

"...la baya de san mateos [Northern Ecuador, bay of San Mateo, close to the Santiago River] y de nacabez y de tovirisimi y conilope y papagayos y tolona y quisimos [Cojimies] y coaque [where the equatorline passes and just south of Pedernales] y tonconjes y aranypaxaos [Cabo Pasado next to Canoa] y pintagua [could be Tosagua?] y cara lobes [Bahía de Caráquez] xamaxejos [Jaramijo adjacent north of Manta] came [Same] y amotopce docoa..."

We are certain these are the aboriginal names of all these sites. From there to the south, they found an island next to the villages [possibly the Island of Salango] where they located a temple to pray at, made like a tent with rich and beautiful textiles, where there was an image [clay statue maybe] of a woman with a child in her arms. Anyone sick would make a copy of their compromised area [part of their body] in gold and offer it in the temple. With this final information the Samano-Xerex account ends.

The information of the seaworthy skills of these coastal cultures that we have received from archaeologists and historians can be compared to any other civilization that used the seas for commerce. We know that with the balsa found in Ecuador, they were sailing to long distance destinations like pre-Columbian Chile and Mexico. This account of one of Pizarro's captains [Bartolomeo Ruiz] having such an encounter with this native vessel is a strong indication of the importance of Ecuador's coastal cultures for the integration of pre-Columbian South America and Mesoamerica. It is the native vessel described in most detail by the Spaniards when they reach this part of the Pacific of the Americas. A replica of this balsawood sailing vessel can be seen in the Archaeological Museum of the Ministry of Culture in Bahía de Caráquez.

Returning to Pizarro's journeys, we know that Ruiz came back to the camp where the conquistador had stayed, and also that Almagro came in with new fresh recruits. They headed south and reached the bay of San Mateo [St. Matthews]. There, they saw that the thick mangrove coasts [usually on the Pacific side of Colombia], turned into lands which were more populated and cultivated. At Tacanez [Atacames, Ecuador] they found 3,000 houses and their ships were visited by 14 large canoes with warriors armed with gold and silver, showing a gold mask as a banner or ensign and displaying acts of defiance. The Spanish could not capture them because their ships could not reach the sandbars that the canoes quickly paddled towards.

Once Pizarro landed on the shore, there with his soldiers and horses, with the hopes to negotiate and draw back any hostilities, there were 10,000-armed warriors that were eagerly waiting to spring into action. Then they had an experience that the accounts state saved their lives. Out of the book, History of the Conquest of Peru by William Prescott, directly quoted from the Spanish accounts (I translated from Spanish):

"Once they broke formation, one with the other, one of the them fell from their horse; and the Indians, seeing that animal divided into two parts, believing that it is just one thing, felt such fear that they turned their backs and told the others assembled behind them that the creature turned into two, causing much admiration of the incident."

We have to remind our readers that horses were not present in pre-Columbian America at the time of contact with the Spaniards.

So upon seeing that it would not be worth the venture to come into those lands, Pizarro headed back. All the Indians along the way were very menacing and of course knew of the invader's intentions. One of the mistakes that Pizarro made on this second expedition was to cling to the northern coasts of what we know now as Colombia. These are very humid and non-inviting coastal zones. So his men again went through much suffering before finally arriving to the Island of Gallo, near the coast. With this, Pizarro dispatched the ships towards Panama, to get more reinforcements and to tell of the gold they had seen. But many of the soldiers were discontented and sent letters to say that many lives were lost and they had not found the riches that were promised them. Diego de Almagro confiscated these letters, but one got through that was hidden inside a ball of cotton, and it reached many eyes, including those of the Governor.

Seeing this, the governor did not want to help and send resources to Pizarro, so he sent 2 ships to pick up the rest of the men under a cavalier named Tafur. Pizarro received letters from Luque and Almagro to prevail and not to surrender his conquest to another person.

The Famous 13

This is where the famous quote of Pizarro is heard on the Island of Gallo (from the History of the Conquest of Peru, I translated into English).

"So obeying the resolution of his partners and unsheathing his sword, and with notable encouragement, using the point, he drew a line from East to West, and signaling the midday [midday sun, probably south towards the equator], which was part of the news and his course, said: "comrades and friends, [probably pointing on the north side of the line cut in the ground], this is the part where death lies, of work, of famine, of nudity, of the downpours and helplessness; the other side is of pleasure: because this way you go to Panama to be poor, over there to Peru to become rich. Choose as a good Castillian what best fits you."

After he says this, he crosses the line and is followed by Bartholemeo Ruiz, Pedro de Candi, natural of Candia [and others]. The names of these thirteen faithful companions are preserved in the convention made with the Crown two years later, where they are suitably commemorated for their loyalty. Their names should not be omitted in a history of the Conquest of Peru. They were "Bartolome Ruiz, Cristoval de Peralta, Pedro de Candia, Domingo de Soria Luce, Nicolas de Ribera, Francisco de Cuellar, Alonso de Molina, Pedro Alcon, Garcia de Jerez, Anton de Carrion, Alonso Briceño, Martin de Paz, and Joan de la Torre].

Bartholomeo Ruiz was ordered to go back to Panama to coordinate with Luque and Almagro for another expedition. What we know is that Pizarro and these brave men [also the 3 natives of the balsawood vessel discovered by Ruiz earlier] waited on the desolate rock (Isla Gallo) for 5 months, and then constructed a raft that took them to the Island of Gorgona, about 25 leagues to the north. As soon as the very small ship came with provisions, he ordered to go south.

They noticed as they went past Cabo Pasado (next to Canoa/Bahía), the lands became less rugged and larger populations were seen towards the interior. Twenty days passed and they reached the Santa Elena point where the actual Salinas in Ecuador is located, and one of the most westernmost points is as well [along with the Cabo San Lorenzo close to Manta, these points jut out towards the west]. From here they were able to enter the smooth waters of the Gulf of Guayaquil and see many villages and also the Chimborazo [on clear days from the port city of Guayaquil you can see this beautiful volcano, at 6310 meters or 20,702 feet]. On this trip they went all the way to Tumbez [just a few miles south of the actual border Ecuador has with Peru] and beyond, recognizing that there was the foundation of what all the Indians were talking about, a great empire. Actually, the accounts state that he reached the 9th degree latitude south past the region where the city we know now as Trujillo is in Peru.

The historian Prescott states that he returned and sailed north, arriving (first picking up a survivor on the Island of Gorgona) in Panama after 18 months of exploration. At his arrival the governor of that time did not want to support the third expedition. Pedro de los Rios, Prescott writes from the Spanish account:

"He had no desire to build up other states at the expense of his own; nor would he be led to throw away more lives than had already been sacrificed by the cheap display of gold and silver toys and a few Indian sheep!"

Pizarro decided to go to Spain, so he borrowed 1500 ducats from his friends and went to Spain in the spring of 1528 (with Pedro de Candia) to get support from the King, who, after telling him of all the marvels of the new empire, did support him. But it was Queen Isabel who gave Pizarro complete authority of the newly found land (the new Castile) as Governor, Captain General and the rights to the conquest of Peru.

Third Expedition (1530)

Returning to Pizarro's journey through pre-Columbian Ecuador, according to the writings of Miguel Estete (1535), in 1531, Francisco Pizarro left Panama [on other accounts it states on the last days of December of 1530] with his 3 brothers, Gonzalo,

Juan and Hernando Pizarro. They arrived at the bay of San Mateo [Northern Ecuador] in 7 days [Francisco de Jerez says it would take 13 days]. Modern sailboats with good headwind make the journey from Panama to Northern Ecuador in about 5-6 days, around 100 nautical miles daily on a 30-foot boat]. So this prediction was very reasonable.

According to Alonso de Mena (1534) they had left Panama in February 1531 with 250 men and 80 horses. When they landed on the coast of what we know now as northern Ecuador, [Bahía de San Mateo, possibly where we have La Tolita Pampa de Oro in the northern part of the province of Esmeraldas] in Estete's account it states that it was the best land they had discovered in 3 years.

They finally disembarked there with horses (some dying in the sea) and, after they had rested, made headway south to Tacanez [what we know now as Atacames in the province of Esmeraldas]. They passed Cojimies on the march [a beautiful peninsula that now has amazing coconut plantations and beautiful beaches].

Coaque

A village that I am very fond of, it was part of my Grandfather's Hacienda in the last century and now belongs to my uncle. It is a place of much pre-Hispanic and conquistador history, there is actually a pre-Columbian culture named Jama-Coaque after this region of the Pacific Coast of Ecuador.

When Pizarro and his men reached Coaque, they decided to raid the village before coming in to negotiate. The result of earlier events did not favor them, so a surprise attack was the best plan. Miguel Estete (1534) writes:

"The village of Coaque is next to the sea, in a good location, and consists of 400 houses. They say that the equator line passed above the village and that there were fine Emerald mines there, ones that were found in the remains of the village, so abundant and pure, if the people would recognize this, there would be more wealth than all the gold that was found afterwards. The natives of this province were fugitives and indomitable, they left their houses and went to the mountains. The people of Coaque used a scale to measure about half a vara in length (1.5 feet) to weigh gold and silver. It is believed they used this scale only to weigh the precious metals because of their small size and for the other things they must have had another scale". (Miguel de Estete, 1534). [So this account happens in 1531]

Another account from De La Gama y Espinoza, 1534

"The explorers found another city called Colliaque, [Coaque] whose lord also had the same name. The houses of this city [400] were made of very well built stone and their exterior was comprised of grass [possibly the roofs too that went down around to the ground]. Once the Christians arrived to the city the assault began. The lord of Coaque was brave and experienced in war. Being alerted of this case and not having ever seen

a Christian or ever having heard of them, he sent 20,000 castellanos of fine gold with other beautiful jewels. They found in this place a great quantity of emeralds and because the Christians did not know about them they broke and wasted them. In this same place the Christians halted for 6 months, resting and eating" [one of the longest base camps Pizarro took before capturing Atahualpa, the last Inca. Coaque is actually only 1-hour drive time north of Bahía de Caráquez].

Lopez de Gomara in 1552 writes:

"…he sent 20,000 gold pesos to Diego de Almagro so that he could send to Panama and Nicaragua for more men, horses, arms and provisions, and to fertilize the ground of his conquest, which had a bad reputation."

What we know is that the time up to Pizarro's conquest had brought death and few riches. I have always thought if Pizarro did not find Coaque, the name of a new conquistador could have been marked as the one to conquer the rich cultures of the eastern Pacific in South America. We have a special account in Prescott's writings from after they invaded the deserted dwellings and found many gems:

"Some of the jewels that fell into the hands of Pizarro in this neighborhood were as large as a Pigeons egg. Unluckily, his rude followers did not know the value of their prize; and they broke many of them in pieces, pounding them with hammers. They were led to this extraordinary proceeding it is said, by one of the Dominican missionaries, Fray Reginaldo de Pedraza, who assured them that this was the way to prove it was a true emerald, which could not be broken. It is observed that the good father did not subject his own jewels to this wise experiment; but, as the stones, in consequence of it, fell in value, being regarded merely as colored glass, he carried a considerable store of them back to Panama."

"The gold and silver ornaments rifled from the dwellings were brought together and deposited in a common heap. A fifth was deducted for the Crown, and Pizarro distributed the remainder in due proportions among the officers and privates of his company. This was the procedure invariably observed on the like occasions throughout the Conquest. The invaders had embarked in a common adventure. Their interest was common, and to allow everyone to plunder on his own account would only have led to insubordination and perpetual broils. All were required, therefore, on pain of death, to contribute whatever they obtained, whether by bargain or by rapine, to the general stock; and they all were too interested in the execution of the penalty to allow the unhappy culprit, who violated the law, any chance of escape." [This information is retrieved from Pedro Pizarro; Relaciones del Descubrimiento y Conquista de los Reynos del Peru].

The following writings from the account of Miguel de Estete (1535) state that from Coaque going south, they went by land with the ships following closely. They reached Pasao, [Cape of Pasao] giving the troops valor:

"...little by little, they entered a province called Pasao, which is on a mountainous plateau next to the sea. Warlike people and great worshippers of many idols and gods inhabited it. In this village they saw great novelties in rituals that were very detailed; the most notable one was that in the mosques where they bury their dead; they skin the body and burn the meat. The skin was cured like leather. They stuffed (with the meat already out) the bodies with straw, the arms in a cross, and hung them from the roof of the mosque. This is where they were when they entered the plaza, hanging in crosses. They thought these peoples had news of our Lord Jesus Christ and had his image, until they saw and understood what it was. The naturals of this province were fugitives and indomitable (rebel) and so they left their houses and they went to the mountains. These people and the peoples of Coaque used weight and measure in roman scales, about half a yard in length with the number on them and its weight [for counter balancing]. The only thing they saw that was weighed with them was gold and silver, and so it is believed that this was their only use."

"The heads of the deceased were conserved with a certain balsamic substance in this manner: After the cranium was taken out through the back of the neck, leaving the face with its entire form; nose, eyes, eyelashes, eyebrows and hair, the body was cured with certain preparations to conserve the skin so that it did not rot and to preserve the cartilage of the nose and to ensure the hair, eyebrows and eyelashes remained attached to the skin. They gave so many baths in such a manner to conserve the bodies that they ended up reduced to the size of a child just after birth. They were so small that they saved them inside chests within the mosques and they lasted without rotting many years, up to 2 to 3 ages. This is truly a thing of admiration and never seen before. When they laid eyes upon it, they were certain these were the faces of midgets, until they learned the truth of this ritual." [I have personally seen good examples of Tzantzas - of Amazon origin at the Municipal Museum of Guayaquil] http://bit.ly/tzantas.

From the village of Pasao, moving forward on the coast [towards the south], the governor departed with his people [Francisco Pizarro was named Governor of New Castile from 1528 to 1541, including the territories from the border of modern Colombia and Ecuador all the way to Chile] and arrived at a branch of salt water that was one league in width and named Bahía [bay] de Caraque; because this is the name of the province of where it came out."

This is where I was born, Bahía de Caráquez, a beautiful ocean and bay front city on the north-central coast of the province of Manabí. Many of the locals don't know when and who named the bay for the first time, and I hope to translate this chapter into Spanish for their enjoyment and education. The archives, chronicles and accounts are documents that I highly treasure and hope that many will do the same.

Coaque, the village right on the equator line, where later my grandfather's hacienda was built, is where Pizarro made one of his first base camps and found the largest bounty of gold in what we know now as the territories of Ecuador.

Evidence of the Coaque camp

In 1971, an English treasure hunter, Howard Jennings, made various cuts on the right side of the Coaque river mouth and in a hill directly located to the east. Here he found burials of the Jama Coaque culture with funerary remains being:

"copper bells, 2 copper axes, and one golden plate. However, my greatest reward was the find of 2 objects that proved without a doubt that Pizarro visited the site 443 years earlier. There were 2 parts of an iron bridle and I knew that it could only come from one of the 26 horses that Pizarro had with him during the conquest of the Inca Empire" (Moore and Jennings, 1976).

A good friend of mine, the archaeologist Jose Chancay from Guayaquil, told me in 2008, *"all of this evidence is convincing in relation to the temporal settlement established by Pizarro and the interest existent for the discovery of his emplacement."*

I have just recently spoken to Florencio Delgado, a renowned archaeologist in coastal cultures. Along with the North American archaeologist James Zeidler, they are conducting an investigation to dig the actual site of the Pizarro camp.

My hometown Bahía is such a historical city, with the Bahía Culture and the Caras being their proud legacy. It was one of the favorite ports of the Spaniards. It took them only 16 days on horseback to travel from the Andes into Quito. There are so many beautiful historical markers for Bahía de Caráquez that I would like to share one with you, which I thank one of my favorite aunts, Dr. Carmen Dueñas de Anhalzer, a grand historian of our region, for sharing with me.

The Discovery of the Galapagos Islands describes Bahía de Caráquez.

Thomas de Berlanga was a friar of the Dominican Order who discovered the Galapagos Islands on March 10, 1535, and afterward set sail towards the mainland, reaching Bahía de Caráquez. Quoted from his letter to the King taken from "1535. Carta de fray Tomás de Berlanga, obispo de Castilla del Oro al Rey" [where he details the discovery of the Islands], he writes [my translation]:

"Thinking that we were only 20 to 30 leagues away from this land of Peru [remembering Peru was called all the new land discovered from Colombia all the way to Chile] we were content with all the water we had recovered [on the Galapagos Islands] so we made sail and with average weather, we navigated 11 days without seeing land. The pilot and the master of the ship came to tell me that they did not know where we were and there was no more than 1 barrel of water left. I tried to take the altitude of the sun that day and found that we were 3 degrees latitude South, and I saw with the course/direction we had taken, that we would be engulfed by the current rather than reaching land because we were going South. I made the ship turn to the other board [to tack is a normal sailing maneuver, meaning to change direction or to come about behind the wind, from the position they were in, from going south, they changed towards the northeast, our southwest prevailing winds would have helped for this], and we

divided the water in this manner: ½ we gave to the animals and with the other half we made a brew that the wine cask swelled. We were certain that we were not far away from land; we navigated the eight days that the brew lasted. Although we were calmed for two days in which we drank pure wine, we were very thankful when we finally saw land.

We entered in the bay and river of the Caráquez on Friday the 9th of April, and we found the people of the galleon from Nicaragua that had 8 months before set sail from Nicaragua, so we considered our trip good compared to theirs. This bay of the Caráquez was located half a degree latitude South but in the maps it is at 3 degrees. From this bay to Puerto Viejo there were 9 leagues along the coast [south]. This bay [Bay of Bahía] could be one of the most beautiful ports of the world. It could have ships arrive to dock and they could go up 3 to 4 leagues, maybe even more. Adelantado [honorable title] Pedro de Alvarado entered the bay and destroyed a village there that was inhabited by Indians, and disturbed others wherever he went with his men. It is a pity to see the destruction."

We have to note that Pedro de Alvarado conquered Guatemala with great cruelty and entered the Bahía de los Caráquez with one of the greatest fleets that the Southern Seas had seen. It was a direct menace to Pizarro. He had left Nicaragua with one galleon of 300 tons named San Cristobal, another galleon of 170 tons named Santa Clara, another of 50 tons named the San Buenaventura, another ship of 150 tons, a caravel of 60 tons and 3 smaller ships holding 500 well armed soldiers, 227 horses, and Central American Indians [some reports state that it went up to 2,500 natives and also 200 African slaves] that were well trained for war. So the havoc wreaked by Alvarado was considerable. Another account states that right before Alvarado hit Bahía with this formidable force, the Indians had been in rebellion for 20 days and that Hernan Ponce had destroyed 5 villages in the area. Slaughter and the pillage were without precedence for the natives of the bay of the Caráquez.

Finally, the pass of the conquistadors through this area of the Pacific Coast was well documented and I believe there is still many a treasure for history lovers of my country like myself to investigate. For example, at the General Archives of the Indies in Seville, Spain there still is a sad feeling for what happened almost 500 years ago and I wish that the cultural exchange and colonization could have been different, but it is proven that our modern liberal thinking of human justice did not function in that era, specifically in the more "developed" of the European empires. Blessed be the souls of all the humans who lost their lives defending their territories or were turned into slaves in this wretched experience.

For the Crown, in the name of God, it is still happening.

CHAPTER SEVEN

Chocolate of Paradise

During the time I served as Regional Manager for the Pacific Coast of Ecuador for the Ministry of Tourism I helped implement the Ruta del Cacao (the Cacao Route) project. This was meant to attract national and international travelers to visit Cacao Plantations and become familiarized with the techniques of growing Cacao while experiencing the elements of culture and gastronomy.

Nowadays many tourists go to the area of the Route of Cacao, which is from Guayaquil to Cuenca in an area close to Naranjal. It is a very lush area in the plains right before the foothills of the Andes. This area is actually where the Andes are closest to the Pacific Coast in Ecuador. Jumping away from our focus on Cacao for a moment, because of the way Ecuador is geomorphologically positioned jutting out on the northwestern corner of South America, the rain on these mountains, which are so close to the Pacific, must travel a long way out to the Amazon River mouth in Brazil.

Coming back to Ecuador as a Cacao producing nation and a diverse destination to the traveler looking for an authentic experience, especially on the Pacific coast, we will examine the haciendas that produce Cacao. There, one can learn the history and is shown how the plants grow and how the bean is fermented and readied to export. I went on one of these tours to the Hacienda Cañas at the beginning of Agritourism development with the famous Jack Hannah (Jungle Jack), the zoo expert. I saw how many travelers and famous personalities truly enjoyed the experience there.

I also went to an organic plantation where the production was being sent to a factory where it was being used in the manufacturing of Paul Newman's Organic Chocolate. Later I will explain what we are doing with Bo Rinaldi, Edward Berr and Carl Wescott in a historical site of cacao production close to Bahía de Caráquez.

It is important to note that these investigations and implementations of Agritourism projects for Ecuador are mainly for strategic development in the rural territories, which often suffer backwardness development and cause major migration from the countryside to the large cities. Ecuador has suffered mass migration not only to the large cities of our country but mostly now to foreign lands. I have seen personally how family's fathers and wives separate from their children for years. Now the situation is getting better but in the year 2000 we had more than 158,000 Ecuadorians leave the country to look for jobs elsewhere.

The proposal for developing tourism will benefit the rural areas of Ecuador due to the correct timing and general appraisal of Ecuador as an emerging destination with the world famous Galapagos Islands. Chocolate and Roses are very romantic conceptually and also big items of exportation for Ecuador. Why not visit the plantations and the haciendas where your favorite chocolate comes from? Leave your dollars in the areas most needed, so as to support sustainability and our great investment. We need to build on these industries, particularly in the rural areas.

The Cacao boom

Ecuador has had various economic booms throughout its history. First, the straw hat or Jipijapa (erroneously called Panama Hat) was the first grand product of exportation from the mid-18th century up to the mid-19th century. Then the Cacao boom from 1889 to 1926, as Ecuador exported one of the best cocoa beans of the world. There was also Rubber and other products being exported around this time. All together these would not reach the amount of cacao exported - during 1915 it comprised ¾ of all the Ecuadorian exports. After this came the banana boom and the oil production era in the 70's, (of course with prices over 100 USD a barrel, we could say it has returned) and the shrimp farm boom in the 80's and 90's. Now we are experiencing the tourism boom, especially with the baby boomer market coming to see the beautiful beachfront properties in Ecuador.

Thus far, this chapter has been about why we started the Ruta del Cacao as part of the Agritourism (rural) travel offer from the Ministry of Tourism and have touched on the importance of Cacao and the Ruta del Cacao for the Pacific Coast of Ecuador.

Cacao (Kah-Kow) and Chocolate (Cho-ko-lah-te)

Where does chocolate come from? The culprits are the beans (cocoa) from the fruit that live in the cacao pods of the tree with the same name. The famous Swedish Scientist Linnaeus, the father of Botany, named this species *Theobroma cacao*, which means in Greek "*Food of the Gods*". Cacao was cultivated by the pre-Columbian cultures of the tropical South and Central America thousands of years ago (the Mayans 1500 yrs. ago).

The original native strain of Cacao, scientists declare, comes from the upper Amazon of Ecuador and Colombia. This area is considered the center of origin of Cacao. Early man involved in tropical agriculture spread it and introduced it into Central America. Please read "*Cacao domestication I: the origin of the cacao cultivated by the Mayas*".

Cacao Beans

Christopher Columbus discovered for the Old World the Cacao Bean on his fourth visit to the New World. Below is a written account by one of Christopher's sons, Fernando, *"They seemed to hold these almonds at a great price; for when they were brought on board the ship together with their goods, I observed that when any of these almonds fell, they all stooped to pick it up, as if an eye had fallen".*

This account was near the now known territories of Honduras when Columbus robbed the cargo of a Mayan trader.

How much was the bean really worth then? We know that during the times of the Aztec ruler Montezuma, one slave was worth 1,100 beans and a mule 50 beans.

Was there a potential of wealth for anyone who lived in the Amerindian territories of the tropical humid zone to grow a tree in their parcel of land? Probably, due to actual agricultural extensions that exist in Central and South America.

Did the nobles only grow it? Probably not. History books say Montezuma had great quantities of it stored. And now? Numerous companies capitalize on our resources. In 2003, Mars Inc. alone had sales for over 8 billion United States dollars. Discovering cacao was one of the greatest finds of the New World.

Fernando Gonzalez de Oviedo, a Spanish writer and colonist, details many of the events that run from 1492 to 1549 in his most famous book *General and Natural History of the Indies, Islands, Mainland and Ocean Sea* (the first text printing of the first part was done in 1535, the second part was interrupted by his death in 1557, the full text was printed in 1851 and 1855). I translated his writing about cacao into English:

"... Each cob has about 20 and 30 almonds. This is how the fruit ripens, it juices around the pulp between the almonds and they stay loose in this box, where they are taken out and saved. They have the same price estimation that the Christians and other peoples have for gold and coin, because this is what these almonds are worth to them [the natives]. With them they buy everything. In the province of Nicaragua; a rabbit is worth 10 of these almonds and for 4 almonds they give you 8 jugs of excellent fruit that they call munongapot [a very sweet fruit]. A slave is worth 100 of these almonds more or less, according to the will of the contracting parties. In these lands there are women that give price for their bodies, the same as public prostitutes for the Christians (such a woman they call guatepol, which is the same as prostitute). Whoever wants them for their lustful use; they have to give them a row of 8 to 10 almonds, however he and she agree. Coin does not flow between these people; nothing is bought or sold in the same manner as the Christians with doubloons or ducats. Even in those almonds there are frauds to trick one another and to mix in false or empty ones. This is done by taking off the shell that these almonds have, just like ours, and filling them with dirt or any other thing, and then closing it so subtly that you don't know. To understand that one is being swindled, when you count them, you feel them one by one, putting your index finger next to your thumb on each one. Even if the false one is filled, you can find out through sense of touch, as it does not feel the same as a real one.

But first I want to speak of the manner in which they raise and cultivate these trees. The trees are planted in fertile earth, in sites where water is near so they can water them regularly. They are planted in lines at intervals of 10 to 12 feet, so they can feed off the terrain better. The trees grow and reach out in such a manner that below them everything is in shade and the sun cannot see the earth, but only in a few areas between the branches. In some years the sun will scald the fruit in such a manner that the fruit comes out empty or does not ripen and it is lost. To remedy this, they put other trees that the Indians call Yaguaguyt in between the groves. These grow almost double the size of the cacao ones and shelter them from the sun, making shade with their branches and leaves. They grow straight up for this purpose; these trees live much longer than the cacao and never rot or fall, and it is one of the best kinds of wood known.

The fruit of the cacao has two other names, coco and cacagual. From February up to the end of April, once they harvest the cobs and remove the almonds, they put them to the sun they are cured and used to make the special drink. When these almonds are toasted, in the same manner as hazelnuts, they can be ground up to create the beverage. A little bixa [red pigment from the achiote fruit] is then added to make it red. After it is finely ground in a grinding stone, a little water is added to it and stirred to create a thick paste. This batter can be saved and made into dough. It has to sit for 4 or 5 hours at least to be good, and is better if made in the morning to wait to drink it until the night, and is even better the next day. It can be stored for 5 to 6 days.

This paste is also put on ones cheek and chin and over the nose. This makes it look like they are covered in mud or clay; sometimes it is very red because they mix it with Bixa. Men attract women with this substance spread over their faces, the more the better. This is the way they go to the market or to do whatever else they want. From time to time they also suck the cocoa oil by taking it little by little on their finger. The Christians consider this dirty, but to these peoples it does not appear disgusting, it actually sustains them. The substance quenches their thirst and hunger, protects them from the sun and air, and is good for the skin on their faces. It has been said that Indians who drink cacao on an empty stomach will not be harmed, even if that day they were bit by a poisonous snake, which there are many in this land, they would be in no danger of dying.

To drink this they put a quantity of 30 ground almonds in a quart of water and dilute it with the hand, creating a thin batter. They then take another cup to drink from and trickle liquid from the cacao cup into it from about 2 hand spans in height. This raises foam to the top and this is how they drink it. It looks like they are drinking vegetable residues, so it appears disgusting to those that have not had this drink. But to those who use it, it appears good; it has a nice flavor and is a very healthy beverage. The foam stays on the lips and around the mouth, and when it is red (with bixa) it is horrendous looking, because it looks like blood, and when it doesn't have bixa it is brown, but in both cases it is a dirty sight. The Christians see it as very beneficial and the Indians appreciate this. They use it for a state or chiefdom, and they say it is the best thing in the world and worthy of estimation."

Balsawood Sailing Vessel Replica

Hernando Cortez leading the Mesoamerican conquistador group and his search for gold wrote much of the history of the first chocolate use. Cortez first wrote about chocolate in 1518 and after conquering the Aztecs, returned to the royal court of King Charles V in 1528 carrying gifts. One of these gifts was cacao (cocoa beans) from the territory that is now known as Mexico. Accounts say that the emperor Montezuma stated: *"The divine drink builds up resistance and fights fatigue. A cup of this precious drink [cocoa] permits a man to walk for a whole day without food."*

Montezuma reigned from 1502 to 1520. From the written accounts there are descriptions of how Montezuma gave this drink to the Spaniards. They say the drink was mixed with water and chili peppers, probably not to the liking of the conquistadors, who most likely had to mix in some sweetness from the sugar cane or honey to better suit it for their taste buds.

Returning to the history, of the original strains of Cacao from the now known territories of Ecuador, we ask the question, "but how was it brought over to Central America"? One of the theories is that man was partially responsible through land-based trade, but more likely it was distributed through maritime trade. Here in this area we have balsawood from the balsa tree (*Ochroma pyramidale*). In modern times, since the beginning of the last century, balsawood has been used for building light aircrafts, airplane models and even now is used partially in the blades of wind turbines. It is a very light wood, and is considered the softest hardwood. Ecuador supplies 95% of all the balsa to the world.

The logs of this tree are very buoyant and were used mostly during the times of the Bahía (500 BC to 500 AD) and Manteño culture (500 to around 1534 AD) for the base of sailing vessels. In 1947, Thor Heyerdahl, the Norwegian adventurer and scientist, used the balsa logs for his ship, the Kon Tiki that sailed from Peru to Polynesia.

As I write in the "*The Magic of the Red Spiny Oyster*", which is the following chapter of this book, these Ecuadorian maritime groups were excellent navigators. I point out that the pre-Columbian sea navigation for the dissemination of tropical crop plants in the Americas along the Pacific coast has been underestimated. Wolters (1999) suggests that the Valdivia culture (3500 – 1600 B.C.), and all successive cultures in western Ecuador, conducted coastal shipping to Peru, Middle America, and southern Mexico from 2200 to 1450 B.C. Presumably, crop plant export occurred from western Ecuador to Peru, Middle America (sweet manioc, Annona cherimola, Carica papaya, early great-grained corn) and to Mexico (tobacco and cacao).

Up until this date, the cultures of the Pacific coast of Ecuador have not received the credit or recognition they deserve in mainstream historical and global perception. The ancient civilizations were based upon incredible maritime navigational skills, traveling aboard balsawood sailing vessels as far north as Mexico and as far south as Chile. As I have mentioned before, I cannot even imagine the network and connectivity they had throughout time. You will find more on this subject in the chapter called "The Magic of the Red Spiny Oyster".

A piece of history mostly forgotten is Francisco Pizarro's journey through Ecuador. It is of great importance to know about the written accounts of Francisco Pizarro's first landings, (conquistador of the last Inca Empire and ruler) and the early descriptions of the coastal region. There is much more detail on this in the section on Pizarro's journey through the coast of Ecuador.

The first voyages of Pizarro to look for El Dorado (the golden city) were unmistakably filled with hardships, such as loosing men to disease, war with the Indians and hunger. Some of the journeys he took south of Panama into the territories now known as Colombia and Ecuador, are when we first hear stories about soldiers surviving on maize, potatoes (sweet) and wild cocoa beans.

Since the time of contact with the New World, the Spaniards said cacao was a divine source of nutrition and also of financial incumbency. Around 1580, cocoa had gotten widespread attention in Spain and then around the world. Chocolate was initially brought to the United States for medicinal purposes and sold in apothecaries. In 1765, Harvard-educated Dr. John Baker and Irish immigrant John Hannon opened a small shop inside a cocoa mill along the banks of a river outside Boston. Cocoa was here to stay!

Once Spain had dominated the trade of Cacao during the 16th century, small plantations started to spring up in coastal Ecuador in the 1600's. According to many sources and stated directly from ANECACAO (National Association of Cacao Exporters-Ecuador), this cacao was a special strain that received world attention due to its typical floral aroma, that today we call Arriba or Nacional. A royal decree in 1789 permitted the exportation of Cacao through Guayaquil and not the Port of Callao [Peru]. This was very helpful for Ecuador's amazing growth in production of this tasty product. During the last decade of the 19th century, Ecuador was the largest producer of Cacao in the world. Afterwards Brazil took its place.

The Haciendas

My aunt, Dr. Carmen Dueñas, is the author of many books on the history of Manabí (province where Bahía de Caráquez was a major port and where I am originally from) and also a lifetime referral source for many of my investigations for the Pacific Coast of Ecuador. She states:

"It would be only in the latter half of the 19th Century that the cacao haciendas are consolidated in the province, mainly in the valley of Chone. This production is exported from the port of Bahía de Caráquez. According to the Commercial and Agricultural Guide of 1909, back in 1899, there was an existence of a total of 6,523,170 cacao trees in the province, the majority of which was found in Chone. The biggest properties belonged to Juan Alvarez del Barco in Hacienda La Clemencia, with 100,000 cacao trees and the numerous properties of Juan Jose Polit with a total of 320,000 trees." (Dueñas de Anhalzer, C. 1986)

Published in 1913, Juan B. Ceriola in his book, *Manabí a la Vista*, gives a detailed description about Juan Polit and the Providencia (very famous cacao plantation owner). This Hacienda was a model for all of Ecuador at that time. This is a direct quote I have translated from the book:

"Its foundation dates back to 1891, when he bought the main hacienda called Providencia. The extension of the area is around 2000 hectares and contained 320,000 cacao trees, of which 200,000 were from 5 to 15 years old. He has planted in a new style with long distances between the trees. This modern system uses a distance of 5m (15ft) to 15m (45 ft.) under the shadow of the Palo Prieto and Bucare Tree. All of the orchards are lined by small streams and are divided from the Garrapata Rios and the Chagualu.

The last harvest of cacao (cocoa bean) was 250,000 lbs. (1908) according to the Accounting Books of the Hacienda. The Hacienda also has 100,000 Rubber trees, which were planted about 9 years ago. Also there are from 60,000 to 80,000 thousand Coffee trees. The estate of the Hacienda possesses 3 valorous buildings. The first one is the owner's house, office and warehouses. The second one is the housing compound of the employees of the hacienda and also the drying area for cacao, made of incorruptible wood and steel that measure 90 meters (295 ft.) long and 10 meters (32 ft.) wide. The third building is the housing compound of the laborers.

The cacao produced on these estates has obtained the highest price in the markets of Guayaquil, New York, London, Hamburg and Genova. The brand J.P. is the one used and the one present in the Commercial Magazines of those plazas.

If there was to be a model plantation for the practical study of agriculture in the province of Manabí, there would be no other better than this hacienda. The old cultivators of cacao in Ecuador have the erroneous belief that a larger number of trees would give more production. So this was the situation for many of them, to plant the most trees in smaller extensions of land and to let them grow with all the development nature has to offer. This has resulted in the planting areas becoming immense forests with dense foliage on the trees that make it difficult and very costly to collect the precious bean, and have also led to the sterile progressiveness of the land, caused by the crowding or agglomeration of the plantings. In that way, the cultivation of the cacao is seasonal. Up until now, there has been just a few owners that have tried the formation of new sown land, following the scientific procedures of pruning and planting each bush a good distance one from another. In this manner, when they are developed you have bushes instead of trees that slightly touch each other's branches at about 5 to 6 meters distance between each plant.

The rich owner Don (out of respect) Juan Polit has been one of the first ones, maybe the first one in the Province of Manabí, to put into practice the procedures we speak about. He has obtained flattering results like we see in the photographs that illustrate these pages, which were taken from his hacienda Providencia in the Canton Chone. In these new crops of cacao, the very well organized workers of Mr. Polit do not need to use the bothersome hoop poles used for tall trees, because his are only bushes. Within the reach of their hands are abundant harvests of cacao pods, which have developed splendidly. Cacao that has been planted according to the old custom, with very close proximity of the plants, generally about less than 3 meters of distance, causes gradual but progressive sterility of the land, which brings about reduction and degeneration of the harvests. Mr. Polit has emended this method with a flattering success. He cut down 1 tree between every 2 of the old trees planted and trimmed down the ones that were left standing so that at least 2 main trunks would serve as stalks. What was the result? Abundant harvests in contrast to the last harvests of other haciendas that have lower productions due to the planting style we talked about before. That is why the Hacienda Providencia is a model of organization, energy, labor and work. Lately, it has been visited by farmers that have gone there to see for themselves the results Mr. Polit has obtained in his large plantations (which also are highlighted by his rubber plantation).

Various peoples have now begun to follow the methods set by Don Juan Polit, who we owe much to for the agricultural improvements of the province and who generously spreads his knowledge of the subject we are dealing with. The experience confirms the efficiency of the method employed by Mr. Don Juan Polit with the surprising results obtained in his hacienda "Providencia", which is serving beneficially as a model finca in the Province of Manabí." (Ceriola, Juan 1913)

The Economics of Cocoa

Some of the cantones (geopolitical districts smaller than a province) had more than 30% of their population dependent on cacao production back in 1902. Just in the province of Manabí alone there were 1,440 Cacao estates that had 6.5 million trees and produced 4,000,000 lbs. of cocoa beans in that year. In Manabí, the largest producers were in Chone, very close to Bahía de Caráquez, where the majority of the product was exported.

According to the book, *Social and Economic Reform in Ecuador: Life and Work in Guayaquil,* by Ronn F. Pineo, the coastal region produced significant quantities of Cacao. For example, in 1900 there were 4827 large Cacao estates with 58 million trees. Back then there were only five provinces, Guayas, Manabí, Esmeraldas, Los Rios and El Oro.

The Ecuadorian National Agriculture and Livestock Census (for the year 2000) states that in the province of Manabí there are 101,000 hectares of cacao, of which 48% pertain to coops or associations. Years ago cacao areas were measured by the number of trees from a plantation or region. Nowadays, the cacao area is measured in hectares.

For comparison with the early XIX Century way of measuring the extension of cacao production, according to Esteves (2011), "If we need to put an approximate number on the amount of trees in production, we should multiply the number of hectares by the average number of planted trees per hectare (which is approximate 1000 cacao trees per hectare). This means that in this past decade the amount of trees in Manabí numbered around 100 million trees. However, this is only an approximate number, since many plantations in Manabí are old and have a low population of cacao trees per hectare".

In the 1920s, the exportation of the Cocoa bean from Ecuador suffered its biggest fall due to the spread of diseases that decimated the crop and a declining market and transport system from the consequences of World War I. In the 1960s, Ecuador started to increase its production by means of the Agrarian Reform the government initiated in 1964. This reform called for vacant land to be redistributed to native farmers and by 1973 there was a total of 213,000 hectares (about 526,000 acres) planted with Cacao.

In 2011, the International Cocoa Organization stated that "prices have almost doubled in five years, from about $1,540 USD per ton in 2005 to $3,135 USD per ton in 2010. In response to this, the cocoa and chocolate industry and most of the major cocoa producing nations have planned significant increases in their production".

Almost 45 percent of the world's cocoa is grown along Africa's Ivory Coast, where average annual yield has been around 1.3 million tons.

On January 9, 2012, ANECACAO reported that there were 415,000 hectares (1,025,487 acres) of Cacao planted in this country, producing 150,000 metric tons of beans with an average price of 2,020 USD per metric ton, generating 350 million USD. According to Rainforest Alliance, certification of cocoa farms began in Ecuador in 1997. Sales of certified cocoa soared to $16.75 million last year, from $4.5 million in 2007. Ecuador harvests 75% of the world's premium crop.

As a destination for travelers who want to partake in visiting plantations and/or fincas, Ecuador is blessed with natural environments and grand luminosity for spectacular plant growth that has led to major production in many areas. You can visit large plantations, co-op community plantations and small family fincas, which provide a genuine experience and are supported through Agritourism. So a USP (Unique Selling Proposition) in this category of travel is definitely seeing the plantations with naturally grown Cacao and the process to make chocolate.

Planting with nature

One of these areas for Ecuador is the Chone area, inside the bay from Bahía de Caráquez. The upper water shed area is incredibly rich for agriculture and historically was one of the best for the province of Manabí. It's a beautiful ride bordering the bay towards this agricultural area; you pass Isla Corazon, which is an outstanding place for marine bird watching and also the La Segua wetlands, which also are an incredible area for viewing migratory bird species. Nestled in a cove of a mountain range, the best land in Chone for Cacao is found here.

In Bahía, we are talking with a couple of friends from the United States to once again transform the area into a great Cacao producing site. There is a small cocoa bean co-op collecting point, which does not produce chocolate. They have small machines there that are not working, plus we need to bring them an expert or a chocolatier to help them get off the ground. We need to change this by developing a chocolate production system so that the 400 families that bring their beans there can gain more income from their raw cacao (usually the beans are sold to Nestle or to a company in Guayaquil that sends them to Europe). Nowadays, even though we have a lot of visitors south of Guayaquil to the plantations that produce Cacao such as the Hacienda Cañas and others, there is still not enough attention paid by the inbound tour operators (which sell these land programs) and the market in general to create an alluring global perspective of Ecuador's modern and historical production of this highly demanded and precious product.

My goal is to bring cacao production back into the area of Chone and help the communities export directly to the major markets of the world. Let us restore the

Hacienda Providencia and revive the Chocolate of Paradise for everyone to savor as part of Ecuador's Ruta del Cacao. The route that we take is the one we build.

***We would like to thank Luis and Roberto Andrade
for showing us the Centennial Cacao Hacienda of
La Providencia in Chone.***

Cacao Plants and Pods
Photos by Reg Galbraith

CHAPTER EIGHT

The Magic of the Red Spiny Oyster

I spent my childhood and up to 9th grade living in the United States, and as I said in an earlier chapter of this book, we never learned about the true North American Indian and their history. Only the forging of the nation through the Pilgrims, and the Revolutionary and Civil Wars were recorded in my hard drive as the earliest events I learned about. Hopefully times have changed and the sons and daughters of my friends have an opportunity to be amazed by the fascinating pre-Colonial history that existed there.

This is the story I want tell you, starting with the hunter gatherer nomadic groups in our pre-Columbian territories of Ecuador with dates earlier than the 10,000 BP mark. It is believed that many of them started crossing from North America to South America at about 13,000 B.P, maybe even back to 15,000 BP. We know that many of the ancient sites that could have evidenced human activity are underwater today through paleo-oceanographic studies. The oceans began to rise dramatically during this period, so the easiest way of migration was along the coastline. Again, much of the very early evidence could be underwater. The El Inga site and the Punin skeleton are probably the Ecuadorian Andes earliest evidence of man. Using common sense, we know that the Andean and Coastal nomads hunted the last Pleistocene megafauna.

We have proof that the megafauna did exist on the Pacific Coast in the now known territories of Ecuador. About 2 years ago in the area I live in (Bahía de Caráquez) there was a Mastodon discovered (could be Stegomastodon waringi or Cuvieronius hyodon). A friend of mine, the archaeologist Erick Lopez of the Universidad Estatal Península de Santa Elena on the southern coast of Ecuador, helped create the Paleontological Museum that was inaugurated in 2008. This after they uncovered a Giant Sloth (Megaterium americanum) when workers from a petroleum company found part of the bones in some sort of tar pit. We know from investigations led by Emily Lindsey of UC at Berkeley, that this animal had died next to a lagoon or river meander, and afterwards the tar had oozed out of rocks in a Eocene deposit right next to where the bones lay, preserving them.

We can predict that food was readily available for the hunter-gatherers in nomadic groups that arrived first in the region and all the way up until the existence of Las Vegas. Not the gambling Las Vegas, but our first culture. After the over killing and the extinction of the megafauna, the groups started to center on marine and land species. The coastline migrations of peoples were accentuated to settlements where the best protected bays and fishing grounds were located and where they had protection from environmental threats like flooding and other factors.

Evidence of the earliest cultures on the Pacific Coast was shown to me by one of my favorite Archaeologists and friend that has worked here, Karen Stothert. I met her in the mid-1990s after I rediscovered Chirije for a new expression of travel that I named Eco-Cultural Tourism. She had earned her Ph.D. at Yale University in 1974 and worked in Ecuador during that same decade. The National Congress of Ecuador awarded her an honor for her contributions to cultural identity in 1997.

In all the outstanding work Dr. Stothert has done in Ecuador I believe the investigation with the Las Vegas Culture in the Santa Elena province of Southern Coastal Ecuador [3.5 hours south of Bahía], is the most relevant. This culture was discovered by E.P. Lanning in 1967, but thoroughly investigated in detail by Karen in the late 70s until present. She speaks almost perfect Spanish, and has helped many other archaeologists that have investigated the cultures here in Ecuador.

One of the prized discoveries was the "Ancient Lovers of Sumpa" burial. In 1977, Karen Stothert was asked by the late Olaf Holm (then the director of the Anthropological Museum of the Central Bank Museum, who also I made contact with for Chirije) to excavate a pre-ceramic site in the peninsula of Santa Elena. She found 200 skeletons buried between 8,000 and 6,700 years before present (B.P.). One of the tombs that were found had two embracing skeletons, a woman and a man that died approximately 7000 B.P, thus the name of the burial and the museum. From her work with paleobotanical remains of the Las Vegas culture, Stothert states, "the late Vegans were using maize (Zea mays, this cereal plant-corn dried by sun grinded produced flour) at 7000 years B.P.".

Her work was important in that it came right as Ecuador's communities started recognizing their past with this new information. She states from her report to the Society for American Archaeology:

"In the late 1970s and 1980s the indigenous movement in Ecuador and the ideology of the left contributed to the development of the connection between the existing campesino communities of the coast and their aboriginal and archaeological past. For example, in the town of Valdivia a celebration of "6,000 years of Valdivia" became, the next year, a celebration of 6,001 years, and then 6,002 years. A small museum celebrating the ethnic identity of the people of the Valley of Chanduy with ethnographic, historical, and archaeological materials was opened at an important Valdivia archaeological site. In the town of Agua Blanca archaeologists Colin McEwan and María Isabel Silva began working together with the residents in an integrated program of archaeological research and community development, making it possible for the community, which once survived by making charcoal from the forest and digging up ruins to sell ancient artifacts, to find a new, sustainable economic focus in Eco cultural tourism."

With the Real Alto, Agua Blanca, Amantes de Sumpa onsite museums and of course what I am trying to do at Chirije, there has been a construction of a new level of ethnic pride that was missing since the Spaniards colonized the Pacific Coast. This is true with new information from scientists and people who, by making discoveries and the building of good will, interlace a community asset of their cultural identities with their unknown ancestral heritage.

There is still so much more to investigate and to assert value to in Ecuador and especially on the Pacific Coast. We need more funds for the many sites that require further investigation, like Chirije. There are so many sites already, just in our province alone there were 800 archaeological sites registered in inventory by the Instituto Nacional de Patrimonio Cultural (National Heritage Institute). There are spectacular sites like Chirije and one close by called Japoto, amongst others. I wish at some point to bring in Karen to the La Dibujada, a site near Chone (only an hour away from Bahía). I have invited her but the circumstances of her work limit her to only the most extraordinary tasks that she is working on.

La Dibujada means "The drawing". This is a site I promoted when I was director of tourism for the Manabí province (2000) that I was told about by Gina Molina, a great team player. A cave with petroglyphs inside a beautiful green forest made it seem like the site pertained to the pre-ceramic period. I had the funds to help bring the site to life, but was negated by a government official in a higher rank than I was, saying that this was a project for the Universities and the Ministry of Tourism needed not initiate nor offer help. In the project, apart from all the multi-components for community capacity building, trails and infrastructure, I had specified that we needed to contract a good archaeologist to research the first levels of occupation (specially for C-14 dates) at the bottom of the cave. With that we could start preparing the design and the script for interpretation that the site needed, so it could begin being visited. This included an onsite museum, etc. Chone, which has nothing prepared for Tourism (but has so much potential) could have had this product already formed (it has been 10 years since I started pushing for this). The area outside the city is marvelously appreciable for the best agriculture in the province. The incredible history of cocoa bean production used in chocolate is one element of its Agritourism visitation portfolio that would be amazing. I am trying to work with a couple of partners on this. Not being able to complete a dream with the archaeological project of La Dibujada was frustrating.

Luckily, I was blessed to have the idea of the Ruta del Spondylus Bi-National plan with Peru; this means if this plan is executed correctly, La Dibujada and many other sites are on the list to become known to Ecuador and the world as sacred sites within sacred landscapes. Let's hope the future authorities in tourism and cultural heritage construe the dedicated time necessary for this.

Spondylus (The Sacred Pacific Red Spiny Oyster)

Ecuador's pre-Colombian past outdates the Incas by thousands of years. On the coast of Ecuador, cultures were thriving as early as 9,000 B.C. Some of the later cultures like the Bahía and the Manteño were among the most maritime of all. These could have been the "Phoenicians of the Americas", sailing on Ecuadorian balsawood vessels all the way north to Mexico and as far south as Chile, trading one of the most important sacred items of all time, "The Red Spondylus Shell". This shell was also known as "Mullu" in Quechua (the native language in much of the Andes).

On October 26, 1998, the presidents of Peru and Ecuador met in Brasilia to sign a peace agreement ending over 50 years of often-armed border dispute. In his speech at Brasilia, Ecuadorian President Jamil Mahuad made the first public reference to Spondylus in the context of the new integration between our country and Peru. Addressing Peruvian President Alberto Fujimori, he said "The history of our countries is much closer and tighter than the problems of the last decades; when the Lord of Sipán was found, he had among his ornaments gold, silver, and the Spondylus shell (*Spondylus princeps*), which is only found in Ecuador" [we know that Spondylus has wider habitat, but it flourishes magnificently off the waters of this country].

Spondylus is also known as the Red Pacific Thorny Oyster; however, it is more closely related to scallops than oysters. From recent studies it has been observed that the two species found in Ecuador, *Spondylus princeps* and *Spondylus calcifer* are found from about 12 to 60 feet deep. Up to the juvenile stage they are mobile, and afterwards they adhere themselves to rocks.

This shell was one of the most demanded items in pre-Hispanic times, traded and highly valued by the Ecuadorian Andean and Peruvian Chiefdoms. They have been found in almost all of the most important archaeological discoveries of the west coast of South America, for example in the tomb of the Lord of Sipán in northern Peru. The shell has also been found in Mesoamerica and it is proven scientifically that the route of trade was extended to these areas. Some scientists say that the demand from the Peruvian Chiefdoms was so high that maybe they overfished the Ecuadorian beds and had to extend their fishing/diving areas up to the territories of pre-Columbian Mexico.

*Ceremonial cup from Chirije inserted in a beautiful
red spiny oyster or Spondylus shell*

For generations upon generations of divers, the harvesting of this primary and sacred product existed up until the Spaniards imposed their economic system and culture on the natives. I cite from Pablo-Martin's work "*En Busca del Spondylus, Rutas y Simbolismo*" the following chant that was sung by the natives 100 years after the contact, when the importance of the shell and diving for it disappeared:

> "*Muchachos a trabajar [Lads, to work],*
> *si quieren tener mujer [if you want to have a woman]*
> *pues no la han de mantener [well you won't be able to maintain them],*
> *con las conchitas del mar [with the shells of the sea].*"

English Map of Ruta del Spondylus

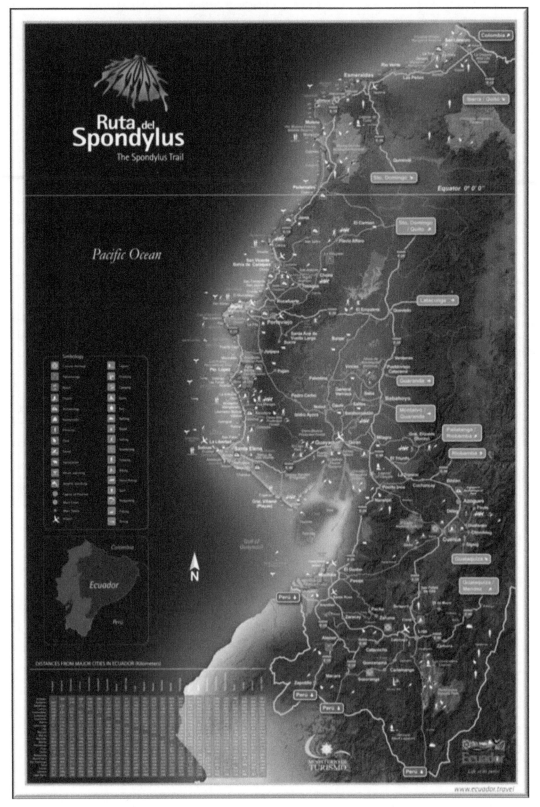

Map Courtesy of Ministry of Tourism of Ecuador
Graphic Artist: Chino Flores

Another reason why mass free-diving on the coast disappeared is that the Spaniards forced the natives to look for pearls. As soon as the shoals were fished out they would push them to more depths, probably out to 100 feet deep. Imagine doing this with only one breath of air, not all could, and old archives say that predators killed most of the divers. The line of many of the generations of specialized divers came to a halt. As I said earlier, the economic importance of the shell between the coastal cultures of pre-Columbian Ecuador, the Amerindian Chiefdoms and Incan empire gave way to the European economic mode of life.

Reviving the Ruta del Spondylus

The Ruta (route) del Spondylus was originally the trade route utilized by our ancestors. I brought it back into use, as symbol for coastal and national pride and as the base for this fabulous tourism project. It was a pretty big sacrifice for me, taking away from my quality family time. With 2 small cute kids it really hit me (especially after the time I had invested being the first director for Ecuador's private and public tourism promotion board), I hope I am kind of done with this - which is why I get up at dawn to write this book.

The idea of creating the Ruta del Spondylus came about when I was the director for the Pacific Coast for the Ministry of Tourism in the year 2002. I was attending the BITE, a travel business-to-business event in Cuenca, Ecuador. I was acting as a supervising official for a group of Peruvian tour operators and, as I was immersed in trying to start development and promote the cultural attractions of the coast, I realized the richness of the ancient civilizations, and put two and two together.

First, the rich pre-Hispanic history of both pre-Columbian Peru and Ecuador is very intertwined and integrated with the use of the Spondylus seashell. Second, the tourism attractions symbolize the very ancient civilizations of Ecuador, and combined with the large and beautiful archaeological sites of northern Peru make for an incredible multi destination product. I saw that the hotel sector of the beaches in northern Peru and of the Ecuadorian coast had very low yearly occupation levels. I noticed the grand positioning of Peru in archaeology, and yet our ancestral heritage sites were not well known. I have to say that even though Peru, Mexico and most of Mesoamerica have monumental archaeological sites, which you can still see, built in stone and whose remains have weathered through time, so does Ecuador. Since our sites are not comprised of stone (bases of housing, temples, yes), it is so rich here in biodiversity, forests, and wood that all the settlements (except for the few years of the Inca invasion in these territories leaving stone structures, like Ingapirca near Cuenca) have decayed over time.

I have a base of specific information from our scientists about most of our coastal sites, concluding that we had a long and continuous occupation from our ancient cultures; from very early stages of human settlements in the Americas all the way up to contact (with the Conquistadors). They had been excellent navigators, skillful farmers, hunters and craftsmen. Dr. Jean Francois Bouchard, archaeologist and professor of pre-Columbian art/history for the Louvre Museum of Paris, told me once that the ceramic artwork during the Chorrera culture (1500 B.C to 500 B.C.) was as beautiful as any Greek ceramic.

It was great to try and see how far I could go with this project, like any grand challenge. I passed this idea to a group of Peruvian agencies and they responded positively. On this trip I met a delightful personality that also catalyzed my passion for this project. His name is Henning A. Nilsen, editor of the travel magazine "Reiser & Ferie" Norwegian travel magazine (until retirement 2002). He has travelled to approximately 80 different countries all over the globe. We went to see the places in Manabí and Chirije which showed him the potential for archaeological tourism on the Ruta del Spondylus [which was not named yet, as the project was still on the drawing board] and of course, I was thrilled with the stories he had and also of his meeting with Thor Heyerdahl and the work he had done in Northern Peru. Henning liked the coast of Ecuador so much; he decided to settle here and now is the proud owner of the Faro Escandinavo, a nice boutique hotel south of Bahía.

Now back to the historical process of the Ruta del Spondylus. In 2004, I had written up the project proposal and passed it on to the Peruvian government through Michele Levi, our foreign spokesperson. The minister of tourism of that time was Gladys El Juri, a very successful businesswoman from Cuenca. I have much gratitude for her.

Apart from the help I had from the Ministers of Tourism, Gladys El Juri and others, I had much support from the Minister Veronica Sion (now Minister of Industries 20120). I was appointed by Veronica director of the national priority project Ruta del Spondylus, and worked with Maria del Carmen Burneo and her consulting firm. This was from summer to fall of 2008.

On October 27, 2008, Veronica Sion, Minister of Tourism of Ecuador, signed with Mercedes Araoz, Minister of Foreign Commerce and Tourism of Peru, (another lovely and intelligent woman) a Memorandum of Understanding to develop the Spondylus Route as a bi-national project.

I had great collaboration with many technicians for the final project of the Ruta del Spondylus in 2008. One of them was Amos Bien, a pioneer of world sustainable tourism and a good friend. In the executive summary of the main document of the final plan that I wrote and translated it states:

The Ruta del Spondylus (The Spondylus Trail) is a Project developed in 2008 by the Ministry of Tourism as part of the Strategic Plan for Sustainable Tourism Development PLANDETUR 2020.

The Spondylus princeps or Red thorny oyster, was a pre-Columbian symbol of the cultural and natural richness of the coast, belonging to a sacred trade with most of the complex societies of the northwestern coast of South America (also there is evidence that the Balsa sailing vessel and the ancient maritime coastal cultures would trade this shell up north to Mexico and south to Chile). Today this symbol represents the same richness and is the icon and presentation to the region towards national and international tourism through the Ruta del Spondylus (The Spondylus Trail).

The design and implementation of the Spondylus Trail (Ruta del Spondylus) of Ecuador, has a central objective to catalyze sustainable tourism and to contribute in a direct and most effective way to community development. This will be accomplished within the framework of Sustainable Tourism, which the Ruta del Spondylus (Spondylus Trail) bases itself on, adding the restoration of value of the cultural, historical and archaeological heritage with the strengthening of natural resources and attractions that will generate more dynamic local economies. With this in mind, the rest of the foundation is based upon environmental conservation, respect to the social and cultural fabric and the best management practices.

The Spondylus Trail is based on 4 Pillars of incidence and actions, and each one of these is associated with requirements that pertain to product development, capacity building and development in infrastructure and promotion. The 4 strategic pillars are:

1. *The restoration of value of the historical, cultural and archaeological heritage in relation to the ancient peoples and the Spondylus Shell.*

2. *Sustainable Tourism: Conserving the environment with local based participation, with business responsibility, social opportunity and respect to the communities settled in these areas.*

3. *To develop and supply services with excellence, based on the best managerial, environmental, social and business practices.*

4. *Development of Gastronomical and Handicraft activities based on traditions and special products for each province.*

The Spondylus Shell is a symbol of historical, cultural and archaeological heritage of all the pre-Columbian cultures before the arrival of the Spanish conquistadores. It was obtained at different depths off the Ecuadorian coast and has been utilized since the Valdivia culture (3800 B.C.) in the Formative Period and onward, through the cultures of the Integration Period (500 to 1534 A.D.). When the Spaniards arrived, it was documented that the use of the Spondylus shell was to show power and instill hierarchy; they described it as the Red Gold of the Incas. The origins of the Shell, being from the coast, allowed it wide distribution, symbolizing the natural and cultural richness of Ecuador and the importance of the coast, with a strong emphasis on intercultural commerce during 4000 years, which is the base foundation of tourism.

The Spondylus Trail (Ruta del Spondylus) differentiates itself from other tourism products and previous routes in various aspects, highlighting the attractions of the Coast and the Andes together with those of Northern Peru. It is based on principles of sustainability through time and on social, environmental and cultural aspects. It incorporates cultural elements of the ancient past of this region and of the live cultures, highlighting this as one of the main assets, and also spanning over archaeology, history, culinary heritage, handicrafts and the modern and traditional cultures of the coast. Other features to note are the natural attractions of the coast and the Andes. This macro product includes other products and existing routes inside the framework of sustainability and quality.

As the Spondylus Shell is a natural product and a cultural symbol, the dangers that come upon this species of bivalve due to mass exploitation are very imminent. This consulting group recommends using the Spondylus in the project as an all-purpose icon of a) the beauty of nature threatened from actual human predation, b) pre-Columbian cosmology, based on the concept of the equilibrium between human society, nature and the spirit world and c) the effort to conserve natural resources for future generations.

On this last point, the Spondylus Trail pleads for the reinforcement of aquaculture rearing in hatcheries for the Spondylus princeps to develop reliable techniques and protocols to cultivate the species in Spondylus farms in the ocean. Also the plead goes to promulgate a ban on the diving for this specie in the area of the Machalilla National Park and in the areas where you find healthy Spondylus banks on the sea bottom off of Ecuador's coast. [For example, in 10 years the demand for the food and the adornments from this shell will be huge, especially if the country promotes this travel route aggressively. I know the coastal and Andean restaurants, hotels and handicraft outlets will need this product, not only in Ecuador but also in Peru. I can see the exportation of farmed Spondylus in the near future. A friend of mine, Monica Fabara, who I admire for her work with the Spondylus shell, has been able with her team to spawn successfully this species 3 times. The problem is that we need the grow-out phase studied. How long will it take, can the communities work on a cultural identity booster project for sustainable business? This means that are many areas to be researched. I have included in the government proposal (2008) the projects for this to happen. It will be a necessity. Aquaculture of the Spondylus Shell is what it will take for this sacred item to replenish its stocks for present and future demand].

I hope we can revive the sacred realm of this shell and reconnect it with the coastal communities through public and private partnership efforts, moving towards a grass roots appreciation for developing sustainable tourism. Most of the ancestral communities now understand this. This is how it was born, as an idea for promoting our beautiful coast and culture from a movement that was initiated by the information collected from a handful of dedicated scientists from their field and lab work, both foreign and national. Kudos to the devoted work of these women and men in our country!

Spondylus Shell

There is still so much here in this area of the province of Manabí, and almost everywhere on the coast and other regions, that I believe Ecuador is just one solid archaeological site. With this being said, I want to take you to see the chronological timetable of what we have evidence of.

Cultural Chronology of the Pacific Coast of Ecuador		
Development Period	Time Period	Cultures
Paleo-Indian/Preceramic	10000 to 4400 BC	Las Vegas (8800 to 4600 BC)
Formative	4400 to 500 BC	Valdivia (4400 to 1450 BC) and Machalilla (1350 to 850 BC) and Chorrera (850 to 300 BC) these are new dates
Regional Development	500 BC to 500 AD	Bahía-Jama Coaque 1- Guangala-Daule- Tejar Guayaquil- La Tolita
Integration	500 AD to 1534	Chirije - Guancavilca- Manteño -Milagro Quevedo-Jama Coaque 2
Incas invade territories of Pre-Columbian Ecuador approx. 1450-1463 AD		
Time of Contact with the Spaniards 1531 (landing at San Mateo)		

The information with the dates provided is fairly new for the coast of Ecuador. During a conversation with Jose Chancay, a good friend who has worked at the National Heritage Institute (INPC), he told me that Dr. Marcos had worked with universities from Spain and Italy, and that Valdivia has an earlier date of appearance than what was dated from previous investigations.

CHAPTER NINE

The General of the Galapagos

My great, great, great, great grandfather was General Jose de Villamil y Joly. He was born in Louisiana in 1788, and was one of the national heroes of the Republic of Ecuador. He was also one of the founding fathers of the nation. He had much to do with the Independence of Ecuador in 1820; he was acclaimed one of the principal leaders of the revolution. My great (x4) grandmother was Ana Maria Juana de Garaycoa y Llaguno, born in 1793. She sewed the first blue and white flag of independence, which is still up today, displaying the proud colors of Guayaquil, a city where I have lived and have many friends.

General Villamil also consolidated the Galapagos Islands to the new Republic of Ecuador. In 1833, he was the first governor of the Galapagos Islands.

Taking excerpts from the studies of the *Ecuadorian historian Rodolfo Perez Pimentel* and from the biographical dictionary of Ecuador, I have the following information to share:

In October of 1831, General Jose De Villamil y Joly sent an explorer commission to the Archipelago of Galapagos to investigate the existence of a plant named "Orchilla", which was used as dye for textiles and was exported to Mexico. On the 14th of November of the same year he constituted the "Colonizing Society of the Archipelago of Galapagos" and he claimed some land on Charles Island, later named Floreana.

In January of 1832, the General formed a Military Corp to repel the attack of the Flores Battalion that had rebelled against the government. On the 20th of the same month an expedition was sent to Galapagos led by Coronel Ignacio Hernandez. In 1833, the General worked as the General Consulate of the United States for a few months and embarked to the Galapagos as the Governor of the Archipelago. There, he governed with "sound judgment, shrewdness and great practical spirit". He resigned in 1837 because the number of colonists had reduced on the islands. In his place, he left General Pedro Mena to take care of his properties. In 1841, he was called to military service in the Pasto campaign with General Juan Jose Flores. He returned to Galapagos and with money borrowed from his daughter Ana de Alarcon, and transferred his cattle from his property to evade conflicts with the colonists of Floreana.

At the beginning of August in 1842, the General was in Galapagos when he found out about the yellow fever epidemic in Panama. He set full sail to communicate the news and declare quarantine to all ships coming from the north, from the Mexican, Central American and Panamanian Coasts. Though he tried to warn them, it was too late.

Just a few days before, on the 31st of August, an English ship called "Queen Victoria" came from Veraguas and anchored with various sick people onboard.

In 1845, his first report from Galapagos states: "Delicious Temperature 60-65° Fahrenheit. Good and abundant water. Land is fertile and can produce crops from the two zones. A population of 12,000 inhabitants can be maintained here. Today there are 48 cultivated parcels of land and 51 cabins. There should be a population of 400 people. There is a road of 3,000m in length and 10m wide and it is projected for 400 additional meters. There is a natural spring that gives 80 gallons per hour and water can be conducted via bamboo pipes, but President Flores in 1833 ordered that criminals be deported to the Galapagos and since then the colony became a dangerous site".

During this time his daughter, Maria Colombia Villamil Garaycoa, was married in Montecristi to Nicolas Alarcon with numerous descendants. In 1849, the General left for California, attracted by the fever of the Gold Rush. The ship he was traveling on went down, but he saved many of the passengers in small boats that he directed to port.

He returned in 1854 and visited the Galapagos with the Consul Mateo P. Game in search of Guano deposits [very profitable in that time, it was used for fertilizer] in commercial quantities, but they found none.

He returned to Ecuador in 1862 bothered by bronchial asthma. He was always suffocating and was cardiac. In 1866, he knew of the Spanish armada's aggression towards Chile and Peru and offered his services to this last nation, but because of his bad health he could not travel to Callao has he had intended. On the 11th of May, news of the Peruvian Triumph reached Guayaquil. "It was his last day. Due to the activity of the people who were close to him, he understood that something remarkable had occurred. He asked for all the details of the event, sat up, made his observations and his predictions and on the next day he ceased to exist". He died at 77 years and 11 months of age, and left all his money to his granddaughter, Ana Luz de Ycaza Villamil.

In 1863, he requested to have his famous novel published in Lima, "Account of the Political and Military Events of the Province of Guayaquil from 1813 to 1824", which was printed in various editions.

According to Rodolfo Pimentel, "*The General died after 50 years of service without any sort of pension for his elderly years*". His daughters appealed to the government for ownership of the third part of the Island of Floreana, but this was not granted. His grandsons and granddaughters authorized individuals to gather up the wild cattle of the islands, which had descended from the cattle brought by Villamil in 1832. [One of his granddaughters was Alcira Alarcon Villamil, born in 1861 (my great great grandmother) and married to Manuel de Jesus Mejia, these were my grandmother's (Natalia Mejia Dueñas) grandparents].

I have combined the history of one of my ancestors with what my beautiful grandmother Natalia said to me just a year before she died in 2003 at the age of 89.

Miguelito in Bahía de Caráquez

Could Miguelito, a Galapagos Tortoise that is at the school Escuela Mixta Miguel Valverde in Bahía de Caráquez, have come from Floreana? Could he be the last of his species, a Geochelone nigra elephantopus, due to the over killing by colonists and whalers? Miguelito is the icon for the new recycling program of Bahía (Miguelito Reciclon), and also very loved by all the kids and the rest of us who once were and still are kids.

So this is how the story starts…

Alcira Alarcon Villamil was one of the granddaughters of General Villamil that were authorized to bring in cattle from the Galapagos. My grandmother said that her grandfather, Manuel de Jesus Mejia, had brought Miguelito in 1920, and they had kept it with them for a long time (I can vouch for that; when I was 8 years old and lived in the United States, I came to Bahía on vacation and saw the tortoise in my grandmothers yard, which was right next to the market. My grandmother's dad was named Ramon Mejia Alarcon, and her uncle was named Manuel Mejia Alarcon. He had a grand house in the sector of the city called San Roque that was burnt down by a fire, and on his land the old school Miguel Valverde was built. Through this sequence of events, it is logical to conclude that Manuel, my grandmother's uncle, had the tortoise from the start.

At one point my great grandmother, Maria Dueñas Giler, had the tortoise in her yard (when they lived next to the market) and this is where I saw it around 1967. My grandmother Natalia told me that my great uncle, (my grandmother's brother) Raul Mejia Dueñas, a professional dentist, had a sea captain of a commercial ship (that was docked in Bahía) interested in buying the tortoise. One late afternoon, the turtle was carried out of the yard, up past the house (they had Miguelito in an interior yard) and taken to the shoreline where my Uncle rented a canoe. When he saw the size of Miguelito, the ship's captain said no, he did not want to buy it. They came back ashore and left the tortoise in the canoe. Evening came and there was no one around to carry him home. The next day they came to get Miguelito but to their surprise our tortoise was gone.

How he got out of the canoe, we don't know, but probably with his weight he could have toppled it to one side and was able to scurry slowly but surely around the beach and into the forest (or was he picked up then? We do not know).

Back then the beach was not as far out as it is now. The sea wall they built in 1936 to protect San Roque was key in causing the transportation of sediments, which lengthened the peninsula.

In the end, people found the tortoise on the beach. Someone told me that Miguelito had arrived at the school by swimming from the Galapagos, but we all know that a marine turtle swims and a Galapagos tortoise is a land tortoise, so that he swam

600 miles is out of the question. After being picked up on the beach, Miguelito migrated from house to house (due to not too many families being able to feed him the great quantities of greens he needs each day) and finally he was taken to the new Miguel Valverde School where he lives now. They have done the best they can to help the tortoise live and there is a general fondness for Miguelito.

We still need to do a lot more investigation. I would love to create a small park and a Galapagos Islands Interpretation Center (there is not one in the whole coast of Ecuador) at the Miguel Valverde School. It would be nice to have a biologist trained and paid to take care of Miguelito. I'd also like to create a Miguelito Friends Foundation or Club, to see if we can collect funds for the small park infrastructure and information graphics needed. This would be great for Bahía, its citizens, and for Miguelito. We would greatly appreciate your help in these endeavors.

Facts about the Galapagos Tortoise

- ❖ They can live over 150 years old. Harriet the Galapagos Tortoise, which was held at the Australia Zoo in Queensland, lived to the estimated age of 175. Some scientists say that she is one of the specimens Charles Darwin (1835) brought back to London on the HMS Beagle.

- ❖ They can weigh over 300 pounds.

- ❖ Apart from hunting, habitat clearance has been the major factor of the population diminishing. Intensive programs of clearing the introduced grazing animals, like the wild goats have helped return the population on some of the islands.

(The following facts are from Pete Oxford and David Horwell's book, *Galapagos Wildlife*):

- ❖ Galapagos Tortoises reach sexual maturity between 20 and 25 years of age.

- ❖ In order to mate, the male tortoise climbs on to the females back and reaches under her shell with his long tail, which houses his penis. His plastron (the under part of the shell) is highly convex so that her carapace fits snugly into the depression and he does not roll off. Mating is a very lengthy and noisy process and the loud, rhythmic grunts of the male can be heard 100 meters (328 ft.) or more. When hormonal levels are running high, male tortoises have even been known to try mounting rounded rocks resembling females.

- ❖ Some female tortoises dig up to 2 to 3 nests per year and lay 20 eggs each time.

- ❖ The tortoises are vegetarians and feed on over 50 species of plants in the Galapagos.

I wrote this small chapter for Maya (*without the Galapagos facts*), the daughter of Ruth Berkowitz, who was writing for her travel blog on Miguelito. Hers is a sailing family, like many that are welcomed here in Bahía. After they left, they went to the Galapagos and showed a picture of Miguelito to one of the scientists. She wrote me to tell me that our giant tortoise might be from the Isla Santiago (from the subspecie darwini).

Thank you Maya!

Miguelito, the Galapagos Tortoise

Miguelito,
the Galapagos Tortoise,
In
Bahía de Caráquez

Photos of Miguelito by Michaela Maissen
(Cerro Seco Reserve)

FAMILY TREE

General José Maria de Villamil y Joly B.1788/ Ana María Juana de Garaycoa y Llaguno B.1793

Mariano Nicolás Alarcón Ureta/Maria Colombia Villamil Garaycoa B.1817

Manuel de Jesús Mejía Moncayo/Alcira Alarcón Villamil B.1861

Ramón Mejía Alarcón B.1883 y Maria Dueñas Giler B.1888

Manuel Mejía Alarcón y Sra. Becerra

Joaquín Tamariz Talbot / Natalia Mejía Dueñas B.1914

Patricio Tamariz Mejía B.1934 / Flor Maria Dueñas Argandoña

Patricio Tamariz Dueñas B.1960 / Juliana Zedeño Zambrano

Son and Daughter

Patricio Tamariz Zedeño B.2005 and Melissa Maria Tamariz Zedeño B.2002

On the other side of my family, the Tamariz name comes from Colonel Francisco Tamariz, a Spaniard who fought against Napoleon, came to America in 1815, and arrived in Ecuador to fight against the revolution in 1820. He lost a key battle and was asked by Jose Antonio de Sucre (closest general and friend to Simon Bolivar) to become a citizen of the new republic. He later became Minister of Finance in 1835.

From the book, *Rank and Privilege: the military and society in Latin America*, by Linda Alexander Rodriguez (1994) states:

"The best-known foreign military men who settled in Ecuador: Marshal Jose Antonio de Sucre (Venezuelan), General Juan Jose Flores (Venezuelan), General Isidoro Barriga (Colombian), Colonel Francisco Tamaríz (Spanish), Coronel Bernardo Daste (French), Colonel Ricardo Wright (English), Colonel Juan Illingworth (English)".

As I can be proud of my ancestors like General Villamil and Colonel Tamariz, I aspire that my Amerindian ancestors can also be proud of me.

CHAPTER TEN

The General of the Galapagos

I began learning about the forest that surrounds Bahía de Caráquez back in the late 1980s. The Dry Tropical Forest at Chirije (the archaeological site that we own www.chirije.com) made a long lasting impression on me. This specialized forest is adapted to its extreme environment, jungle green during the months of January through May, which is our green season, and when the occasional rains end during the dry (brown) season, it turns it into a dormant forest.

A feature to note is the omnipotent beauty of the fabulous Ceibo tree. This tree has a similarity to the African Baobab tree, when its leaves drop it looks like those fairytale trees that resemble mystical human shapes. The famous Ecuadorian painter, Eduardo Kingman, said it exhibits with grace the sensuality of a woman. He has passed away now, but we have beautiful paintings of his creation in Casa Grande, he even dedicated a painting to my mother with a flower in her hand. I remember he had a great time with me at Chirije while I explained to him the wonders of the ancient cultures and the forests of this site.

It produces an awe for discovering incredible amounts of mysteries that you behold when you enter this type of forest. There is so much we still don't understand. I believe there are elements in these forests that can catalyze the science of many plants into future medicinal usage.

There are mysteries to us in this époque however, the properties of these plants were known for millennia by our ancestors that thrived in this region and transmitted this knowledge from generation to generation. They knew how to treat anything from healing wounds, surgeries, ailments and more, using a different plant or a mixture of them, either macerated and/or squeezed. The medicinal properties were, and still are, outstanding.

One of the more important elements of life was how the community respected and dealt with their surroundings. The Amerindian cultures were highly skilled in the use of these plants for food and medicinal purposes. I cannot locate the source, but there was a book I read about 20 years ago which was written by one of the first friars (maybe Franciscan or Dominican) just after the conquest of the New World.

He wrote on the first page as a dedication; "I thank the Lord for being able to witness that the natives use all the plants in this forest. Not even a shrub or any plant we think is not of use, they have a use for each and every one of them".

The seasonally dry forests of coastal Ecuador are the most unique and biodiverse forests of the world. They are part of the Tumbesian Region. This region stretches out from northwestern Peru to the central coast of Ecuador. This is where you find an incredible amount of bird species for avid birders. Many of the ancient cultures thrived in this area knowing how to capture and retain rainwater for the dry seasons through the use of albarradas or earthen ponds that were created by native engineers that knew the water flow of the region, their hills and slopes, etc. In Chirije you can see these.

I was returning from our archaeological site (Chirije) and driving on the beach towards Bahía, when I found my friend Marcelo Luque putting up a camp about 1 mile south of it. Marcelo and I have been friends since the time I got back from the United States (1983). He has been working with me in ecotourism at Chirije at Isla Corazon and we also worked together on a whale watching operation from Bahía. He is one of those guys that has vision and respect for everything. This marks our partnership and shared passion for conservation of the local natural systems that surround us, which is why he owns Cerro Seco. Marcelo started a beautiful project for protecting the fauna and flora of the mountain range that goes from Bahía de Caráquez to San Clemente (where Chirije is also). This mountain range is called Cordillera del Balsamo, which has around 22 kilometers of beachfront, including the Punta Bellaca, Mesita, Punta Gorda, Pajonal, Chirije and Balsamo.

While we were saying hello that late afternoon close to Chirije, out of the corner of my eye I saw a humpback whale breach about a kilometer off the beach. The students and volunteers that were working with Marcelo started to hoot and holler. What a spectacular way to end the day. As we were enjoying the sunset and the ocean breeze while standing there watching the show, next to me was a volunteer I did not recognize. I said hello and quickly established a nice friendship with her.

Her name was Nathalie Pyrooz. I found out that her background was in environmental studies, involving multidisciplinary research, program coordination, data collection, analysis, ecology, plant identification, sustainability studies, environmental education, and visual communication. I was so inspired by this young woman who had come to volunteer her time to work with Marcelo and protect our forest that all of a sudden it dawned on me I should ask her if she wanted to write up a chapter on the Dry Tropical Forests of our region. I needed the vision of a North American scientist to outline a similar perception of what all of you would experience here in the Bahía area. The next pages are her account on some of the treasures of this not yet promoted forest. My commentaries are in brackets.

Getting lost and gaining respect

I got lost in this forest once, in my first week here. We were on a sort of biological reconnaissance, a group of biologists headed into the forest to see what we would find. We each had our own specialty: plants, insects, reptiles, mammals; in this outing, however, we were hoping to have an encounter with Howler monkeys (the western Ecuadorian genus Alouatta palliata aequatorialis). In previous days we'd cleared a trail with a machete and walked up to a certain point a few times. After resting in this place, we decided to venture further in, armed with a machete and two GPS units, which we had used to collect a few points indicating interesting observations.

It was recently the dry season, and many leaves had already fallen from the trees, but the forest was still thick in a tangle of vegetation. We waded through it, swimming in its layers of small and large shrubs, trees armed with spines, thick vines, and roots suspended in the air but reaching for the ground, avoiding spider webs and prickly things. Finding mushrooms and tarantulas, reptiles and birds, we were increasingly enchanted as we moved further in. The hills in the Cordillera Balsamo undulate in twisted cerebral wrinkles, and are much steeper than they appear, and we continued in every imaginable direction following the guidance and limitations of the landscape and vegetation.

Before we knew it we were lost. Although we had the GPS units, we hadn't recorded data in a while, and base maps in rural Ecuador were not available so we could only see our location in reference to our earlier points. In whatever direction we tried to go to return to our primitive trail, we were halted by terrain or impenetrable jungle. We descended a steep hillside clinging to roots and branches in order to enter a ravine to help guide us to the ocean, our only reliable 'landmark'. Unfortunately, it was too narrow and swollen with greenery to pass with our solitary machete. Frustrated and confused, we began to argue about what to do and which direction to go.

Then, the GPS unit batteries went out. Thoughts raced through each person's mind about what we would have to do should we not find our camp before nightfall – in no way were we prepared to sleep in the forest: without food or very much water left, lacking any warm clothes, or light. Cell phones were without reception. Eventually we realized that the batteries in my camera would work to power one of the GPS units. Still, the going was rough, and the mess of vegetation very disorienting. At times when we thought we were heading back to the camp, we would find we were moving away from it, or we would find that we'd gone in a circle. Along the way we found scat and tracks of several types of endemic wild animals, skeletons of tarantulas, and heard the calls of uncountable birds, all of which heightened the sensation of being deep in a wild place, with no clear or definable method of getting out.

We did eventually find our way back to camp, just as the dark was creeping in. But when I emerged I was filled with a sense of wonder, awe, and respect for this forest that I'd not known before.

Stepping into the Bosque Seco

The tropical dry forest at Cerro Seco, the Cordillera Balsamo and along the coast of western Ecuador represents one of the most threatened habitats in the world. Much of it is deciduous woodland: the dryness caused by the cold Humboldt current causes vegetation to lose its leaves seasonally. It is dry for about 7 months each year, from May to November, and the plants that exist here have specific adaptations enabling them to survive the lack of precipitation. Many drop their leaves, and are deciduously dormant like a temperate tree in the wintertime. Others close their leaves at night, stopping respiration. Some have swollen roots or stems acting to store water from the few misty rains that occur during this season. Being from a temperate zone, it's strange to think of this dry and dormant season as summer: it's colder and there are not leaves on the trees. Seasonality is a whole different being than I am accustomed to: spring wildflowers, summer heat, autumn decomposition, winter stillness. Instead, the start of the rains in December initiates the first green buds, the decomposing winter leaves give a boost to this nutrient-poor sandy clay soil for everything to grow rapidly in tropical style. The concentrated flowering time is during the final rains as the plants expend their final energies before retreating to dormancy, these flowers then morphing into fruits over the course of the dry period.

Dry tropical forest is in greater danger of extermination than tropical rain forest, though at one point worldwide it was more widespread than rainforest. Less than 2% of dry tropical forest remains in Ecuador, in part because the land is very desirable to convert to cropland and grazing. This loss of habitat, coupled with the high endemism rate of most organisms here (more than 20% of plants and birds), means that a number of species are in danger of extinction. Though not as diverse as tropical rainforest, biodiversity is quite impressive: between 50 and 70 species of woody plants can be found in a tenth of a hectare, 200-300 different birds frequent these forests, and amphibians and reptiles are abundant.

The Grand Ceibo

When you first begin to arrive to the dry tropical forests of Manabi, after emerging from the dramatically steep mountains of the western Andes, which to rolling hillsides that are increasingly agricultural, the first thing you begin to notice are the grand ceibos. The ceibo, Ceiba trichistandra, is a tree of a certain stature that makes it feel humanlike, with a rounded belly and outreaching arms, and buttressed roots indicating a stance of firmness. Some sit like Buddha, peaceful and at rest with their view of the mountain, their buttresses affirming their place connecting earth and sky. Others tower like princes, commanding and valiant, twisted and complex. Indicatory of its ability to photosynthesize and therefore process sunlight into nutrients and grow in the absence of leaves, its bark is the deep green of an emerald, which from far away is distinct in a duotone that changes form as the sun moves throughout the sky. The ceibo towers over all the other trees in intact forest, and stands solitary amidst farmlands and cleared areas, commanding respect and awe.

Less valuable for its wood than other dry tropical forest species in the area, the ceibo has not been completely exploited for commercial value; therefore, there are many remnant trees in forests where the most commercially valuable species have been extracted. Instead, it has been valued for its 'kapok', which is a white, fluffy, cottony material surrounding the seeds, all of which is contained within a hard shell. The kapok has been used to stuff pillows and mattresses, and has been spun into a wool or yarn. While they don't last as long as synthetics, this cotton has been used for ages and is a great substitute.

The ceibo has an incredible capacity to bring water up from deep within the earth, one factor enabling this tree to survive the long dry season. If you take a machete to its buttressed roots, you can drink this sweet fresh water from them – good to know if you are lost in the woods. When young, the tree protects itself from animal browsing with a density of thick sharp spines arming its trunk. Fewer spines protect the tree as it ages and presumably becomes less tender and susceptible to herbivory. Butterfly larva often use Ceiba species for food plants. Specifically, the leaf-miner butterflies, or *Bucculatricidae,* exclusively use this genus for sustenance. According to my great uncles and grandfathers, the silky cotton-like kapok fiber was exported from Bahía de Caráquez in great quantities for life vests during World War II. It is a product that is under-exploited and ancient cultures used it in cots and pillows.

Abundant Muyuyo

While the ceibos are dominant from afar, as you spend time in the countryside and the forest, you will begin to notice a shrub that seems to be everywhere, and is almost always flowering somewhere. The yellow flowers are in large and showy and in clusters, leaving behind fruits that start out green but mature into a translucent white. The rounded leaves are sandpaper-like, a distinct texture due to stiff, short hairs, which for me are always an identifier even when the form of the plant can vary quite a lot. Though abundantly found on the sides of roads as well as in the forest young and shrub like, the muyuyo can actually grow into a tree form over 20 feet tall, the bark of its trunk becoming strong and furrowed.

Muyuyo, whose scientific name is Cordia lutea, is in the Boraginaceae family. Its genus Cordia contains about 300 species of shrubs and trees. It has a sweet and delicious smell while in flower, and provides nectar for butterflies, especially as its flowering time is extended. The pulp inside the fruit is very sticky, giving it the nickname 'glue plant'. The uses for this are quite broad: it's utilized more or less like gum Arabic, and to seal envelopes. When you're headed out on a last minute date you can use it to style your hair! Trying to sweep the fallen fruit off of a cement staircase can be a tricky job.

Native to coastal Ecuador, it tolerates exceptionally well the harsh climate of the coast, growing abundantly in these nutrient-poor, stony, clay-loam soils, with almost no precipitation for 7 months of the year. And while it survives on roadsides, dusty and slightly sullen, it thrives in the forests laden with leaves and beautiful yellow flowers, which has led to its use in live fences, and has even exported as an ornamental.

People have had an extensive relationship with muyuyo for quite some time and in varying capacities. In the countryside, it provides shade for livestock, such as pigs, goats and cattle, and the animals can forage on the fruits, seeds, and leaves. It also is commonly used as a living fence, and serves well for this purpose as it has a quite shrubby habit of growth. The flowers, in an infusion, help the liver and kidneys. They also help wounds to heal. With the change of seasons, from winter to summer, from hot and wet to cool and dry and windy, many people come down with gripe, the flu – muyuyo leaves and flowers made into an infusion are an excellent treatment, and just about any coastal Ecuadorian will tell you so. The young shoots are used to prepare an infusion that helps to calm a cough, and the fruits are made into a syrup that is an expectorant and helps to clear the lungs. There are also accounts that it properties to cure wounds and minimize scarring, as well as to reduce stomach pain. The wood of this tree is also used quite widely, from posts, to firewood, to packing boxes, to broom handles. Its arching medium sized branches are often seen decorating the wraparound decks common to coastal homes in the region.

Palo Santo: Scent of the Gods

Continuing a walk through the forest, perhaps we pause at a mirador to look out over the vast Pacific Ocean. You lean against a tree (after checking to make sure it doesn't have spines, as so many things here do), and begin to notice a strong, fragrant, resinous odor filling the air. You've found the palo santo. Adapted to the extended dry season, palo santo mainly occurs in Ecuador on the coast beginning in the Cordillera Balsamo and extending southwards as the aridity increases, as well as in other dry forests in Central and South America.

The odor you smell is characteristic of Burseraceae, and can be an indicator in identifying species in this family. Burseraceae also includes frankincense and myrrh, so you can imagine just a bit what palo santo might be like: rather thick and ambrosial. An important tree to the Ecuadorian coastal areas, Palo Santo (scientific name: Bursera graveolens) has a number of ethnobotanical uses associated with its deep reddish brown resin. It can be applied to styes to cure them, and when macerated in alcohol it can be used to alleviate rheumatism; diluted with kerosene, it helps with pain in the joints and bones. With newborn babies it is applied to their belly button to help the umbilical cord fall off easily.

However, the most common use is associated with its branches. When burned, their smoke keeps away mosquitoes and other irritating bugs. This fragrant smoke, heady and heavenly, is also considered cleansing to the soul and spirit and is used to cleanse a room or a house to clear away bad energies and to bring good luck. Throughout Ecuador, in markets and shops selling natural medicines and incense, you can find pieces of the branches for sale.

When you walk through the forests of Chirije you can smell the scent in the air and on the old trees you can see the resin oozing out. Once I had a Japanese group of scientists here that said that you could make a plantation of this and make a living selling this that it was probably worth more than Frankincense. We know that the Spaniards during the conquest saw the natives use this "holy tree" especially for the incense of the temples.

It's Just Chemistry: Inside the Guayacan

The wood of guayacán (Tabebuia spp.) is one of the most important in the dry forests of western Ecuador. Even in the dry season without its leaves it becomes evident as you familiarize yourself with the forest, with its trunk strong and deeply furrowed, standing out amidst the thinner shrubs, and in direct contrast with the cascol, smooth and white. There are several species of guayacan: guayacan blanca (with whiter bark), guayacan negra (with darker, blackish bark) and guayacan de la costa. The bright yellow flowers come out on trees of three years and older during the dry summer season and stay for almost a month; they provide nourishment to a number of insects and animals in this season with limited food and water resources, and as the trophic levels proceed on up, insectivorous birds also benefit.

Valued for its extreme durability and resistance to termites, the guayacán has been logged extensively, and you will often see distinctive stumps with young shoots persistently sprouting from the base. The strong wood is commonly used for furniture, doors, and support posts. I've seen wooden support posts almost 100 years old holding up a new two story building, still compact and strong, even after being exposed to weather year after year, and even after laying discarded in an estuary for an unknown amount of time. This is even more stunning if you consider the power of the termites here: a great number of the woods here fall prone due to infestations of these fascinating insects in just a couple of years.

The guayacan offers something more intriguing and useful inside its bark: a naturally occurring organic compound called lapachol. First discovered in 1882 from the tree Tabebuia avellanedae, a close relative of guayacan, lapachol has had favorable results in experiments in controlling the growth of cancerous tumors. A great variety of medicinal properties have been attributed to lapachol and its derivatives, including: anti-abscess, anti-ulcer, anticarcinomic, antiemetic, anti-inflammatory, antimalarial, antiseptic, antitumor, antiviral, bactericidal, fungicidal, insectifungal, pesticidal, termiticidal, and viricidal. Though isolated first from Tabebuia, lapechol has since been found in other plant families such as Verbenaceae, Leguminosae, Sapotaceae,

Scrophulariaceae, and Malvaceae. It works as an anticancer agent by inducing changes in the protein profile of cancer cells and slowing their invasiveness.

There have been some problems associated with side effects, and there is some question about the effectiveness of lapachol. However, there is still a lot of potential for investigation, and there are a great number of plants which have not endured any type of testing of their biochemical compounds; therefore, if the forest disappears before we really know what is in it, how are we to know if we haven't already eliminated a cure for an as yet incurable disease?

Soothing Sábila

Though not an Ecuadorian native, sábila (better known in English as aloe vera, scientific name Aloe vulgaris) is hard to ignore in any discussion of important medicinal and otherwise useful species in this area. Sábila is cultivated widely in the Ecuadorian coast, has many uses and is commonly known. Its thick, fleshy, succulent leaves are spiny, and it sends up shoots topped with a cluster of bright yellow tubular flowers. You'll often see this plant in gardens throughout the coastal areas, and it is especially custom in rural areas and occasionally in the cities to put a plant in the entrance of the house or to tie up to the front door as a prevention against curses or as a good omen. Bees and other happy pollinators cluster around the spike of flowers to bathe and benefit from the sweet nectar.

A gelatinous substance, known as acibar, is contained in the leaves of sábila. When blended with water and applied on the hair, it helps to prevent hair from falling out. Blended with alcohol, this substance helps to combat problems with skin fungus. Alone, the interior of the leaves of the aloe helps to cool and heal burns – particularly useful in coastal areas where it is tempting to stay in the sun on the beach for maybe a bit longer than your skin wants to. It has also been used to heal malignant tumors and skin cancer. Pig farmers in the country rub their feet with the interior of the leaf to keep them from getting bitten by mosquitoes or niguas, a type of flea found in tropical America that burrows under the nails.

Creative Persistence: Surviving Against the Elements

Adaptation is a necessary element for existence in any species, anywhere, in any sort of setting in the world. Each form of being exists because it has developed a special adaptation allowing it to live within the context of everything else around it. The basic theme in Charles Darwin's theory of natural selection is that speciation occurs as the genetic material transferred over generations, as influenced by increased survival or reproduction, eventually leads to the evolution of distinct populations. Adaptations take on any number of forms in any part of the plant, affecting chemical makeup and physiological responses, root systems, flower shape, type of leaf or stem, type of seeds and dispersal systems.

Some plants are able to withstand extreme heat or cold, others can endure long periods of drought or inundation; some take advantage of high levels of disturbance; some become widespread and general, and others only survive in very distinct niches. The tropical dry forest in coastal Ecuador requires adaptations to very long periods with very little to no water, soils generally poor in nutrients, strong ultraviolet rays of the equatorial sun, and in some parts exposure to the constant saline mist blown in from the sea.

To avoid further water loss through transpiration, some plants close their leaves at night. A couple of trees in the pea family have earned the common name Dormilón, because the locals have interpreted this as if the plant is sleeping (dormir means 'to sleep'), which in a way, it is. Other plants have modified roots, which are swollen to capture and hold water when it comes and transmit it slowly into their systems when it is dry. Examples of some of these are bulbs, like a tulip, or tubers, like potatoes. Succulent stems, most commonly seen in cacti, also help to capture excess water during heavy rains while allowing the plant to contract and live off of this stored water in arid times. Aerial roots allow plants to capture more easily moisture in the air during mists and periods of high humidity.

With the dry and deciduous nature of this forest, plants are subject to a high rate of herbivory in the rainless months. Those that keep their leaves are few, and therefore greater targets to herbivorous mammals, leafcutter ants, and other insects that feed on or grow their larvae in leaves. Deciduous trees and shrubs are still subject to browse of their bark. In defense, many plants develop spines and thorns, thorns being a sharp pointed stem or shoot, while a spine is technically a modified leaf. Both help to reduce herbivory, and spines also minimize water loss being that their surface area is reduced.

Seed dispersal strategies are also dependant on how a plant is adapted to its environment. You find more wind-dispersed plants in tropical dry forest than in tropical rainforest. This is probably due to many plants go to seed during the dry summer, when few plants have leaves, and there is generally a strong afternoon wind to carry them. The seeds of the kapok trees, ceibo, jaboncillo (in the Bombaceae family) are encased in a white, fluffy, cotton like material, which the wind catches and carries through the web of leafless branches and to their resting and waiting places. The vine modroño has a fleshy orange fruit with a single seed inside, and the shrub perlillo has a translucent berry, both of which are eaten by animals and distributed in this manner.

Water stressed conditions see plants that close their stomata to inhibit excess water loss. Stomata are miniscule openings in the leaves, which permit water to pass in and out of the plant, called evapotranspiration. This slows the flow of CO_2 into the leaf, but since the enzyme which is different in C4 photosynthesis (PEP carbolxylase) has a greater affinity for CO_2 than the one used in C3 photosynthesis (RuBP carbolylase), in these lower CO_2 conditions, the initial fixation of the CO_2 is more efficient, and is more concentrated. One common example is corn (Zea mays). CAM plants are generally succulents, CAM (crassulacean acid metabolism), minimize water loss due to evapotranspiration. Initial CO_2 fixation at night, which, opposite of other plants, is when these plants have their stomata open, and closed during the day, when it is further processed.

The Forest is Bigger than the Trees

Until this point, we've talked mainly about the plant kingdom and the fascinating world it presents. But what about the animals? They also make interesting changes owing to the nature of the dry forest.

Many animals are forced to migrate as they accustom themselves to the waterless season. Considered by many to be the loudest land animal, howler monkeys cluster in the more humid ravines during the dry season to be closer to water and food. Their vocal calls, which can be heard for 3 miles, are a deep, guttural, ethereal cry. Normally these monkeys roam distinct territories, with one male to every four females, but as they search further for food, such as leaves, fruit, buds, flowers and nuts, and for even scarcer water, they share small and more humid areas without confrontation.

Frogs and some insects find damp muddy areas where they can burrow or create small holes where they can go into 'estivation', which is basically hibernation in the summertime. This strategy lowers their metabolism and needs for energy and water so they can live on their excess storage tissues during the dry months. When moisture levels raise with the coming of the wet season, these animals become active again.

A Plea to Save the Forest

As you can see, the tropical dry forest of coastal Ecuador holds a number of secrets and surprises. Deciduous tropical forest worldwide is a specialized ecosystem, and in Ecuador this forest is particularly unique due to the numerous microclimates, leading to a high degree of endemism and specialization of its inhabitants.

Patricio looking at the magnificent Ceiba Trees present at Hacienda Palo Alto

Manabi actually has fewer documented species than most other Ecuadorian provinces. On one hand this is surprising considering the topographical and climactic diversity in this 6th largest province of the country; however, given the extent and duration of human disturbance compounded with the lack of scientific investigation here, it is possible that: a) many species have been eliminated long ago due to the extensive deforestation and human manipulation of the region, and b) since isolated remnant forests have not been well-surveyed there could be undiscovered beings residing in them. In Ecuador, since 1975, there have been an average of 165 new species found each year, 91 of them being endemic – as yet there is not any presupposition for this trend to discontinue.

With the high rates of deforestation due to the inclination to farm the land and raise cattle, as well as the high value of many of the woody species it contains, it is a forest that needs to be greater recognized in light of conservation, reforestation, and research efforts. The forest as a whole as well as the species it contains are rather poorly understood: due to the greater diversity and compounding pressures of deforestation and contamination the Amazon basin and humid forests, most of the international attention is focused on these regions, while the topical dry forest receives much less attention and is equally valuable. Deforestation heightens the rate of erosion, readily apparent as you move through the hillsides and see some of them crumbling into dust.

Though valued highly for its wood products, it is important to direct conservation efforts to develop sustainable harvesting for species that continue to be utilized locally in the region so that they can continue to provide decent habitat and intact ecosystem to support the niches needed by the mammal, bird, reptile, and insect species it contains. A great number of plants are ethno botanically important, some of which have been described here (and others of which have brief profiles in the appendix), and one solution is to determine sustainable methods of wild crafting that use the forest for its non-timber products. This places greater value on the forest as a manner of sustaining the population around it economically while maintaining the forest as a living and complete system.

Because much of the land has been considerably altered, conservation of existing forest is not enough to maintain the dry tropical forest. Reforestation efforts, combined with environmental education of area landholders, are an important component to maintain the ecosystem. Some local reforestation projects include efforts by Planet Drum and the Cerro Seco Biological Reserve, who in separate projects have planted native and endemic trees and shrubs around Bahía de Caráquez and the greater area.

Ecotourism, enacted responsibly, is another option that can help to sustainably exploit and even improve the condition of these interesting places. For a traveler in Ecuador and much of Latin America, although there are many places that provide access to rain forest and cloud forest, few feature seasonally deciduous forest, allowing an option for these visitors to see a distinct and interesting ecosystem. Birders will be astounded by the diversity of birds here and excited by the endemics they can check off their list, which they can find nowhere else in the world. Well thought-out and organized efforts in eco-tourism provide an opportunity to financially sustain the population in the region, in a manner that protects rather than destructs natural resources.

Environmental education of the native people as well as of the national and international visitors to the region is both an opportunity and a necessity. Many of the locals are familiar with the basic uses of the most common medicinal and edible species, but do not necessarily embrace a conservation mentality to protect forested areas. Exploitation of the land to raise cash crops or cows is common, and compounded with the economic poverty in the province, it is sometimes difficult to explain to someone who has forested land why they should not use it in order to earn a living. However, it is rich with prospects for investigation for university students of ecology and biology, and provides the basics for the beginning of an environmental consciousness for those in the younger grades.

Appendix: List of other selected useful plants

Anacardiaceae
Hobo
Spondius mombin
The fruit is edible straight off the tree (although its better with a bit of salt), in jelly, or made into a drink. The wood is used for firewood, boxes, matchboxes, and boards/planks.

The hobo is a tree that walks the line of domestication. Sharing the same family as the cashew, Anacardiaceae, hobo produces small fruits that are sold in stands and markets throughout Ecuador. Unripe, they are also eaten by the locals with a bit of salt. The fruit can also be made into refreshing drinks, as well as jams or jellies. Though native to the tropical Americas, Spondius purpurea is also found and cultivated throughout numerous tropical regions worldwide, including the Philippines and Nigeria, and in Central America, and cultivars have been developed to select for fruit size and flavor.

Formed as though it was made to climb, the fairly smooth and white trunk begins branching horizontally at about 3 feet, tempting for anyone who likes to play around in trees. The deciduous leaves are pinnately compound, only emerging during the wet season, leaving the tree a labyrinth of white topped with immature green fruits for several months of the year. The fragrant flowers, emerging directly from and close to the branches are an indicator of the color of the fruit to come, which can vary from red to purple or yellow.

Hobo is native to Ecuador, and is found throughout the coastal areas. While it isn't cultivated in orchards in Ecuador to my knowledge as one would with a tree specifically grown for its produce (though reputedly in Mexico and Venezuela there are plantations), it is often found in populated areas, as well as in the forest. Interestingly, once I was following an ancient path through the forest south of Bahía de Caráquez , one which was no longer marked by any sort of trail but known by the local guides I was with, and we encountered hobo trees at every couple hundred meters or so, seemingly marking certain turns in the trail. They were old and grand in the midst of the sleeping dry forest, calling as places to rest. Additionally, these trees sprout easily from cuttings, and so are often used for living fences.

Medicinally, the hobo has astringent qualities, and the fruit and leaves can be made into an infusion. A decoction of the fruit is used to clean wounds and cure mouth ulcers. It is also a diuretic and antispasmodic, and a syrup made from the fruits is said to relieve diarrhea. The juice from young leaves helps to cure ulcers, and a decoction of the fruit or bark of the trees is good to bring down a fever.

Annonaceae
Anona
Annona glabra
The fruit is edible and medicinal against dysentery. It makes a very light wood used to hold up fishing nets.

Guanabana
Annona muricata
The large, fleshy aggregate fruit is very good raw or in drinks. [It is a fantastic thirst quencher, tangy and sweet].

Chirimoya
Annona squamosal
Very delicious fruit. Although there has not been a phytocheical analysis of the leaves, in some places in Los Rios province they place the leaves under the pillows of niños so that they don't wake up at night. In Colombia they use barbasco for this. [In the summertime, the season of the harvest of Chirimoya, here in Bahía de Caráquez you can see local families who have plots of land in the forest, will be selling them in the afternoons, hand-size greenish with black sees surrounded by pulpy white tangy flesh].

Apocynaceae
Perlilla
Vallesia glabra
Used medicinally to take a juice from the fruit which helps to reduce inflammation in the eyes.

Areaceae
Tagua
Phytelephas aequatorialis
Garden ornamental, you can also make a drink from the fruits. The mature seeds are used industrially to make buttons, dice, chess pieces, and a variety of adornments [very hard like ivory]. Before plastics, the amount of Tagua (Vegetable Ivory Nut) exported was a considerable source of new revenue for the country. The leaves are used as roofs for houses. [This is called Cade and you can see them on the roofs of the cabins at Chirije and in the rural areas of the Pacific Coast. They say 200 pounds of worked adornments have the same street value as an Elephant's Ivory Tusk. There is a legend in Bahía de Caráquez where it says that the exportation of the Tagua nut was such that

there was always such a great demand but when this went down, for example during the Victorian Era, the exporters would go with bags and bundles of money and push them under the table to the stylists in Europe so they would put one more button on the dresses driving the price up again. We know that during the World Wars this nut was exported for the buttons of the uniforms of different countries.

Phytelephas macrocarpa
The tender young fruits are edible, as are the shoots, and the mature fruits are used to make buttons. The leaves are used for the roofs of buildings. The roots have diuretic properties when they are boiled. The stems are also used to make floors.

Bombaceae
Ceibo
Ceiba trichistandra
Large tree, with a green trunk and stems, prop roots, and dominant in tropical dry forest ecosystems of the Ecuadorian coast. Young trees have spines. The wood is not very valuable, but is used for boxes and firewood. The kapok that surrounds the seeds is used to fill mattresses, pillows, and the like.

Balsa
Ochroma pyramidale
Very lightweight wood, used to build boats. During the world war, Ecuador was the leading producer of lifeboats and war craft. The characteristics of the wood make it suitable for making games, packing boxes, etc. The seed capsules also contain a wooly, silky fiber used to fill pillows or mattresses, and the fibers of the bark help to strengthen and decorate boats. [Our ancient cultures had the most impressive balsawood sailing vessels that navigated up to the territories of pre-Columbian Mexico and down to pre-Columbian Chile]

Cactaceae
Pitajaya
Hylocereus polyrhizus
This climbing ephiphytic cactus has a distinctive three-sided stem. Its mature red fruit is edible raw or made into a drink. [Many of the animals of the forest feed on these]

Capparidaceae
Sapote de Perro
Capparis angulata
The resin of this small tree can be mixed with lime and used to paint houses. It's also used for firewood and carbon.

Chrysphalanaceae
Icaco
Chrysobalanus icaco
Cultivated in Guayaquil, Bahía de Caráquez and Chone, the fruit of this shrub or small tree is extremely nutritious, and deserves greater cultivation and distribution.

Euphorbiaceae
Piñon
Jatropha curcas
Tree with lobed leaves, heart-shaped base, and yellow flowers, cultivated for living posts. Used medicinally, the leaves are made into poultices to relieve skin inflammations. In small doses, the seeds are purgatives, though in large amounts they are dangerous. The seeds are oily but also contain the toxic protein cureina. [Many businesses look for biofuels with this plant].

Malphigaceae
Cerezo
Malphigia puniofolia
Survives in all types of soil and is native to much of northern South America, and is common in dry areas and bad terrains in Santa Elena. This small tree has an edible fruit that can be eaten raw or preserved. Containing an elevated amount of ascorbic acid (vitamin C), the American Medical Association recommended its cultivation in developing areas of the world.

Mimoisadeae / Leguminosae
Tierra Espina
Pithecellobium dulce
The white pulp that surrounds the seeds is edible. The wood is used for construction, posts, firewood and carbon. The skin has a high tannin content por lo que se lo ha usado en las curtiembres. The resin can be used like gum arabic. Medicinally, the leaves are shredded and applied to ulcers to heal them very quickly.

Algarrobo
Prosopis juliflora
The green fruits can be used against diarrhea. The veins have 27% glucose. There is a cocktail in Peru that is made from this concoction. In addition, it is a valuable wood tree, used for doors and windows, erosion control, and reforestation.

Algarrobo
Prosopis pallida
The young shoots can be heated and applied to problems with the eye. They have a high caloric value and are used for firewood and carbon. This is also an important species in reforestation.

Musaceae
Banano o guineo
Musa acuminate
Of paleotropical origin, with propagation completely clonal and the only source of variation has been in somatic mutation. (*somatic mutations (also called acquired mutations) involve cells outside the dedicated reproductive group and which are not usually transmitted to descendants, however, If the organism can reproduce asexually through mechanisms such as cuttings or budding the distinction can become blurred. For example, plants can sometimes transmit somatic mutations to their descendants asexually or sexually where flower buds develop in somatically mutated parts of plants – Wikipedia*). A fruit that is largely exported. Ecuador is the primary producer and exporter of bananas in all of South America. All varieties can be eaten raw or cooked

into a jelly. Vinegar can be obtained in two ways. 1) You can strain very mature bananas in a strainer over a bowl where little by little the drops of vinegar will emerge. 2) In the countryside, they gather the mature fruits and strain them into an earthen bowl and cover it, and after three days, the resulting mass floats in a transparent liquid.

It can also be made into a sweet liqueur or wine. While isn't done in Ecuador, in Africa they make a beer by drying the mature guineas in the sun, and then cooking them and leaving the mixture to ferment. After adding water, the beverage is ready.

Recently the flour has been used because it is cheaper and nutritious to feed children. It contains water, starch, cellulose, sucrose, glucose, gum, fats, tannins, proteins, and ash. The peel is toxic and contains bananadina, which has hallucinogenic properties when it is smoked like a cigarette. Additionally it's been found to contain other alkaloids such as psilocybin and serotonin, the last of which is a calming agent. For medicinal purposes, the stem of a banana is cut and left overnight with sugar added to it. When taken as a drink the following day, it is used to cure for bad cases of diarrhea.

Platano
Musa sp.
There are three varieties of platano [plantain]. El dominico, which has many racemes of fruit. El barraganete, a medium size, which has big fruit but with a smaller number of them, and el maqueño, which has recently been propagated and produced.

Platano is a very important food for much of Ecuador. It is consumed green or mature and is prepared in an infinite number of ways. The flour is also used extensively. Simmonds 1973 in the work Los Platanos indicates that the platano contains calcium, phosphorus, iron, water, carbohydrates, proteins, fats, ash, fiber, Beta-carotene, thiamine, riboflavin, niacin, and ascorbic acid.

The leaves are also used to wrap tamales, hayacas, muchines, and other treats. [At the Isla Corazon, the ecotourism model with community management only 20 minutes away from Bahía, where there is an incredible amount of bird populations, the local guides prepare a Tonga for you, this is freshly cooked rice with seafood (shrimp or fish) in peanut sauce, wrapped with these leaves. Gives it a special flavor.]

Sapotaceae
Paipai
Prodosia nutans
Used for its wood, for walls, floors, firewood. Medicinally, the people of Iseras in the Guayas province use the latex as an eyewash to clean and reduce inflammation in the eyes.

Sterculiaceae
Cacao
Theobroma cacao
The provinces of los Rios and Guayas have had large exportations of cacao, although now the amount of exportation has decreased, in part due to the impact of El Niño. Its fruit is eaten in a number of ways, using the seeds to make chocolate in a variety of forms, cocoa powder, and cocoa butter. The cocoa is made with its husk or shell, and mixed with a quantity of other seeds. Medicinally it is commonly used in the Los Rios

province to cure sourness chewing a cacao seed. Cocoa butter is used for suppositories and inflammations of the sinuses.

Urticaceae
Ortiga
Urera baccifera
Used medicinally against arthritis or cramps by hitting the affected area with the plant. Can also be used to calm hemorrhages or stop the flow of blood if one is injured with a machete in the forest.

From the Author:

We have to give thanks for the contribution of the American Indian and the knowledge passed on through generations on the medicinal plants found in the forests of the tropical forests. An important opportunity still exists for many plants and fruits to be investigated inside the Bosque Seco. There are probably thousands of metric tons of the fruit of the Moyuyo that ripen and are lost every year here. The silky cotton fiber of the Ceiba tree also is usable and there are many ways to use these special elements for the human body that can be harvested naturally.

However, due to cattle farming and carbon production we might lose what little is left of the Dry Tropical Forest of Ecuador. There is a great movement here in Bahía, led by Marcelo Luque and many of the activists that have gotten involved. Peter Berg and the Planetdrum Foundation also have supported our forests here through their grand work on revegetating hillsides.

If our forests do not go into a process of conservation, we will lose the diversity that once lined the territories of our ancestors. The loss of habitat of the Howler Monkeys, Deer, Cuchucho, Anteater, Silver Fox, Puma and many more species of wildlife present can accelerate their extinction.

We cannot turn back time and see the same forests Francisco Pizarro did when he was discovering this part of the Pacific Coast almost 500 yrs ago, but we can still explore what has been left and protected by many communities and private owners.

El misterio del Bosque Seco!

A Magnificent View of
Chirije's Pacific Coastline from the
Whale Observation Site

CHAPTER ELEVEN

The Mystery of the Lights

Growing up in the United States in the 1960's, I watched movies like "War of the Worlds", "The Blob, Earth vs. the Spaceships" and others of the sci-fi genre. They were scary as heck and left a big impression on me. I still remember sitting at our rented house in Long Island, NY hearing sirens from ambulances as they went howling past and thinking they were sounds from UFOs and dangerous aliens.

When I was 7 years old and went to Ecuador on summer vacations, I remember at night I would shiver every time a night guard walked by on the street with a whistle, making a horrific shriek every 5 minutes. Now I understand the primary purpose of this was not to warn robbers that they were patrolling, but rather to wake up the family bosses to make sure they had the money to pay their wages. I think those sounds from the guardian's whistles would have made great sound effects for a UFO movie.

What really blew my mind was when I was in Ecuador at family reunions and they would talk about this subject, as it was a hot topic at the time. I distinctively remember the adults saying there had been a mega sighting of lights over the Pichincha Volcano in Quito and elsewhere. What struck me odd was they acted as if it was an everyday thing.

When I moved back to my homeland in 1974, I started viewing life in a different way. This altered perspective was influenced by everything I saw, heard and felt, from enamoring a Latina to the very ancient pottery I saw, to hearing about el Mal de Ojo (evil eye), which in folk culture is caused by a hex from the gaze from a more powerful or stronger person looking into a weaker persons eye.

This would be not your everyday topic of conversation in the United States. Talking about UFOs became a common thing here. Where do I begin?

It has to be with my sister, Veronica, who has an immense passion for this subject. In the latter half of the 1980s, Veronica formed a pop music band called *Anexxo*; she was an avid musician, songwriter, electric guitarist, and a percussionist. Her band was very talented and quickly became quite popular. In our province of Manabí, a song she had written called "*Tu eres para Mí*" was in the top rankings for a few weeks. This catapulted the band into first place, displacing the famous song of Luis Miguel's, "*La Incondicional*", which was first place in all Latin America. The group was great!

Can you guess who the manager was? Yes, yours truly. Boy did we have fun! I loved it when we played concerts, our mix of Latin Rock and Pop music jived. My mother had to pay the price since we had group practices right next to her bedroom door at Casa Grande (the neighbors were also at the front door all the time complaining). Veronica had some of her songs mixed in Miami and they were on a great trip upwards, but the group broke up and that was the end of her musical career.

In 1992, she started to collect and read books on UFOs. In 1993, she joined Mission Rahma, a group of people on a mission for humanity. They try to contact extraterrestrial life through the Cosmic Plan, which is none other than the will of the "Profound Love of Cosmic Consciousness", or God within Creation. The Mission Rahma seeks to help beings achieve their Christification, or consciousness of the essence. Utilizing faith and love as tools of evolutionary ascent does this. There is a large interest of this here in Ecuador and in the rest of the world.

In 1993, Veronica met Jaime Rodriguez, the number one specialist on this topic in Ecuador. He is one of my favorite people, a good friend and my sister's partner through many investigations in this area. He has been an Ufologist since 1979 and has made 156 documentaries in 23 countries around the world about the UFO Phenomenon and the great enigmas of humanity. He is the creator and Director of CEIFO (ECIUF-Ecuadorian Comisión for the Investigation of the UFO Phenomenon). Jaime has also developed special documentaries abroad and on Ecuadorian national TV. He started to look into cases with the military back in 1983 and just convinced our President, Rafael Correa, to sign an agreement declassifying all the military documents. You can see these and many interviews with military personnel online on YouTube.

Jaime Rodriguez says that on the several occasions he and Veronica have visited the Astro Tourism Resort situated in Chirije, they have shared intense moments with the people there. Veronica has also dedicated a great part of her life to investigating the UFO phenomenon in the province of Manabí, where she was born. Later on in this chapter, we will hear Veronica's views on this phenomenon in Chirije.

I have done much exploring with Jaime Rodriguez; later on in this chapter, there is an interesting account of one particular adventure in Chirije. Once I helped Veronica with a conference Jaime had in Bahía. You really must listen to him and see his documented presentations; they are so interesting, even if you are not a UFO believer. The conference Jaime had in 2010 in Bahía filled up the Universidad Eloy Alfaro's main auditorium (around 330 people), proving there is marked interest in the subject. The presentation was impressive, but the most striking part was afterwards, when a large amount of people came up to him to share their experiences with UFOs in the Bahía area. There were so many accounts, one could write a book on it!

Accounts of Encounters

I will return to Jaime a little later. Now it's time to focus on the amount of incredible sightings friends, family and staff have had in Ecuador, particularly at the archaeological site in Chirije. Let's begin with the accounts of a friend of mine, Arturo Zedeño, who has had two incredible encounters with unidentified flying objects. By the way, Arturo Zedeño became my brother in law about 10 years ago when I met his beautiful sister, Juliana.

I must first describe Arturo. He is a grand person with a great personality and a vast knowledge of life. As a serious fellow and did not want to talk much about this subject, but he was kind to share this with me. His first encounter was when he was 15 yrs. old at about 11pm at night. My brother in law states his encounter as follows, "Four of my good friends were sitting with me on a park bench in front of the ocean promenade at the Parque del Indio (park where the Cara leaders' monument is located). We were joking around and telling stories of our past conquests when, all of sudden, one of my friends screamed, *"Whoa"!* He was pointing diagonally up. I thought he was joking but…

About 150 meters (almost 500 ft.) away, right over the ocean and between where we were, there was a street lamp at about 75 meters (246 ft.). We were looking at the horizon and what immediately caught our attention was a big, dark shape parallel to the sky and ocean, just sitting in midair. I could make it out to be a craft that was above the ocean and the sand, and with the light from the street lamp, I could see the underbelly was a grey color with some geometric designs that were constructed with rivets, similar to an aircraft. The ship was about 80 meters wide (262 ft.) and round with no lights. There was a low frequency hum that was definitely coming from it. I stared at it for about 10 to 15 seconds and once I knew it wasn't ours (human) and it started moving, everyone jumped and ran in different directions. I took off running to my house that was only a block away. One friend followed, because it was the closest safe haven for him as well.

Arturo later told me he had been so scared that he and his friend almost broke down the door of the house and ran over his mom. When they looked out the window, they saw the object had moved towards the ocean and there were now lights at the back of it. The next day, many people had also seen the lights over the water, but did not have the encounter they did. His account was so intriguing to me, a ship coming out over the water towards the beach and back out to the ocean, how fascinating!

He had another interesting account in 1996, in which he was driving back from the shrimp farm with his son Arturo Jr. who was around 12 years old, and with Robertito, his nephew who was 9 (now both my nephews). Arturo told me that sometimes at night on the shrimp farm, when he made rounds to make sure everything was in order, he would see lights in the sky. He was sure that these were not airplanes or satellites because of their movements. This added to his belief after his first experience when he was a teenager that life existed outside of this earthly plane or realm.

So that night, as they were slowly coming down the curves of the road where you can see Isla Corazon at about 11:30pm in his pickup truck, Arturo remembers, "*I slowed down the car when I saw an object about 120 feet wide with green, red and yellow lights hovered above Dr. Parra's Chicken Farm over a small hill*". Dr. Parra is a well-respected Medical Dr. who I play doubles tennis with and the father of a surfer friend Chicho and Johnny, another tennis friend. When Johnny was younger, at about the age of 12, he beat the famous Ecuadorian Tennis player Andres Gomez. Johnny is also one of the best Lear jet pilots in Ecuador, and once had an object fly right next to his wing for almost all the trajectory from Quito to Guayaquil. The most amusing thing for me is that he says since then he carries a camera with him all the time.

Back to Arturo's encounter - driving the last curves of the Bahía-Tosagua road, he reached the same horizontal height as the object. He was watching how it displaced itself from the left to the right, about 30 ft. each way, and as he passed the last curve going down, the object was angled to him at 90 degrees.

Robertito was asleep and Arturo Jr., his oldest son, was drifting off. Arturo then told me he got a sudden urge to stop his car and flick his lights, in an attempt to communicate, but all of a sudden his motor died and his lights went dim. He remembers the only light he saw in the car was the car's clock. Then he saw the green, red and yellow lights that had been still start to fire up like a blender or a police siren. He said the object was like two dishes oppositely stuck together and the lights were not at the edges but were on the diagonal part down the side towards the bottom.

When the lights start firing up, he woke up Arturo Jr. and asked him, "*What do you see?*" He asked this because of his earlier experience and needed someone else to confirm what he was seeing to know that he was not just hallucinating. Arturo Jr. immediately said, "*lights dad*", and after a long pause, "*No dad, that's a UFO*". At that moment Arturito started panicking.

Right then the object started to move a little towards Bahía and when this happened Arturo's car lights went back on. He started his car and drove quickly about 500 yards to the gas station right off the road. The object switched direction towards the Corona Road (which goes toward Chirije) then shot away. Arturo said that the beam of light from the speed launch of the object was pretty impressive.

Now the most interesting part is that throughout this entire ordeal, before Arturo woke up Arturito, he was receiving a message over and over, "*You are not alone, we are here, you are not alone, we are here*".

Chirije

As I mentioned in the preface and in the chapter on The Conquistadors, my family and I were blessed with the beautiful land of Chirije (Chee-ree-hey).

I consider my loyal staff part of the family, as they work with us during the good and the bad times. One particular staff member, Chino Juan Jose Rodriguez, is one of those unsung heroes who helped more than 30 children when they were swept by an El Niño event into the bay. He is an electrician, plumber, maintains pools, air conditioning expert and driver. He is amazing. I could write a whole chapter just on him. His dad was an amateur archaeologist and found many pieces on the Chirjie site before I bought it, and in the valleys close by. Chino asked him to help us by donating these native ceramics and stone objects to our onsite museum (which is also comprised of objects found by archaeologists who studied the site).

One of these pieces is of much interest. As I was navigating the Internet for documents or photos of drawings and evidence of ancient aliens, I found one with depictions drawn from different sources around the world. There was a picture of a NASA astronaut and a clay pre-Columbian figurine from Ecuador that were laying side by side for comparison.

A detail caught my attention; this figurine was standing with monkey like ears coming out from the sides of its helmet. This caught my eye because we have a very similar figurine sitting in the front of a vessel crafted by an ancient native from the times of the Bahía/Chorrera culture. This is one of the pieces Chino's dad gave the Chirije onsite museum. It has no utilitarian use, and is probably a ceremonial vessel. With a thin spout in the back, the main object looks like a flying saucer! *(See photo on next page.)*

Pre-Columbian artifact found in Chirije
Many say… possible astronaut on flying saucer?

The first sightings at Chirije

We bought Chirije in 1994 and started building an eco-cultural tourism lodge. As I had mentioned before, my mother, Flor Maria, was the first woman in Latin America to grow farmed shrimp (this in the mid-seventies) and also the first woman in the world to get an organic certification for this commodity of the aquaculture industry. She was of great help in the creation of the project in Chirije. Her staff from the shrimp farm worked on the cabins and with general construction. Once one of the cabins was finished, we had a guard live there and protect the 30 hectares of the beachfront archaeological site and the 210 hectares of surrounding dry tropical forest.

Samuel Zambrano, our dedicated Shrimp Farm administrator, is a smart person who maintains very good political relations with the country folk and many other people in the business. My mother asked him to supervise the workers at Chirije.

He has a good relationship with Veronica and myself and is supportive of new ideas and global interaction. One day he came to me and said he had something to tell me, so I listened. Samuel said I must to go to Chirije to hear what the guard's wife has to say.

I immediately left for the 15-minute beach ride from Bahía. Once I got there, I asked her what had happened and she very timidly started telling me. Before I start this account I want to explain the geographic location of Chirije. Chirije is located 15km south of Bahía de Caráquez and about 7 km north of San Clemente. The only way to reach the place is by the beach. There is no settlement on the beach between Bahía and San Clemente. Before we owned it, the old proprietors had rented it out to an Ecuadorian businessman (or so they thought). They later found out this man was one of Ecuador's biggest Drug Barons. Luckily he was eventually captured. While he was renting Chirjie, he used the long airstrip for small planes on one of the sides of the cliffs. The strip was bombed twice by the Ecuadorian air force in the late 1970s. I mention this so you can gain perspective on how secluded this site is, even though it is only 15 minutes along the beach from Bahía, the prettiest city of the Ecuadorian coast.

Returning to the account from the Guardians wife in 1994, "*Don Patricio (Don is used as respect throughout Latin America), last night as my husband was making his rounds, I saw a pretty blue light come down and suspend itself in midair at the back of the house towards the hill (about 300 ft. from the house). It was beautiful and I watched it for more than 10 minutes, but then I got scared because the fishermen who come to this area are always seeing what they call "colorful ghosts", which come in and out of the valley of Chirije. So I went inside and locked myself in, and later on it was gone*". This was the first encounter with something unexplained in Chirije.

There have been many other accounts since then of people seeing lights in the sky and coming in and out of the valley.

A particularly interesting account was back in 1997, when the Chirije staff (we had 2 members on site then) saw lights up on the hills and briefly mentioned it to me. A few days later, I walked by as they were talking effusively outside of my Bahía Dolphin Tours office about the lights. I said to them, "*You guys are talking about the lights you told me about the day before yesterday?*" They answered back, "*No Don Patricio…these were last night*". I said, "*Wait a minute; come into my office one by one*". They both told me essentially the same story, but the accounts do not differ and one of them, Celestino Molina, was the night guard and the other was the gardener (a temporary worker whose name I forgot). They were in two different places when it happened, Celestino was in the hammock and the gardener was at the house in the back of the compound.

Gardener's account:

"*After the sun had set and we had finished dinner, I showered and was brushing my teeth when I was illuminated by a big red light. The red light was huge and it lit up all of*

Chirije. About every 3 seconds it shrunk to the size of a very large ball. The light was about 90 feet from me to the left of the museum. At that time the area didn't have any forest because when we bought Chirije in 1994, the fishermen who were living in the area had cut all the vegetation down to grow corn. I saw that it was hovering at about the height of my waistline and swaying just a little bit. After a couple of seconds I screamed out to my wife, and she and her sister, who was visiting, came out. We panicked then ran towards Celestino."

Celestino's account:

"Because the tide was high, I was taking a short nap in the beachside hammock up in the reception area when the gardener and his family came to wake me up. They said, 'Celestino, Celestino, look! Look at that strange light'! I answered back, 'come on guys, I know you are trying to trick me and that is just a big campfire you have lit back there'. 'No, it's not!' they exclaimed. When I saw it surely wasn't and observed it for a few minutes, I got scared and called Chino on the radio and asked if he was at the back of Chirije with his truck. Chino said that he was at the shrimp farm and since it was high tide, no other truck could come in (Chirije has 2 open windows of 6 hours on each low tide during the day, there are 2 low tides in the 24 hour period).

Once we armed ourselves with valor, we ventured towards the object. When we were at least 50 yards away, we realized it was not from here, and what if it picked us up and tried to shred us like picked meat and scatter us in the mountain?! (Referring to some scary movie or program they had seen).

I had a shotgun and when I pumped it, the light disappeared immediately. In a matter of seconds, I saw the bright red object at 300 meters (900 ft.) in altitude and then it disappeared".

We have another two accounts from that night. I will start with the one from the fishermen who were on the beach when it happened. This one outlines the real beauty of that fateful night in Chirije's UFO history. The account of Celestino and the gardener were so convincing that I immediately called Jaime Rodriguez and he came to our house in Bahía as soon as he could. He started an investigation and saw burn markings on the ground, but the most interesting part of the investigation was the following.

After Jaime interviewed the gardener and Celestino, something new came up. Both of them said there was a group of shrimp larvae fishermen on the beach the same evening of the event (this was a malpractice that caused a lot of damage to the environment back then, killing many species of marine life when they swept the near waters of the beach with plankton nets). The fishermen had seen the red dish that had swooped over them. They were probably from San Roque, where there were many of this type of fisherman.

Jaime started investigating in the San Roque area, asking all the larvae fishermen, but none had been in the Chirije area that night. A friend of mine, Juan Moreno, that I had just happened to have been talking to during that time, told me that same night he and his wife and children were eating empanadas near the Church, when he looked up and saw what he described as *"a red light in the form of an American football"*. He also was interviewed and filmed by Jaime Rodriguez.

On the days after this event, I was very busy. I was manager and tour guide of Bahía Dolphin Tours and usually had Isla Corazon or Chirije trips on a daily basis. During that summer of 1997, which was the vacation time for the Andean schools, we had many families staying with us. I remember a friend of the family from Quito (she booked trips for her whole family) came in and asked for a tour to Chirije. With the encounters fresh in my mind I told her about them.

I hadn't noticed her daughter in the background, who was quietly listening. When I said 'red light', she jumped up and exclaimed, *"You see, I told you so! I told my husband and he wouldn't believe me. I told him I saw this red oval light on top of the ferry* and he just didn't believe me". [Now Bahía de Caráquez has the longest bridge in Ecuador, crossing over to San Vicente, but for decades it had only a 17-car ferry that made folkloric crossings. We do miss it, but don't cry over it, as it would take up to three hours to wait for due to all the lines of cars waiting on both sides of the bay]. I could not believe this at first, but it became more intriguing a couple of months later.

One early evening, I was waiting in a beautiful place called Las Delicias for new workers for a harvest that night at the shrimp farm. It was far from Bahía, about an hour into the mountains. Usually, we use temporary workers specialized in harvesting shrimp who live close to the shrimp farm, but they were all busy since every company was harvesting that night (the harvest is usually done when the moon is at its fullest or is a new moon and up to 3 days after. During this time the shrimp are more active and swim faster to the nets).

So there I was in the back of my pickup truck, waiting for the wives of the workers to cook up their dinners and tie them up in banana leaves for them to take to work. On this clear night, all of the sudden I saw one very small star on a straight course west towards the ocean. I immediately acknowledged this sighting as a satellite. We are on the equator and the sun had just set, so this metal object (appearing little in the distance) was reflecting sunlight as it flew speedily on. The area was so clear and beautiful (I was on a high plateau settlement near the coast). I asked the guys if they had ever seen any pretty or odd lights there.

The answer I got lit my face up with a smile and then with awe. Behind the truck, there was a bamboo house with a nice terrace. An older man with his feet dangling over the edge just having a good old time started to say:

"Si Señor, one day we were at Chirijo (he said it with an O and not an e, and definitely did not know that I owned Chirije), on the beach when this beautiful red dish came up to us after we had just finished fishing for larva. It flew very close over us and we threw ourselves on the sand".

Boom! These were the guys Jaime and Veronica were looking for in the Bahía area months ago. They were so isolated up here in this village, it was an amazing coincidence that I found them. Arturo, my brother in law, had told me several times that when Jaime Rodriguez interviewed him, the Ufologist always told him, "*Nothing is a coincidence*".

The larvae fisherman who was there that night when Chirije lit up started explaining that this red dish was dancing over the beach. I asked him what else had he seen, and he responded, "*A mirror inside the dish*" and I asked again, "*And what else did you see?*" "*A Cristiano (Christian) inside the mirror*" he said. Here in the countryside, Cristiano means human, a person very much like you or me.

There are many other accounts like this in which other staff members at the Chirije Eco lodge and archaeological site have had the incredible opportunity to experience. One of them is from Francisco Paladines, another loyal worker and a part of our family, as I feel about all the collaborators over the years with our businesses here. He has been a guard and gardener for many years at Chirije. He is very native looking, and as a teenager was paid 20 cents per day by North American treasure hunters to dig huge holes in search of beautiful pre-Columbian pottery and gold/silver crafts. Is it a coincidence that he works with me? He is now the protector of the entire archaeological site of Chirije.

Here is one of the many sightings Francisco has had…

One night at about 8pm, he was looking over the dark ocean from Chirije. It was right before the new moon when everything is a little darker. All of a sudden he saw all the gardens and the cabins on the other side light up just like it was daytime. He figured there couldn't be a truck there that late; Chino couldn't have come with the high tide (Chino brings in water to the site). He left the lodging area and walked out to the gardens. When he looked up he saw "a round white lamp" on top of him. Francisco shuddered and looked down, and when he looked up again it was gone, but he saw a small point way up in the sky that was certainly the same object. How did it move so quickly in a fraction of a second?

I could go on and on with the sightings at Chirije, but to tell you the truth I have never seen a UFO. Do I believe in them, apart from the millions of galaxies, the right combinations of amino acids in meteorites, asteroids and hydrogen possible compounds that could be in the universe? Yes I do. Hearing the stories of many of my friends and people I do not know (of course not even one tenth of them are included in this book) also helps, but just being in Chirije on a day to day basis is enough to convince me that we are not alone. Nothing wrong or bad has happened with the people that have interacted with extraterrestrial life, we are just two different life forms interested in each other. I hope that both will be interested in sustainability on a universal level.

In all the accounts that I have been told about over the years, no one has ever been hurt, killed, taken away, etc. Do they come in peace? Are they studying us? Are they just our more advanced brothers that have the knowledge, updated data, or telepathic perception of our human and environmental condition on earth to help us during the critical moments in which we need a higher energy form to show us the right path?

Could it be that because we are a beautiful blue planet lit up by a star in the immensity of dark space and make so much racket with our radio and TV waves we are too visible? Alternatively, does the lack of extraordinary evidence (videos not captured and transmitted by national TV chains and such), show that we are only supposed to make a slight contact and vice versa? For example quoting from a TV interview, Stephen Hawkings said:

"To my mathematical brain, the numbers alone make thinking about aliens perfectly rational. The real challenge is to work out what aliens might actually be like. If aliens visit us, the outcome would be much as when Columbus landed in America, which didn't turn out well for the Native Americans."

He advocated that, rather than try to establish contact, man should try to avoid contact with alien life forms.

I want to end this chapter with some words from my sister Veronica who was persistent in her search for extraterrestrial life.

Tec. Veronica Tamariz:

Worked with Jaime Rodriguez in various projects, especially in the province of Manabí, Ecuador. Became a member of a contact group called Mission Rahma, founded by Peruvian contactee Sixto Paz Wells. Attended the World Encounter of Contacted Persons in Costa Rica in 1995. Made first documentary in 1996 in Switzerland, interviewing Edward Billy Meier on his contact experience. With Jaime Rodriguez interviewed astronauts in NASA during a special TV coverage of Teleamazonas TV during the STS 91 Space Shuttle Launch. In 2005, visited Claudio Pasten in Chile, a former UFO contactee. In 2007, experienced a sighting at Talara, Peru. In 2009, the first sighting for Veronica in Chirije with experience of a light beam from a craft on her body, with witnesses around.

Veronica states:

"Chirije is an important archaeological site due to the sheer size of the land mass and because of the varied cultures found there. Being close to the equator might explain the magnetic energy field it has. We can combine archaeology with ufology – both have a connection with the past. We have been visited in the past – far before we even thought of existing. It is time for the human race to understand the truth and significance of mankind evolving in this third dimension, towards the fourth and fifth dimension.
To become an ufologist, I had to go through many steps. The first steps were trying to describe the meaning, wanting to know more, tracking these objects in the skies.
The next steps were trying to understand some questions: Why are they here? Why do they visit us? Who are we? Understanding the nature and the role of our existence in this brotherhood universe, and most importantly, the telepathic messages they are sending. The universe is huge. Imagine our creator, God, as an architect of billions of solar systems and planets beyond our infinite galaxy and universe. We cannot be selfish and think we are the only ones. Even in every sacred and ancient writing, the Bible, and other sacred scriptures, we find evidence of extraterrestrial beings that have interacted with the human race".

I want to ask these people who experienced the encounters, "were you just at the right place at the right time"? Is there anything else beyond the human 3D plane that makes this visual linking with them? If you have been blessed to see incredible spacecrafts, more power to you! I will spend more nights at Chirije in hopes that I might see one of these objects up close, fulfilling my dream.

CHAPTER TWELVE

The Secret of Paradise ~ Ecuador

As I started to write this book, I felt the need to raise the question; "How much does the world know about Ecuador?" I remember back in the 60's and 70's when I lived in the United States what little I knew of the country in which I was born. What I can remember is from the few summer vacations we could afford to travel back and see my grandparents. The news on television was what I knew the North Americans were seeing (if anything at all) of this South American nation.

Ecuador, named in 1830 due to being located on the equator, is a small country that gained its independence from Spanish rule in 1822. It has always struggled to survive, and was constantly at war with Peru. Luckily that era is now gone. The name Ecuador only came up when on the news the anchormen would say that another US tuna fishing boat was caught off of our coast in one of many *"Tuna War"* scenarios. Ecuador had pledged to protect their 200-mile territorial water limit. Other news would probably be pertaining to another overthrown military dictatorship which would appear one day in the news and the next day not. Being such a small country with no political interest to anyone outside of it, it seemed to not deserve the attention of the press.

Where I lived in New York was filled with Ecuadorians, I remember them just like my dad, working to the bone. The US census of 2000 stated that 600,000 Ecuadorians lived in the United States and almost 70% of them lived in New York. It was hard, but a great time for my family in the land of liberty. I was blessed by having a good education in English. This helped immensely later on in life.

I was also blessed to have been the first Executive Director for the Promotion Board of Ecuador (Fondo Mixto de Promocion Turistica del Ecuador) and back in 2005 was honored to present the first integrated tourism campaign to attract North American visitors to Ecuador in a beautiful setting in New York. I remember more than 100 press journalists present, with a great exhibit of the 4 worlds of Ecuador (Pacific Coast, Andes, Amazon and the Galapagos Islands) nicely done by our Ecuador office in New York and led by Nathalie Pilovetzky, later to become a lifelong friend. In the middle of my presentation, I was so proud of the country I was representing that I had a tear in my eye. I always remember this was the country where I grew up and now it is such a grand destination for everyone to visit.

A couple days before I started to write this chapter I received one of those Ecuador Google Alerts (I like to be always informed). It contained one of the first good international press editorials on our country that I had seen. It was from *The Guardian*, an important newspaper from the United Kingdom. It contained an article written by Jayati Ghosh (economics professor from the University of New Delhi) on January 19, 2012, stating many things that, as Ecuadorians, we are proud to see. The article is as follows:

Could Ecuador be the most radical and exciting place on Earth?

A decade ago, Ecuador was a banana republic, an economic basket case. Today, it has much to teach the rest of the world.

Ecuador is one of the most exciting places on Earth right now, in terms of working towards a new development paradigm. It shows how much can be achieved with political will, even in uncertain economic times. Just 10 years ago, Ecuador was more or less a basket case, a quintessential "banana republic" (it happens to be the world's largest exporter of bananas), characterized by political instability, inequality, a poorly performing economy, and the ever-looming impact of the US on its domestic politics.

In 2000, in response to hyperinflation and balance of payments problems, the government dollarized the economy, replacing the Sucre with the US currency as legal tender. This subdued inflation, but it did nothing to address the core economic problems, and further constrained the domestic policy space.

A major turning point came with the election of the economist Rafael Correa as president. After taking over in January 2007, his government ushered in a series of changes, based on a new constitution (the country's 20th, approved in 2008) that was itself mandated by a popular referendum. A hallmark of the changes that have occurred since then is that major policies have first been put through the referendum process. This has given the government the political ability to take on major vested interests and powerful lobbies.

The government is now the most stable in recent times and will soon become the longest serving in Ecuador's tumultuous history. The president's approval ratings are well over 70%. All this is due to the reorientation of the government's approach, made possible by a constitution remarkable for its recognition of human rights and the rights of nature, and its acceptance of plurality and cultural diversity.

Economic growth

Consider just some economic changes brought about in the past four years, beginning with the renegotiation of oil contracts with multinational companies. Ecuador is an oil exporter, but had benefited relatively little from this because of the high shares of oil sales that went to foreign oil companies. A new law in July 2010 dramatically changed the terms, increasing the government's share from 13% to 87% of gross oil revenues.

Seven of the 16 foreign oil companies decided to pull out, and their fields were taken over by state-run companies. However, the others stayed on and, as a result, state revenues increased by $870m (£563m) in 2011.

Second, and possibly even more impressively, the government managed a dramatic increase in direct tax receipts. In fact, this has been even more important in revenue terms than oil receipts. Direct taxes (mainly corporation taxes) increased from around 35% of total taxes in 2006 to more than 40% in 2011. This was largely because of better enforcement, since the nexus between big business and the public tax administration was broken.

Third, these increased government revenues were put to good use in infrastructure investment and social spending. Ecuador now has the highest proportion of public investment to GDP (10%) in Latin America and the Caribbean. In addition, social spending has doubled since 2006. This has enabled real progress towards the constitutional goals of free education at all levels and access to free healthcare for all citizens. Significant increases in public housing have followed the constitution's affirmation of the right of all citizens to dignified housing with proper amenities.

There are numerous other measures. Expanding direct public employment; increasing the minimum wage; legally enforcing social security provisions for all workers. Diversifying the economy to reduce dependence on oil exports; diversifying trading partners to reduce dependence on the United States. Enlarging public banking operations to reach more small and medium entrepreneurs. Auditing external debt to reduce debt service payments and abandoning unfair bilateral investment agreements. Other efforts include reform of the justice system.

Creating a Biosphere

One exciting recent initiative is the Yasuní-ITT biosphere reserve, perhaps the world's first attempt to avoid greenhouse emissions by leaving oil underground. This not only protects the extraordinary biodiversity of the area but also the habitats of its indigenous peoples. The scheme proposes to use ecotourism to make human activity compatible with nature.

All this may sound too good to be true, and certainly the process of transformation has only just begun. There are bound to be conflicts with those whose profits and power are threatened, as well as other hurdles along the way. However, for those who believe that we are not condemned to the gloomy status quo, and that societies can do things differently, what is happening in Ecuador provides inspiration and even guidance. The rest of the world has much to learn from this ongoing radical experiment.

(The Guardian, UK, 2012)

Nation branding

Simon Anholt is one of the first experts on Nation Branding; he is the founder of this idea, meaning there is a national image, identity perceived by the public. He says in his book, *Competitive Identity: The New Brand Management for Nations, Cities and Regions*:

"Just as brand management has proved to be one of the most potent instruments for devising strategy and creating wealth in the commercial sector, so its application to the development and competiveness of states, regions and cities could have enormous and far-reaching impacts in the years to come".

He created a hexagonal mode, which depicts what he calls the Natural Channels of National Communication, which are:

❖ **Exports**
That determines the public's image of products and services from each country and the extent to which consumers proactively seek or avoid products from each country-of- origin.

❖ **Governance**
Measures public opinion regarding the level of national government competency and fairness and describes individuals' beliefs about each country's government, as well as its perceived commitment to global issues such as democracy, justice, poverty and the environment.

❖ **Investment and Immigration**
Determines the power to attract people to live, work or study in each country and reveals how people perceive a country's economic and social situation.

❖ **Culture and Heritage**
Reveals global perceptions of each nation's heritage and appreciation for its contemporary culture, including film, music, art, sport and literature.

❖ **People**
Measures the population's reputation for competence, education, openness and friendliness and other qualities, as well as perceived levels of potential hostility and discrimination.

❖ **Tourism**
Captures the level of interest in visiting a country and the draw of natural and man-made tourist attractions.

In the elements presented by Anholt, Ecuador has considerably progressed and it can't be long until we arrive at the door of international recognition and a more favorable worldwide perception of our country brand.

In a way, it is a positive aspect that Ecuador, up until now, has had no country image in the mind of the average world citizen. Being a small country that many people around the world do not even know the location of, this is easy to understand. However, we are expanding in different areas and we, as Ecuadorians, feel that we can place ourselves at an innovative level of emerging nations in the world, with a tendency towards accepting a growth and peaceful order.

Here is a little information on the elements Anholt's hexagon describes and where Ecuador's status is on each one, and how the country can deal with each category, what it should produce for the latter perception of the citizens of the world.

Ecuador Exports

Even though Ecuador still remains the world's largest banana exporter, we have made considerable advances in added value product exportation (an area in which we need more industry investment). Ecuador exported 19.3 billion USD in 2011 (according to Ecuador's Central Bank statistics). Petroleum, which is our most important product of exportation, produced close to 10 billion USD in exports in 2011.

In exports of non-manufactured products, one of the world's most consumed fruits is the banana from Ecuador. This fruit generated a little over 2 billion USD. Following this item, 1 billion USD is produced from the exportation of shrimp (mostly farmed). Then follows 624 million USD in flower exports, 420 million USD in Cacao (cocoa), almost 270 million USD in coffee (Anecafe) and 183 million USD in fish exports, followed by another 138 million USD in timber.

Though Ecuador still exports in majority raw or prime materials, (we are a primary product producer), more than ever the government is looking at the strategic service and industrial areas. For example, last year there was 30 million USD of exported software.

Due to Ecuador's prime geographical position on the equator (sun's luminosity), this small but distinctive and diverse country presents a grand variety of microclimates and altitude levels with the Pacific Coast, Andes, Amazon and Galapagos regions. Having a stable warm and mild climate all year long, there has been a diversification of fruits exported from Ecuador. They include mango, pineapple, prickly pear, naranjilla, tree tomato, Tahiti lime, blackberry, uvilla, guayaba (guava), guanabana, passion fruit and granadilla.

In manufactured products, we are only at 4.5 billion USD in exportation. The mistakenly known Panama Hat, originally from Ecuador, fits into to this category along with petroleum derivatives, other seafood products, cocoa and coffee manufactured products. The straw hat, such an important object weaved into Ecuadorian history, is a product that should be better promoted. It would give the country one of those unique and distinct products helping to build the awareness of Ecuador's native products and exports in the world markets.

Ecuadorian Governance

The domestic opinion of how Ecuador is being governed varies from the heavier taxed group of people who have had more opportunities than the rest of the population who have had fewer options for education, jobs and business entrepreneurship. It's a love-hate situation, where 70% of Ecuador's peoples favor all the changes that are occurring. The rest of the population has had to cope with the beginning of a tax culture for our country. Many people saw this as harmful to the possibility of becoming prosperous, but it is an inevitable change for the well-being of the population at large. The payment of taxes is used to fund infrastructure, education and better services for their overall well-being. A better redistribution of funds collected by government and better options and opportunities for the general public is an objective. Many people started to think erroneously that this was the beginning of communism.

I had the opportunity to talk with our President when he was visiting our Eco lodge at the archaeological site of Chirije.

When we came to the subject of governance and the projection of our country, the President told me he wanted Ecuador to become the best economic model possible with aspects similar to a European socialist democracy, and that the Ecuadorian private business sector was to take the country to the next level. As we finished our talk, the head of the security team that always accompanied him told me that many people think that the President talks about communism, that he thinks like Hugo Chavez, that he is against prosperity. That in all Rafael Correa's essence, there is only a brand new Ecuador to be developed and undeniable prosperity for a good quality of life to be attained by all of its people.

The National Plan for Good Living (Plan Nacional de Buen Vivir) is the strategy proposed by the government to create a better (happier) life for Ecuadorians, which in turn will create a positive domestic and worldwide opinion of Ecuador. This push towards sustainability starts with the views of the Andean indigenous peoples proposing the "sumak kawsay", or life at its fullest.

The notion of development is non-existent in the cosmovision of these peoples, since the future is behind us, it is that we cannot see, that we do not know, meanwhile the past we have in front of us, which we can see, that we know, it has made us and with it we go forward on the path. On this path we are accompanied by our ancestors that are made one with us, with the community and with nature. We share then being together with all these beings, beings that have life, and are a part of us. The world of above, the world of below, the world outside, the world here, connect and make part of this whole, inside a spiral time perspective and not a lineal one.

The ancestral thinking is eminently a collective one. The conceiving of Good Living necessarily resorts to the idea of "us" because the world cannot be understood by the "I" of the west. The community shelters, protects, demands and is part of us. The community is the support and the base of the reproduction of that collective individual that everyone and each one of us "are". From here, the human being is conceived as one part of this all, and should not be understood as the sum of all the parts, rather the whole expressed in each living being and each living being expressed in the whole.

Kichwa thought: "The universe is permanent, it has always existed and will always exist, and it is born and dies inside itself and only time changes it".

Then to hurt nature is to hurt ourselves. Every act, every behavior has cosmic consequences; the hills get angry, or get happy, they laugh or get sad, they feel...they think...they exist (they are there).

The sumak kawsay or life at its fullest, expresses this cosmovision. To reach the full life is the task of the wise and consists in arriving at a level of total harmony with the community and the cosmos.

This is one of the main values for our country. Our focus is not on gaining more and more wealth, instead we take the course of constructing a society of "*good living*", which includes a better understanding and harmony between all beings and to live a happy and more fulfilled life.

The objectives of this plan are:

1.   To foster equality, cohesion, social and territorial integration in diversity.

2.   To improve the capacities and potential of citizenship.

3.   To improve the quality of life for the population.

4.   To guarantee the rights of nature and to promote a healthy and sustainable environment.

5.   To guarantee sovereignty and peace, to boost Ecuador's strategic insertion in the world and Latin American integration.

6.   To guarantee steady, fair and worthy (decent) work in all its diversified forms.

7.   Build and strengthen areas that are public, intercultural and communal.

8.   To strengthen and to reinforce national identity, the diverse identities, multinationalities and interculturality of Ecuador.

9.   To guarantee the validity of rights and justice.

10.   To guarantee access to public and political participation.

11.   Establish a social, supportive and sustainable economic system.

12.   To build a democratic state for good living.

Please do not assume this is all too poetic and romantic, there is an actual 520-page plan that I invite you to read. The national strategies are based on all the programs, projects and actions that need to be taken to accomplish this, at least in this first phase during 2009-2013. Another area in which we will build brand awareness around is environmental conservation.

Ecuador Rights of Nature

Ecuador's government has taken the first actions required to protect the environment in their new constitution, in effect since October 20, 2008. From the Georgetown University Political Database of the Americas we have the following translated chapter:

Chapter 7: Rights for Nature

Art. 71.   Nature or Pachamama, where life is reproduced and exists, has the right to exist, persist, maintain and regenerate its vital cycles, structure, functions and its processes in evolution.

Every person, people, community or nationality, will be able to demand the recognitions of rights for nature before the public organisms [organizations]. The application and interpretation of these rights will follow the related principles established in the Constitution.

The State will motivate natural [individual] and juridical persons as well as collectives to protect nature; it will promote respect towards all the elements that form an ecosystem.

Art. 72.   Nature has the right to restoration. This integral restoration is independent of the obligation on natural and juridical persons or the State to indemnify the people and the collectives that depend on the natural systems.

In the cases of severe or permanent environmental impact, including the ones caused by the exploitation on non-renewable natural resources, the State will establish the most efficient mechanisms for the restoration, and will adopt the adequate measures to eliminate or mitigate the harmful environmental consequences.

Art. 73. The State will apply precaution and restriction measures in all the activities that can lead to the extinction of species, the destruction of the ecosystems or the permanent alteration of the natural cycles.

The introduction of organisms and organic and inorganic material that can alter in a definitive way the national genetic patrimony is prohibited.

Art. 74. The persons, people, communities and nationalities will have the right to benefit from the environment and form natural wealth that will allow wellbeing.

The environmental services cannot be appropriated; its production, provision, use and exploitation, will be regulated by the State.

We have another important project that is just getting worldwide recognition. If you have seen the movie Avatar you can understand to the comparison to the Yasuni-ITT project deep into the Ecuadorian Amazon. Due to the importance of this project for the country and for the world, I have included the following overview from the United Nations Development Program:

The Yasuni National Park is one of the most important and diverse biological reserves in the world. It is home to the Tagaeri-Taromenane indigenous peoples living in voluntary isolation. Ecuador decided to maintain the crude oil in the ITT field indefinitely underground in order to put social and environmental values first. Ecuador will forgo 846 million barrels of heavy crude reserves and, in turn, become the first developing country to propose an effective, quantifiable and verifiable carbon abatement model.

President Rafael Correa's vision of this pioneer proposal, unprecedented in the history of an oil-dependent country, has been received favorably by several governments, organizations and global citizens. The initiative proposes a new cooperative model between developed and developing countries. It is an opportunity for the world to consider an equitable paradigm of sustainable development, which in Ecuador is referred to as "sumak kawsay" or life at its fullest.

The Yasuni Ishpingo Tambococha Tiputini Trust Fund was established for receipt of contributions from supporters of Ecuador's historical decision to permanently forego the extraction of the Yasuni ITT oil fields (about 846 million barrels). The contributions will finance renewable energy and sustainable development investments such as avoidance of deforestation and conservation of ecosystems.

Through this unique initiative, Ecuador is addressing the challenges of climate change and sustainable development and is gradually changing its energy matrix from fossil fuel to renewable energy sources. The Yasuni initiative will avoid the emission of 407 million metric tons of Carbon Dioxide (CO_2) by forgoing extraction and burning of fossil fuels, protect one of the most bio-diverse regions of the world and maintain the livelihoods of the area's indigenous people. In addition, it will lead to savings of 800 million metric tons of CO_2 from avoided deforestation and reforestation it will promote nationally.

In the spirit of co-responsibility, Ecuador is requesting the world community to contribute 50 percent of the income it is forgoing, amounting to 3.6 billion USD (over a 13 year period), with the balance being the contribution of the people of Ecuador to global goods.

Yasuni Guarantee Certificates (CGYs)

In exchange for contributions, the Government will provide a guarantee to maintain the ITT field oil reserves within the National Park underground indefinitely. The Government will issue Yasuni Guarantee Certificates (CGYs) in US dollars equivalent to the face value of each contribution equal to or above 50,000 USD. Where the contribution is below 50,000 USD - the present minimum threshold established by the Steering Committee, it shall constitute a donation to the Yasuni ITT Trust Fund and will not entitle the Contributor to CGYs. The CGY is an instrument that does not earn interest and does not have an expiration or maturity date as long as the Government maintains its commitment not to exploit the Yasuni ITT oil reserves.

Governance of the Yasuni ITT Trust Fund Steering Committee:

The Yasuní Fund will be governed by a Steering Committee chaired by a representative of the Government. The Steering Committee will have six full members comprising of: (i) three representatives of the Government, including the Chairperson; (ii) two representatives from the Contributor Governments; and (iii) one Ecuadorian Civil Society representative, with UNDP Resident Representative/UN Resident Coordinator and the UNDP MPTF Office Executive Coordinator participating as ex officio members. The Committee will make decisions by majority aiming at consensus, with the Chairperson casting the deciding vote in case consensus is not reached.

The key functions of the Steering Committee are to provide overall leadership of the Fund and set its strategic direction and oversight; review and make fund allocation decisions; authorize the release of funds; and oversee effective monitoring and evaluation of financed activities and ensure transparency. It will also ensure coordination with other relevant international initiatives such as UNCBD, UNFCCC, UN-REDD, etc.

The Yasuni Fund Technical Secretariat:

The Technical Secretariat is an impartial entity providing administrative, technical and substantive support to the Steering Committee. It shall undertake four functions under one management structure: (i) Technical support; (ii) Project appraisal; (iii) Monitoring and evaluation; and (iv) Administrative support.

The Government Coordinating Entity:

As the Government designated Government Coordinating Entity, the Ministry of Heritage through the Yasuni ITT Coordination Office, in cooperation with the National Secretary of Planning and Development, is responsible for the development, implementation, monitoring and evaluation of the Yasuni Fund portfolio implemented by national entities. It assumes full programmatic and financial accountability, on behalf of the Government, for activities implemented by the Recipient and Implementing Organizations.

National Recipient and Implementing Organizations:

Through the Government Coordinating Entity, National Recipient and Implementing Organizations will prepare proposals for funding and submit them to the Steering Committee for approval after review by the Technical Secretariat.

I have included this innovative idea of our government in its entirety so we can understand fully what we are proposing for the world. To recap:

❖ Yasuni: One of the most bio-diverse spots on Earth.

❖ One hectare in Yasuni contains more tree species than are native to the whole of North America.

❖ Ecuador indefinitely foregoes extraction of 846 million barrels of oil and more than 7.2 billion USD in income.

❖ Avoidance of 407 million metric tons of CO_2 emissions due to non-extraction and burning of oil.

❖ Avoidance of 800 million metric tons of CO_2 from avoided deforestation.

❖ 78% of Ecuadorian citizens support the Yasuni Initiative. (UNDP)

With the Rights to Nature and the Yasuni ITT initiative, and with the Eco city processes we have started where I live in Bahía de Caráquez, I believe there will be international recognition and a true possibility for this small country to become a model nation for the world.

Investment and Immigration

The Global Property Index, created by *International Living*, recently highlighted Ecuador as a top destination for investment. This makes me extremely proud. See the following article:

Ecuador was named as the best overseas investment destination for U.S. international residential property buyers this week by The Global Property Index, created by International Living.

According to International Living, Ecuador's north Pacific Coast, which was once considered difficult to get to, is now a real development hotspot following the construction of a major new access road. This, along with low property costs and quality housing, are the key factors that put the Latin American country in the top spot.

"This is one of the nicest stretches of Pacific coast you will find," says Ronan McMahon who authored the *International Living* report. "It stayed undiscovered because it was difficult to get to."

Photo by Torsten Loeffler

Concerning immigration, Ecuador is having one of the best years ever, attracting baby boomers for retirement, especially in the areas of Cuenca (a world heritage site), Cotacachi (a very organized native indigenous area) and the Pacific Coast (concentrated in the urban and rural areas of San Clemente, Bahía de Caráquez and up to Jama). In Vilcabamba, the valley of longevity, we have a grand group of Expats that consider this area their home. I was very surprised to see that north Americans were coming down not only for vacation or to stay 6 months, but to pass their golden years living full time in our country.

International Living Magazine for the 3rd year in a row voted Ecuador as the best place to retire in the world:

"And the winner is…"

Flowers bloom everywhere, and not one but four rushing rivers bubble over rocks to feed the lush vegetation. In Ecuador — the country that tops this year's Global Retirement Index — nature is ever-present… and you can enjoy it fully in the city of Cuenca, where those rivers trail amid mountain surrounds.

The colonial churches, grand mansions, shady parks, and fountain-anchored plazas have earned Cuenca worldwide recognition for its beauty. A mild climate makes for comfortable living year-round. Average daily temperatures reach into the 70s F, and the nights are cool and fresh. Ecuador is one of the most affordable countries in the world.

You can rent a furnished, two-bed apartment in an historic center for $220, or buy a large condo for $66,000. You can live well for $600 a month…and like royalty for double that.

To rank our winners this year, we analyzed 37 critical data points for each of our top 23 retirement havens and, for the third year running, Ecuador won. For retirees, colonial Cuenca is Ecuador's most attractive city. The third largest in the country, it offers the relaxed pace of a smaller town with the first-class amenities and health care of a bigger one. However, Cuenca is by no means your only option in Ecuador. This is a country with something for everyone — beaches, rural highlands, jungle escapes, and colonial cities."

"No matter where you choose to live in Ecuador, there is no better place on earth to discover the simple abundance of health, tranquility, adventure, and beauty," says Expat Patricia Farmer. "We chose Bahía de Caráquez on the coast to begin our Ecuador adventure. There are plenty of amenities, including a hospital, restaurants, and frequent Expat get-togethers."

Patricia, her husband Ron, and their two nervous cats arrived at their new beachfront home in February of this year. "We knew no one. And yet we immediately felt at home," says Patricia. "Living in Southern California, we were spoiled by the warm climate and beautiful beaches. Retirement would — or should — have given us time to enjoy all that more fully. Yet, we had no realistic chance of retiring anywhere near a beach in California. Looking back now, we're glad we needed to look elsewhere to fulfill our retirement dreams. Otherwise, the chance of living in one of the most beautiful and exotic retirement havens in the world might have passed us by."

This article from *International Living Magazine* was reproduced in many newspapers and magazines in the United States, including the Chicago Tribune. What a small world it is that Patricia and her husband Ron Farmer are good friends of mine and they had rented my family's apartment in Bahía de Caráquez while they watched their beautiful beachfront house being built. In the hexagonal case of *Country Branding* for investment and immigration, we feel we are on the right path.

Ecuador's Culture and Heritage

Valdivia

Emilio Estrada (who discovered Chirije in 1960) discovered the pottery of the Valdivia phase on the coast of Ecuador in 1956. A that time, this culture was the earliest known that initiated the skillful elaboration of ceramic artifacts in the whole of the Americas. From the original dates of Dr. Betty Meggers to what I was told by Jose Chancay, to the new investigations of Dr. Marcos, these would be 3200 BC and 4400 BC. Just to compare, the earliest pottery in the territories of the United States was found at Stallings Island in Georgia (2515 BC).

Dr. Jorge Marcos, Ecuador's most renowned national archaeologist, discovered a Valdivia site on the northern perimeter at the mouth of the Gulf of Guayaquil in a site called Real Alto in 1971. He has published the book [titles translated] *Archaeology of Coastal Ecuador, Real Alto: History of a Valdivia Ceremonial Center* and other relevant investigations for Ecuador.

In a personal communication this year, Dr. Marcos told me that we had pottery 2000 years before the peoples of the territories of pre-Columbian Mexico and 1700 years before the peoples of pre-Columbian Peru. That is a very long time by any standard; imagine 17-20 centuries before, living on the same coast, but of course in different latitudes. Could the techniques have been introduced?

I believe in being open minded with these theories that to some extent have been already proven. It is logical to conclude there was transpacific contact especially with the Polynesians. With all the documents Betty Meggers sent to me, it is overwhelming and so interesting to see how much contact there was before Columbus. In addition, I believe that we had all the geographical and environmental resources in our favor for a successful venture into agriculture and artistic independence.

Estrada published a pamphlet in 1956 titled *"Valdivia: a Formative Archaeological Site on the Coast of the Guayas Province"*, which detailed the new discovery of ceramic that was earlier than the Chorrera already known for Ecuador.

James Zeidler in his book *Regional Archaeology in Northern Manabí, Ecuador* quotes Betty Meggers (1966):

"Valdivia and Machalilla subsistence can be characterized as mixed systems of fishing, hunting, and agriculture, with maize and root crops under cultivation."

Presley Norton, also another important Ecuadorian archaeologist from Guayaquil, according to Rodolfo Pimentel's biography, was hooked into archaeology through underwater spear fishing. He met Chicho Estrada, Emilio's brother, and they hit it off as good friends. On weekend trips, they would dive while Emilio was working on a beachfront site. He became very interested in all the objects Emilio brought up.

Presley Norton's book, *5000 Years of Occupation,* points to the Bahía and the Manteño cultures (500 BC to time of contact) as being the most maritime of all. Already specialized in navigating the balsa rafts, they were some of the most impressive sea *merchants* of the eastern Pacific. According to Norton the Valdivia culture at 2000 BC were already using balsa sailing rafts.

As for the people of Valdivia, they lived in a tropical environment that probably was even lusher than it is today. Since the colonial period, most of the forests of our coast south of the equator (specially the Dry Tropical Forest) have been deforested for their fine hardwoods. Thousands of hectares have been used since those times for extensive cattle farming as well. The availability of spectacular landscapes, diverse and abundant wildlife with incredible amounts of birdlife, fish and mollusk stocks, magnified the opportunity for successful and sustainable survival of the groups situated from the southern coast all the way to the north central part of the Coast.

Dr. Marcos, in his article *"Woven Textiles in a Late Valdivia Context"* – on comparing cotton-textile samples with the earliest found in Peru, states that cotton domestication and the loom might have been introduced to the Peruvian coast from the north. Experts in hunting, fishing, gathering, agriculture and ceramic arts, they were a people that initiated an important journey that led to maritime and terrestrial exchange that pointed the way towards advances in technologies and environmental adaptation for many cultures of the Americas.

As important as it has been that I have focused on Valdivia's pottery creation and diffusion, nonetheless relevant is the posterior development of cultures on the coast of Ecuador. To write on these would be another challenge and another book. There is a feeling amongst professionals that there are still many fields to explore and many more studies to be done to close the gaps that remain (not on purpose but due to lack of time, number of archaeologists and funding). The essential aspect of focusing on Valdivia is to go back in time to see one of the first cultures to work with ceramic art that is partially dependent of the long period of Paleo-Indian development (especially towards agriculture and sedentary life) and adaptation to the Pacific coast of Ecuador.

The archaeological richness that remains in Ecuador is mostly comprised of skeletal remains, stone tools, shells (since 8,800 B.C.) and evidence of pottery from different cultures dating back to 4400 B.C. Due to the tropical environmental conditions, most of the wood and forest materials used for housing and temples have decomposed, leaving only small traces. Earthen mounds, built by the natives for ceremonial and/or living platforms, have existed throughout the various developmental phases in pre-Columbian Ecuador. Many were created during the Bahía culture (500 B.C. to 500 A.D).

Japoto, a site near Bahía, had an extended mound complex area. I thought the mounds were just platforms until they were pointed out to me by an archaeologist that some of these mounds have ramps and structures inside of them. Due to the organization of the mounds, you can tell an important state of society existed there. In the Chirije Manteño Cultures, (from 500 A.D. to time of contact with the Spaniards), stone was used in quantity, especially for the bases of houses and temples.

Marshall Saville discovered one of the largest cities of pre-Columbian Ecuador, which is located on the hills of Cerro de Hojas and Cerro Jaboncillo, right next to the city of Portoviejo, which is the capital of Manabí. I had already been involved with Chirije since 1994 and had read about the most important discoveries in the area in the books *Antiquities of Manabí and Ecuador* by Marshall Saville *(Preliminary and Final Reports)*.

When I was director of tourism of the Ministry of Tourism of Ecuador for the province in 2002, I was constantly asked to help develop a promenade in Crucita, which has nice beaches and is part of the administrative district of Portoviejo, but I really did not think that would be the star product for the capital. Once I was coastal director for the ministry of tourism, I sent archaeologists like Gerardo Castro up to do a survey and he told me there was a spectacular site on the hills of Cerro de Hojas and Jaboncillo, but that the stone mining was destroying it little by little. I knew that if investigations were redone and if the ceremonial center was recreated, it would become an attraction for travelers and also a point of interest for the cruise ships that would come into Manta.

My work ended with the change of government of that time in 2003 (later on, I would work with the new President and the government as director for the promotion board). I cannot blame my successors for not pushing this project, but for the people of Manabí and me, it was very important. However, later on a friend of mine, Dr. Cristina Castro, took the position of Director of Tourism of Manabí and understood the significance of the project. She is a scientist of marine mammals and teaches environmental education. She asked me as a friend to advise her on her biggest challenge and I told her it was Cerro de Hojas and Jaboncillo, the stone city. I said to her the first thing she needed is to get a team of national press together to report on the site. So I helped organized the press trip and it was a success. They made so much positive noise on the subject that one month later the President of Ecuador Rafael Correa visited the site and started taking action to preserve it.

Another friend of mine, the archaeologist Telmo Lopez, (who went to the Colegio Americano-Senior High School of Guayaquil with me) started working on the site to create a good baseline study. He found a larger area than Saville had found. Now the government has a program to develop the site, led by the renowned archaeologist Dr. Jorge Marcos. Their administrative center is in Ciudad Alfaro in Montecristi, only 15 minutes away. This site currently has more than 800 structures in about 3,500 hectares (8,648 acres). I personally found many interesting structures when I was able to explore about 4 kilometers of the hilltops, the freshwater wells were particularly impressive.

Back in the early 1900s, Marshall H. Saville found wonderful stone structures on the site, including large stone seats (U shaped throne like) with animal and human figures under the "U". No other seats of this nature have been found in North and South America.

The site embodied the Manteño culture, which had contact with the Incas and the Spanish conquistadors on this part of the coast of Manabí. They were the final group to actively trade the Spondylus Shell to the rest of pre-Columbian America.

Ancient cultures

The ancient cultures of pre-Columbian Ecuador are not widely known. Only a small segment of Latin American specialized archaeologists and anthropologists know about the incredible journey that especially the coastal cultures have gone through. Our first culture dates back to 12,000 years ago on the Pacific Coast. This was the pre-ceramic culture of Las Vegas, studied in detail by Dr. Karen Stothert. Here, an important discovery was made with the Ancient Lovers of Sumpa.

Our first culture that worked with ceramic, Valdivia, appeared around 3500-4000 B.C., discovered by Emilio Estrada (who also discovered Chirije). It was the earliest known culture in all the Americas that worked with pottery. This was more than a thousand years before the peoples of pre-Columbian Peru and Mexico would make their first ceramic art manifestation or pottery craft.

One of the reasons why I created the Spondylus Route (Ruta del Spondylus) was to pay homage to the ancient coastal cultures of Ecuador and Northern Peru. The hierarchies of cultural tourism attractions require something very fascinating to qualify as a point for visitation. As a result, we still need a lot of work on this to be able to have global interest in our ancient cultures.

Ecuador's People

Our live cultures are interesting enough, also not well known in the rest of the world. There are 3 ethnic groups called the Chachis, the Awa and the Epera that live on the north central to northern coast of Ecuador. We have also the Tsachilas (Colorados) that live near Santo Domingo. These are our indigenous groups on the coast.

According to the census of 2010, in the country we have 14,483,499 Ecuadorians. The ethnic composition of this population is divided as:

❖ *71.9% Mestizos [mixture of Spanish descent with Amerindian, something interesting that I read occurred after the first conquistadors (around 5 centuries ago) in the first stages of colonization there would be 1 Spanish woman for every 8 or 9 men, hence the large mestizo population]*

❖ *7.4% Montubios [very diverse, emerging from the Mestizo but also of coastal indigenous ancestry, coastal rural farmer and fluvial fisherman]*

❖ *7.2% Afro Ecuadorians [came aboard the first black slave ships, mainly from western Africa (there is a beautiful story to tell from this) and later with Eloy Alfaro's giant infrastructure feat of the coastal Andean train (from Duran to Quito) a smaller group came from Jamaica]*

❖ *7% indigenous [14 different nationalities and 16 different peoples]*

❖ *6.1% white.*

From the book *Blackness in Latin America and the Caribbean* by Norman Whitten, Jr., and Arlene Torres there is a chapter titled "To Rescue National Dignity: Blackness as a Quality of Nationalist Creativity in Ecuador" by Norman Whitten and Diego Quiroga, which has an interesting story:

"Regional blackness as a force of self-liberation in Ecuador begins in Esmeraldas, and its origin occurs during a violent tropical storm and a movement of African rebellion. The documented history of Ecuador establishes the beginnings of Afro-Hispanic culture in what is now Esmeraldas, Ecuador, where a Spanish slaving ship ran aground in 1553. There, a group of twenty-three Africans from the coast of Guinea, led by a black warrior named Antón, attacked the slavers and liberated themselves. Not long after, this group, together with other blacks entering the region, led by a ladino (Hispanicized black person) named Alonso de Illescas, came to dominate the region from northern Manabí north to what is now Barbacoas, Colombia. At this time (late sixteenth century) intermixture with indigenous peoples, to who black people fled to establish their palenques (villages of self-liberated people - some fortified, some not), was such that their features were described as zambo (black-indigenous admixture), synonyms of which were negro (black) and mulato (mixed or hybrid black-white).

By 1599 black people were clearly in charge of what was called "La República de Zambos" or "Zambo Republic". Zambo refers to people of color who are descendants of Native Americans and African-Americans.

In that year a group of Zambo chieftains, said to represent 100,000 or more Zambo people of Esmeraldas, trekked to Quito to declare loyalty to Spain. An oil painting of these chiefs from the emerald land of the Zambo Republic is portrayed by the "Indian artist" Adrián Sánchez Galgue [sic]; it is reportedly the earliest signed and dated painting from South America."

I had the pleasure to meet Norman Whitten at my archaeological site at Chirije, it was interesting to be able to talk with him about the origin of languages in South America and of the work he had done with the Afro Ecuadorians. Also I met with Dr. Diego Quiroga who was interested at the dive site I researched 5 Km off of Bahía, where I found the walls, intersections and round wheel-like stones.

As I was talking with Carmen Dueñas de Anhalzer (p.c.), a dear aunt of mine who is also a grand historian of the coast of Ecuador, I found out this "Zambo Republic" was the first republic in the territories of South America. I was so very proud of this historic event and of course of the painting, that when I was in Spain I went to look for it at the Prado Museum in Madrid. Unfortunately, I could not see it because it was on exhibition in the United States. If this information could be transmitted to the Afro American market of travelers I am sure the province of Esmeraldas would benefit from tourism, and of course all of Ecuador would as well.

The global perception of our ancient and live cultures are not well known, but little by little, I believe the work has started to promote these, especially by the Ministry of

Tourism and our offices that are specialists in marketing and PR in the main outbound markets.

Another point that helps country brand perception is the population's reputation for competence, education, openness and friendliness. Ecuador has been at the top of the list when it comes to the friendliness of its people. This is one of the main reasons travelers say that they would come back to the country and recommend Ecuador as a travel destination.

In many cities within the United States and around the world where Ecuadorians reside, there is a positive perception about how hard the Ecuadorian works. This is the general opinion of the people that are involved in the labor force.

Ecuador's Tourism

Then the last element of the Hexagon is tourism. Tourism captures the level of interest in visiting a country and the draw of natural and man-made tourist attractions. Since Ecuador is an authentic destination it is starting to captivate other markets.

Ecuador has Four Worlds:
- Pacific Coast
- Andes
- Amazon
- Galapagos

Ecuador has everything close by:
- Ecuador is almost the size of the State of Colorado, and flights from one region to another are less than 35 minutes

Ecuador has unique resources at a worldwide level:
- World Natural Heritage sites like the Galápagos and Sangay
- World Cultural Heritage Sites; Quito and Cuenca
- Biosphere Reserves; Sumaco-Napo Galeras, Yasuní and Podocarpus
- National Parks

Ecuador has a Constitution that recognizes:
- Rights to Nature ("Pacha Mama", Mother Earth)
- The right for good living, to recreation and to leisure activity of the people
- A GMO Free Country

In Ecuador you live:
- Unique experiences in each world, with quality international tourism services
- The tradition, its peoples, the live culture, the archaeological, the historical, the colonial, the ancestral and the modernism of Latin America

Hacienda Palo Alto
Photo by Torsten Loeffler

As I participated at the beginning of Ecuador's tourism initiative as the first Executive Director for the Tourism Promotion Fund for Ecuador, I pulled as hard as I could to position our country as a leader in sustainable tourism. I could see it would be a difficult task positioning ourselves as such. Nevertheless, the word got out so much, with Ecuador presented as a travel destination, that I was interviewed in many segments of travel news around the world – three times by CNN, four times by the BBC, and by many others. As difficult as it was, I can see that we positioned ourselves very well in the travel industry segment of our market. Still, there is much to do.

When our President Rafael Correa stayed with us at our archaeological site and Eco lodge Chirije, I mentioned to him that now we have to place the real estate traveler in a priority position. I explained that when a traveler comes in for 12 days, 11 nights to the mainland and Galapagos, they might leave a good 4,000 USD in the local economy. A real estate traveler, on the other hand, might stay at least 4 to 5 times (7 to 14 days each visit). Then when the land was bought, rent a house or apartment until their house is built. Just the building of the house might be in the order of 100,000 USD plus. This the president knew, it is a presidential compromise, especially for the Ministry of Tourism, to position Ecuador as a retirement destination. The project is called Destino Retiro. I know the President will increase government spending in infrastructure and services where he will place the country with incredible connectivity enhancing tourism and also augment budgets for the communication and promotional aspect of this destination.

Let's hope in 2020, the new graphic country brand "Ecuador. Love Life" will be in tune with what the global market perceives of my country. Let us go beyond having a hexagon strategy to the world and let Ecuador be in the top of the mind of the respectful, responsible and enlightened traveler as the place to go…the place to live…the place to make friends…the place to love life.

Travel Agent magazine promoting Ecuador, as a result of the leadership initiative of Patricio Tamariz, during his term as Executive Director for the Tourism Promotion Fund of Ecuador (2004 – 2007).

CHAPTER THIRTEEN

Harmonious Living in Paradise

A couple of days ago, I had a wonderful conversation with *"mi Madre linda"*, (my beautiful mother) who is now in her late seventies. She said, *"even though she is in her golden years, (she is still vibrant with energy and working hard), she is still the engranaje or the main gear of the family. It's like a machine, the wheels (the family members) are dependent on one another, if the main one turns then all the others turn, and the family is the center of the machine. For water irrigation and windmills, it works in the same way, if you don't have those gears, especially the central one, it does not work. If you lose a loved one, they can be replaced because the family nucleus keeps on surging, if I leave, then you become the axel".*

I was thrilled to listen to her, and am proud to be her son. From my perspective, women are the axel of life and family, which may be a new concept for some. When my mother passes, I am sure my wife, Juliana, will become the family axel, and afterwards my daughter Melissa. This is a beautiful thing, I strive to live in harmony with females and hope my fellow brothers feel the same way.

I was brought up in the middle of a matriarchal family, my Great Grandmother mamita Maria, my grandmother Natalia and my mother Flor Maria all served as the main gear or nucleus of our family. The concept of two genders living together peacefully and equally was highly stressed in my childhood. I will be forever grateful for this, as it is an important value I have passed onto my children and they will pass on to theirs, keeping it alive through all the subsequent generations.

The mystique of women's role in society, especially in Ecuador, is truly a proper case of study. I believe we are structured in a global patriarchal society that has been trained to rule over women since the book of Genesis. With all due respect to the reader's religious philosophies and intelligence, the story of Adam and Eve and the notion of God as a male figure with a beard are both ideas we have to shake off as universal truths. Could there be more peace in the world if we evolved back from the Patriarchal to a Matriarchal order of society, or to a more balanced form where both genders hold equal power?

Our ancestors and indigenous groups believed in Pachamama (Mother Earth or Mother World), which is our female deity. She is very sacred, as the supreme mother she represents fertility and provides nourishment for our people and the earth. Through the intellectual and emotional connections our people had with this deity and their cosmovisions with the spiritual world, we have always relied on this superior energy form that looks over us. When Pachamama is upset, she causes earthquakes to let our people know so we can change our attitude towards her and each other to be more loving and compassionate. One of the teachings of Pachamama is to work hard, but with joy and gratitude. In this way, our people have sustained a balanced, harmonious lifestyle while being productive and self-sufficient. She encourages peace amongst all people and with our planet.

This ideology has survived through the centuries and manifested in modern times particularly through the Pachamama Alliance, an organization that my co-author, Bo Rinaldi, is involved with. The Pachamama Alliance has brought indigenous people together with the modern world to create "a conscious commitment to a thriving, just and sustainable way of life on earth" (http://www.pachamama.org/). This wonderful organization is working to shift the trajectory of humankind towards a better future through three main initiatives, Awakening the Dreamer, Pachamama Journeys, and The Possible Futures Film Festival. All of these unique projects are producing tangible changes and helping to shift global awareness. I highly recommend participating in some way with the Alliance, it is truly life changing and incredibly significant for our world as a whole.

In addition to the spirituality of Pachamama, our people also believed in sacred geography. Complementing the Sun, there were the tallest mountains (as the male gods) and the sacred lakes (as the female gods) that had their roles in the ancient peoples' cosmovision. Dr. Johan Reinhard, explorer-in-residence for the National Geographic Society, discovered this principal of Sacred Geography for the Andean peoples. He found, "*the feminine divinity represented in many sacred lakes in the Andean highlands gave birth to many nations and was handed down by generation upon generation*".

The universal view of people in different latitudes and hemispheres differed during the same époques due to many reasons, but at a base level, all of mankind has the same needs and values. The needs of humans in survival mode in prehistoric times are not as different as modern man in the city. Family is family, normally the closest to you is the one that bared you. Due to this, the biological specialization of women centered on conceiving, baring and nursing the young comprise a vast piece in defining a family. The power over the nuclear family is obvious. The power over other social units can be questionable.

Matriarchy is defined as a system of society or government ruled by women and/or a form of social organization in which descent and relationship are reckoned through the female line. Did this exist in times of the Valdivia culture and before?

There is a consensus between historians and anthropologists that the Matriarchal society as such never existed. This does not mean that women did not inherit power, but you wouldn't necessarily call it Matriarchal. When the Spaniards arrived in Bahía (circa 1532), they went up the bay and met with a recently widowed female chief that was viewed as their Lord. (Carmen Dueñas de Anhalzer, 2012). This shows females did yield power, though it is in question whether they held the whole of it.

According to Karen Stothert, renowned archaeologist of Ecuador, in a personal conversation with me, the matriarchal society *"did exist in the mythology of various peoples. What there is for sure are Matrilineal Societies. In this class of societies the position of women are much more pleasant and permits that women reach positions of authority"*.

"Women in Ancient America" (1999), which she wrote with Karen Olsen Bruhns, states:

"It is likely that the skill and knowledge accumulated by Paleo-Indian women became the foundation of the way of life of the less mobile archaic peoples. Some anthropological studies have suggested that males are predominant in situations of migration, but that parity is established with sedentism. The broad-spectrum of foraging of many archaic peoples may have been a good cultural setting for women, and some scholars believe that women may have negotiated equal social power under these conditions. It seems likely that as archaic peoples settled down into areas where the array of resources was harvested, women would have continued to exercise control over their own working conditions and the distribution of the food they produced, a situation that meant great economic power. Under some circumstances, this foraging adaption culminated in women creating new food-producing systems based on the cultivation of plants".

According to K.O. Bruhns and K.E. Stothert on the status amongst foragers:

"Status refers to the relative position of individuals in society. In our society this means ranking on a socioeconomic level and involves distinction between high-status individuals and low-status ones, over whom others hold power. In contrast, under egalitarian conditions there is relatively little exercise over others, although there is social differentiation and several statuses. The old and the young may differ with respect to role, emblems, and access to goods, just as women will differ from men. Talented people may be assigned leadership roles in limited contexts, and elders can be expected to be more central in decision-making, but hierarchy is not a necessary dimension of social organization in all cases. Women's status is variable among hunters and gatherers although some scholars have asserted that women universally have high status in foraging societies.

Brian Hayden and his colleagues have defined several indicators of female status that vary greatly among societies and are difficult to identify in the archaeological record. Some indicators of high status for women include female voice in domestic decisions, female control of children, female control of food they have procured, female ownership or control of the dwelling, female voice in interband affairs, and the possibility of female leaders. Status is interpreted as low if females are frequently beaten or poorly treated, if they are excluded from ritual activity, if (in hunting societies) their participation in hunting is limited by taboos, if there are myths of former female control of males, and if there is a belief in the inferiority of females with respect to males".

Hayden also states that warfare may change the status of women, if warfare is occurring close by, the status of women is reduced, but if the warfare is far away, the position of women changes, giving more power to them.

Varying positions in societies for both genders can be discussed and disputed; however, as cases are built in detail about the exact status for women in the pre-Hispanic period through scientific studies, I wish to find out more about the possible scenarios of gender roles in our past and present in our region of South America. I must begin with our ancient Valdivia culture, which was one of the first cultures of the Americas to work with pottery dating back past 4000 B.C.

According to Bruhns and Stothert (1999), *"the structure of Valdivia Family relations is open to question. It is unknown whether villages were endogamous or exogamous, or whether households were Matrilineal or Matrilocal or had some other form".*

Valdivia is key to understanding the later cultures that arose on the western coast of South America. The position of the female representation in the Venus of Valdivia must have been very important throughout coastal Ecuador. Up to this date, it is the earliest cultural evidence in clay of a female figurine in the whole of the Americas. Was there a Mother-Goddess type cult with the people from Valdivia? Was it that women proved they were magical, and were the ones responsible before everyone's eyes for the miracle of birth, the origin of life? Perhaps there was simply equality between the two genders, a mutual respect that is often lost in current times.

I do not want to be redundant in saying that maybe the woman figurine was just a fertility symbol, although the relationship of bringing forth life and giving maternal love was an important basis for the well being of all members in a community. For the Paleo-Indian groups and the Valdivians, the stronger the maternal communities were, the better their chance of survival was and usually the higher their populations were. It was more probable that a fertile group of humans well adjusted to their environmental conditions with many in their clan would outperform smaller units and would be able to ward off most of their enemies and be healthier with stronger immune systems.

For the nomadic ancestry of the Vegans and Valdivians, there was no doubt that there was some type of cult to the female gender which inspired the Valdivia people to create the clay figurine as an interpretation of sacred femaleness. No other symbol has caught the eye of all the archaeologists that worked excavating this time period and culture on the coast of Ecuador. From human fertility, fertility of the land to good fortune, we can decipher that the Venus of Valdivia represented a woman that had definite supernatural connotations to my ancestors.

Was God viewed as father or mother to these cultures? In most of the world, especially in Europe and Israel, God was seen as "Father". It has been depicted this way since the time of the first writings of the Bible and Jesus. God as "Mother" was a more theme common in the cosmovision of our ancestors here in America (and maybe also in the very ancient societies of the east).

As a true believer of an energy force that created humans (via evolution) and our universe, I view theology as supportive of the Patriarchal ideology "Father". Since maturing in age and thought, the complexity of this "energy force" is such that I put away the gender idea, and focus on it as an omnipotent loving force, rather than a punishing force, which when we do not "go with the flow and love" or we go against the current, we learn. How lucky we are that our spirits can land in a plane of existence where we can use our own will and administer this beautiful planet. The problem seems still that we have not evolved yet or the system does not permit understanding that we need to form a collective conscious for the well-being of all. As such we should accept the law of spirituality that all situations that are brought upon us are perfect. I believe that very enlightened beings like Jesus existed on this planet (and the greatest of probability is that they existed for a purpose and were pure spirits of love). The great Jesus left many teachings for the world and to me the best is "*I am giving you a new commandment: Love each other in the same way that I have loved you*". I pray with my small children to "Papito Dios" and teach them how to love Mother Earth.

Returning to our ancient past, in Real Alto, Ecuador, the investigations led by many archaeologists came up with results depicting a large village of more than 1,500 inhabitants of the Valdivia period. There are scientists that say there could have been a matriarchal society at one time evidenced by skeletal remains of a woman found in one of the burials, with sacrificed humans around her. This could have been some type of fertility ceremonial, or a Cacica (Ka-Si-Ka)/Chief, proving women as a figure of power at that time in Valdivian culture.

Across the millennia, we find the Cañari (Ka-nyar-ee) people of the Southern Andes of Ecuador, who were known with certainty to have had a Matriarchal society. They were one of the fiercest tribes to war against the invading Incas; they probably resisted for decades but were conquered in the 15th century.

Talking with the director of the Los Amantes de Sumpa museum, Beatriz Lindao, the earliest culture of Ecuador was *"the Las Vegas culture" (Vegas meaning a piece of low ground near a river- where the culture was found). She believes that woman in Valdivia had strong positions in society.*

Family structure in Latin America has always been based on close-knit family ties. It is unlike the United States, when you are seventeen or eighteen; you fly out of the nest. Here it is different. You stay with your family, sometimes in extended family units. I would say this is mostly due to economic limitations. A son or daughter will stay more out of necessity than comfort, still living with his/her wife in the family of one's mother or mother in law. This is something that has existed since the early ages of sedentism here on the coast. According to K.O. Bruhns and K.E. Stothert (1999), regarding family relations and the importance of coordinated changes of the Valdivia culture on the coast:

"In one possible scenario, women stayed in the villages of their birth, if that is where they had access to agricultural land, while their brothers sought wives in other villages and joined a new household. Certainly there must have been some mechanism for linking all the Valdivia villages across southern Ecuador because they exhibit both coordinated changes and regional variation in their ceramics through the centuries."

In the following passage from the same book, Zeidler states that both genders of the Valdivia Culture could have had sufficient freedom to exist and rule over their own worlds.

"Based on etnoarchaeological studies of the modern Shuar people who now occupy southeastern Ecuador [Amazon], James Zeidler has interpreted the use of space in the large Middle Valdivia houses. Traditional Shuar houses, like those of many tropical forest peoples, are occupied by extended families, and the interior of the space is differentiated into female and male areas. This differentiation is both conceptual and functional because the sexes maintain spatial separation as they go about their daily activities. This kind of spatial separation of female and male gives both sexes considerable freedom of action. Zeidler has noted that Shuar men, when they are not hunting or clearing forests for agricultural plots, congregate at the front of the house, where they chat, make and repair craft items, receive male guests, eat and if unmarried, sleep. Women spend most of their time at the other end of the house when not gardening or foraging. Here they tend their children, gossip, and cook for their individual and extended families, and here married couples and their young children sleep."

Normally good archaeological work is based on anthropological studies of the live cultures, which show a traditional existence brought to modern times. It is possible that the Valdivia peoples lived in a matrilineal society, where women inherited and were conferred benefits and also where they controlled the family or even the village. It is possible in certain villages that a woman could have ruled over the men if they were given that authority.

On the other side of the Andes, there was an account that veered to the other extreme, the Amazon women met by Francisco de Orellana, (B.1511) who discovered the Amazon River in 1542. He left Quito to discover the land of cinnamon, which was thought to be east of what now is the capital of Ecuador. The account of the expedition offers an interesting and detailed description of a chiefdom led by women warriors that warred with the Spaniards. The Dominican friar Gaspar de Carvajal, chronicler of that expedition states:

"These women are very tall and white and have very long hair, braided around the head. They are very strong and naked with skins covering their genitals, with bows and arrows in their hands. They were making war like 10 Indians together; and it is true that one of these women put in an arrow a palms length through our ship and others also, that made our ship look like a porcupine".

After the skirmish, one Indian that was captured and gave a detailed description of who they were.

"The chiefdom is 150 leagues in extension and they live in 70 villages, all of which have doors with guards and roads between them. The women live in houses made of stone, alone without husbands. When they want to reproduce, they capture male prisoners that they keep imprisoned until they are wanted. When they get pregnant, then the prisoners are freed. If they give birth to males, they kill them [I also read another account that said that they permitted the biological fathers to take them, but also had the first option]. The female young are reared and educated. The queen [chief] is called Coñori and has grand riches. The main Lords (women) ware is of gold and silver while the plebeian women serve themselves with clay and wood vases. In the main city where the queen lives there are 5 temples dedicated to the adoration of the Sun called caranain, or houses of the Sun. Inside their roofs are painted with diverse colors and there are many feminine idols of gold and silver and many utensils of the same metals for the service of the Sun. They dress with very fine wool, because in this land there are many sheep of Peru (alpacas and llamas). They wear tight fitting blankets from the breasts to below and others like buttoned up blankets with many cords. They carry crowns as thick as 2 fingers".

It later says in the same account that the land is filled with llamas to carry all the heavy loads and there is an order that at sunset all the male Indians must leave the cities. Some of the later chroniclers say that this did not happened, that it is a myth. Although Gaspar de Carvajal was eyewitness and the chronicler of this account, it was also Francisco de Orellana that reported the same version, with another witness. Some say that the skirmish they had was possibly because the male counterparts were in the fields or hunting and the women had to defend themselves.

Similarly to the Jesuit priest Juan de Velasco's accounts, which received much critique years after, Gaspar de Carvajal's first account of the discovery of the Amazon River has been questioned, but we must give credit to the first reports made of these places and people. Wouldn't it be an amazing discovery for archaeologists to find the stone remains of these houses and villages?

In modern times, the Chachis (or Cayapas) who are located in the northern coast of Ecuador are one of the remaining Indian groups that have survived with traditional ways. They are part of the Chibcha group that today includes the Awa and Tsachila groups in Ecuador, the Kuna of the San Blas Islands of Panama, and the Koqui of the Sierra Madre of Columbia. Their language is called the Cha'palaa; it comes from a dialect of the language of the Chibchas. The Chachis are people of the river; they live in dispersed villages and seem to be native of the Choco area (Hazlewood, J. 2004).

This nationality is found on the border of the province of northern Manabí and throughout the Esmeraldas province that borders with the coastal jungles of Colombia. According to the Confederation of Indigenous Nationalities of Ecuador (CONAIE), their territory is 105,468 hectares (260,618 acres), where they live in communities that occupy 21% of the land and the rest 79% is basically primary and secondary tropical forests.

My experience with these peoples is of a genuine nature. I remember walking hours along a wet tropical forest riverbank to reach their village (Centro Chachi de Balzar) in the Mache Chindul Ecological Reserve. It is a wonderful area, smack on the border of the Choco, one of the hotspots of biodiversity in the world. When I arrived, I saw these Polynesian style houses and waited for the leader of the community inside the long main cabin that centered right up on a hill aside from the river. I remember (because of the long 4 hour trip there) asking the wife what time she thought her husband would be back from hunting, expecting a response in the form of hours.

She calmly smiled, took a couple of steps and looked out the window over the river and she said, "*in a little while*" (in broken Spanish). A minute passed and I asked myself, what did she see out over the window? Was it the men crossing the river or arriving in canoe? I went to check and saw nothing. All I remember was a couple of birds quickly flying above the river when she leaned out over the window.

Fifteen minutes went by and nothing happened. I had gone there to see if they wanted to explore an alternative source of economy (in ecotourism) than deforesting the reserve. They respect nature but also have many outside pressure groups coming in to entice them.

I was embarrassed to ask again, but had to, because if I didn't, I would be traveling home in the dark. I asked again, and again she gave me a smile and went to the window, looked out and said "*ya esta cerca*", meaning "*he is close*". This time I also looked out the window and saw a huge flock of birds filling the window space, flying in the same direction as before. Five minutes later, her husband came in cleaning his boots. The birds told the time, they were flying down the river opposite from the men walking back from the jungle. I was awed at how in tune these people were with nature.

The chief liked what I had to say about Ecotourism and sent me back in a canoe (which took 20 minutes). I remember seeing a whole family of women paddling their canoes and later found out that in some villages they have more expertise than men. This experience was an incredible journey back through time. I did not go there to see specific gender relationships, but was impressed with what were possibly the last remnants of traditions of ancient civilizations on our Pacific coast.

Years afterwards, while I was writing this book and researching relevant literature on the Chachis, I remembered Julianne Hazelwood, a good friend who did her doctorate on the Chachi culture. There is much to do in preserving this culture and it is my hope we can work together on a project promoting a sustainable development for the Chachis, without the loss of their essence.

Chachi women in dug out canoe handling with expertise the Cojimies River

When thinking about who makes decisions on the communities, one of Juli's linguistic expert friends says, *"it leans towards a Patriarchal society, most of the town officials in Chachi society are men (Floyd, p.c.)."* The question is did the Spanish have an influence here or not?

The patriarchal society of the Spanish definitely had its effect upon the natives, especially through the colonization period (1534-1820). In the 19th and 20th centuries, independence and opportunities for education increased for women, so did their rights to participate in politics. In the late 20th and 21st century, Andean women of Ecuador were more involved in politics and actually served in governing positions. Women from anterior depressed societies catapulted via social change to very important governing positions.

One of the first indigenous women was Dolores Cacuango, (B.1881) who in the 1940's created the Ecuadorian Federation of Indians (Smith, B. 2008). Another native Ecuadorian woman named Nina Pacari (her name in Quechua means "*the dawning of new consciousness*") was vice president of congress and served as minister of foreign affairs.

The valorous contributions of the women who now serve in our President's government have been a main point of value for President Rafael Correa. Forty percent of all the ministerial cabinet is women. Of the five ministers of tourism that I worked under, four were women in the last three governments.

In a public statement he made on International Women's day in front of Independence Square in Quito on the 8th of March of 2012, President Correa stated:

"Women of my country, without you obviously we would be incomplete, without your work the country would not be able to go forward, without your love we could not construct a future of peace".

Finishing our journey together and ending this book, I would like to complement his words with my own:

The love we feel towards women is one, the love of shared time through the endeavors of life together is another, the love of mother and mother-earth another, and the love of the bright and independent spirit that bonds their terrestrial life with their identity in the present and in our past cannot be replaced and should be learnt from.

I have learned from my ancestors, the Valdivia people, that...

The True Secret of Paradise is Living Together as One in Harmony

Patricio with wife Juliana, daughter Melissa and son Patricio Jr.

*A Happy Family Living Harmoniously in the
Paradise of the Pacific Coast of Ecuador*

You're always welcome in Chirije Paradise

Chirije's indigenous style wood and bamboo lodge welcomes visitors
Photographs by Melissa Salter

Aguilar de Tamaríz, María Leonor (2009) *Tejiendo la vida…, los sombreros de paja toquilla en el Ecuador.* 2a. ed. corregida y aumentada. Centro Interamericano De Artesanías y Artes Populares CIDAP. Cuenca.

Alcedo, Antonio de (1786) *Diccionario Geográfico-Histórico de las Indias Occidentales o América: Es a Saber de los Reynos del Perú, Nueva España, Tierra-Firme, Chile, y Nuevo Reyno de Granada.* Tomo I. Imprenta Benito Cano. Madrid.

Alcedo, Antonio de (1788) *Diccionario Geográfico-Histórico de las Indias Occidentales o América: Es a Saber de los Reynos del Perú, Nueva España, Tierra-Firme, Chile, y Nuevo Reyno de Granada.* Tomo IV. Imprenta Manuel González. Madrid.

Alsedo y Herrera, Dionisio (1741) *Compendio Histórico de la Provincia de Guayaquil* (1938). Edit. Uzcátegui. Guayaquil.

ANECACAO (2012) National Association of Cacao Exporters-Ecuador.

Anholt, Simon (2007) *Competitive identity: the new brand management for nations, cities and regions.* Palgrave Macmillan. New York.

Archivo Municipal de Quito (1970) *Libro de Cartas Escritas por los Reyes Nuestros Señores, Sumos Pontífices, Virreyes y otros Ministros de esta Real Audiencia al Cabildo de Quito 1589 – 1714.* Volumen XXXIV. Página 52. Publicaciones del Archivo Municipal de Quito. Mayo de 1970 Quito – Ecuador. (Accessed in February 2012 and found in Wikipedia-Gobierno de Caráquez) Available at: http://es.wikipedia.org/wiki/Gobierno_de_Car%C3%A1quez.

Arosemena, Guillermo (2009) *Estructura y actores del comercio exterior colonial entre Guayaquil y Lima.* Revista Instituto de Historia Marítima.

Balick, Michael and Beck, Hans (1990) *Useful palms of the world: a synoptic bibliography.* Columbia University Press. (Cite)Rich, W.A. (1936). A brief talk about Tagua. Commodities of Commerce Series. No. 21:1-15.

Barrera, Ernesto (2008) *Aportes para Ruta del Spóndylus de Documentos de Investigación.* Facultad de Agronomía de la Universidad de Buenos Aires, Argentina. Ministerio de Turismo, Ecuador.

Batista, Lépido (2009) *Guía Técnica El Cultivo del Cacao.* Centro para el Desarrollo Agropecuario y Forestal, Inc. (CEDAF), Santo Domingo, República Dominicana.

Bauer, Daniel E. (2008) *Negotiating development: Identity and economic practice in coastal Ecuador.* Dissertation for Doctor of Philosophy Degree. Dept. of Anthropology. Graduate School. Southern Illinois University Carbondale.

Beltran, Rafael (2002) *Maravillas, peregrinaciones y utopías: Literatura de Viajes en el mundo románico.* Universitat de Valencia.

Berg, Peter (1999-2009) *Summary of Biorregional Activities in Bahía de Caráquez, Ecuador. Dispatches from Ecuador.* Planet Drum Foundation.

Berg, Peter (2009) *Envisioning Sustainability.* First Edition. Subculture Books.

Bouchard JF. Fuentes Franklin and Lopez Telmo (2006) *Aldeas y pueblos prehispánicos en la costa de Manabí: Chirije y Japoto*. Bulletin de l'Institut Français d'Études Andines / 2006 35 (3): 243-256.

Bouchard, Jean Francois (2008) *Japotó: une métropole régionale tardive dans la province cotière de Manabí (Équateur)*. Les Nouvelles de l'archéologie No.111-112.

Boyd, Richard N. (2012) *Stardust, Supernovae and the Molecules of Life: Might We All Be Aliens*? Springer Science+Business Media, LLC.

Bruhns, Karen Olsen and Stothert, Karen E. (1999) *Women in Ancient America*. University of Oklahoma Press, Publishing Division of the University.

Caillavet, Chantal (2008) «*Como caçica y señora desta tierra mando...*». *Insignias, funciones y poderes de las soberanas del norte andino (siglos XV-XVI)*. Bulletin de l'Institut Français d'Études Andines / 2008, 37 (1): 57-80.

Calderon, Maria Jose (1998) *Oil Transnationals and the Huaorani Community of the Amazon Basin: Redefining Development in the Ecuadorian Rainforest*. University of Maryland. Master of Arts Thesis.

Carter, Benjamin (2011) *Spondylus in South American Prehistory*. Found in Spondylus in Prehistory: New Data and Approaches – Contributions to the Archaeology of Shell Technologies edited by Fotis Ifantidis and Marianna Nikolaidou. Oxford: Archaeopress [British Archaeological Reports, International Series 2216.

Ceriola, Juan B. (1913) *Manabí a la Vista*. Talleres de Artes Gráficas E. Rodenas. Pp.180.

Chancay, José (2008) Aportes personales de investigación y del Instituto Nacional de Patrimonio Cultural del Ecuador.

Chancay, J. and Reinhard J. (2009) Aportes personales de investigación y del Instituto Nacional de Patrimonio Cultural del Ecuador para Laguna Culebrillas.

Chías, Josep 2003 *Plan Integral de Marketing Turístico del Ecuador*. Ministerio de Turismo.

Coleti, Giandomenico (1771) *Dizionario Storico-Geografico Dell' America Meridionali*. Nella Stamperia Coleti. Publicaciones del Banco de la Republica. Archivo de la Economía Nacional.

Cronau, Rodolfo (1892) *América, Historia de su descubrimiento, desde los tiempos primitivos a los mas moderno*. To commemorate the 400 years of Discovery of America. Tomo Segundo. Edición Montaner y Simón. Barcelona.

Dueñas de Anhalzer, Carmen (1986) *Historia Económica y Social del Norte de Manabí*. 1era ed. Abya Yala. 140 p.

Dueñas Santos de Anhalzer, Carmen (1997) *Marqueses, Cacaoteros y Vecinos de Portoviejo: Cultura política en la Presidencia de Quito* (Editorial Abya Yala - Universidad San Francisco de Quito).

Dueñas de Anhalzer, Carmen (2010) *Los Viajes de los Indios de Portoviejo a la Corte Española. Conflictos interétnicos y territoriales*. Procesos, Revista Ecuatoriana de Historia. No.31, 1er semestre 2010. Quito.

Edmund A. Walsh School of Foreign Service: Center for Latin American Studies, Georgetown University (2011) *Republic of Ecuador Constitution of 2008*. Translated into English. Political Database for the Americas.

Estete, Miguel de (1535) *Noticia del Perú*. Boletín de la Sociedad Ecuatoriana de Estudios Históricos Americanos, tomo 1, no. 3. (Impreso en 1918), Quito.

Esteves, Eduardo (2011) Organic Agriculture in Ecuador. Final Report.

Estrada, Emilio and Meggers, Betty J. (1961) *A Complex of Traits of Probable Transpacific Origin on the Coast of Ecuador*. American Anthropologist, 63, 1961.

Estrada, Emilio (1962) *Arqueología de Manabí Central*. Publicación del Museo Víctor Emilio Estrada No. 7. Museo Víctor Emilio Estrada, Guayaquil.

Evans, Clifford and Meggers, Betty J. (1964) *Transpacific Origin of Valdivia Phase Pottery on Coastal Ecuador*. XXXVI Congreso Internacional de Americanistas España 1964. Actas y Memorias. Vol.1 (1966).

Fernández de Oviedo V., Gonzalo (1853) *General Historia Natural de las Indias, Islas y Tierra-Firme del Mar Océano*. Imprenta de la Real Academia de la Historia. Madrid. [Events from 1492 to 1549].

García C., Mariella (2006) *Las Figurinas de Real Alto. Reflejos de los Modos de Vida Valdivia*. 1era Edición. Abya-Yala. Quito, Ecuador.

Ghosh, Jayati (2012) *Could Ecuador be the most radical and exciting place on Earth?* The Guardian (Newspaper) UK. Article published on January 19th, 2012. 2012 Guardian News and Media Limited. London.

Grivetti, Louis E. and Shapiro, Howard-Yana (2009) *Chocolate: history, culture and heritage*. John Wiley and Sons, Inc. Hoboken, New Jersey.

Hampe Martinez, Teodoro (1989) *El reparto de metales, joyas e indios de Coaque: un episodio fundamental en la expedición de conquista del Perú*. En: Quinto Centenario 1989 (15): 77-94. Pontificia Universidad Católica del Perú. Edit. Univ. Complutense. Madrid.

Hidrovo Quiñónez, Tatiana (2006) *Manta: Una Ciudad-Puerto en el Siglo XIX. Economía Regional y Mercado Mundial*. Universidad Laica Eloy Alfaro de Manabí. Procesos, Revista Ecuatoriana de Historia. No. 24. II semestre. Quito.

Horwell, D and Oxford, P. (2011) *Galapagos Wildlife*. Bradt Travel Guides Ltd. The Globe Pequot Press Inc.

Hurwitt, Robert (2011) *Peter Berg Obituary*. San Francisco Chronicle. Printed and Online Edition.Sunday, August 14, 2011.

INEC (2012) El Instituto Nacional de Estadística y Censos. Republica del Ecuador.

International Cocoa Association (2011) ICCO press releases: "Uncoordinated projects could make cocoa's boom and bust cycle worse, the ICCO's Executive Director says". Available at http://www.icco.org/about/press2.aspx?Id=qgu15867.

International Living (2011) *Golden sunsets. Top 5 countries for Americans to retire abroad.* Chicago Tribune. Article published on October 11, 2011. Available at: http://articles.chicagotribune.com/2011-10-11/travel/sc-trav-1011-retire-abroad-20111011_1_ecuador-health-care-cuenca.

iWantSun.co.uk (2012) *Top five eco holiday destinations in the sun.* Published on Wednesday, 14 March 2012. Available at: http://www.iwantsun.co.uk/active-sun/2012/03/14/top-five-eco-holiday-destinations-in-the-sun.

La Condamine, Charles-Marie de (1745) [1962] *Viaje a la América Meridional.* Madrid. Editorial Espasa-Calpe. "Relation abrégée d'un voyage dans l'intérieur de l'Amérique méridionale (Paris, 1745; t2d ed., 1778).

Lila (2006) *Pachamama.* Available at: http://www.orderwhitemoon.org/goddess/Pachamama.htm.

Lane, Kris E. (1997) *Los Bucaneros y la Defensa de la Costa del Pacifico a Fines del Siglo XVII en Quito: El Caso de las Barbacoas.* Fronteras. No. 1, Volumen 1.

Lunniss, Richard (2009) *La Arqueología de la Ruta del Spondylus.* Consultoría para Seproyco - Ministerio de Turismo del Ecuador.

Magasich, Jorge and De Beer, Jean-Marc (2001) *América Mágica, Mitos y creencias en tiempos del descubrimiento del Nuevo Mundo.* Editorial LOM.

Mann, Charles C. (2005) *1491: New Revelations of the Americas before Columbus.* Vintage Books. Random House, Inc. New York.

Marcos, Jorge, (1986) *"De ida y vuelta a Acapulco, con los mercaderes de mullu".* Incluido en "Arqueología de la costa ecuatoriana". Edit. CEN. Quito

Marcos Pino, Jorge y Bazurco Osorio, Martin (2006) *Albarradas y camellones en la región costera del antiguo Ecuador.* CEAA-ESPOL. Taken from Agricultura Ancestral Camellones y Albarradas, Contexto social, usos y retos del pasado y del presente. Coloquio Agricultura Prehispánica sistemas basados en el drenaje y en la elevación de los suelos cultivados. Editor Francisco Valdez. Issue No. 3 of the Colección "Actas & Memorias" of IFEA. Ediciones Abya-Yala.

Markham, Clements R. (1864) *Travels of Pedro de Cieza de Leon, A.D 1532-50, contained in the First Part of his Chronicle of Peru.* Printed for the Hakluyt Society. London.

Martin-Ramos, Pablo (2001) *En busca del Spondylus.* Rutas y Simbolismo. Available at: http://www.scribd.com/doc/13971717/En-Busca-del-Spondylus-Rutas-y-Simbolismo.

Meggers, Betty J., Clifford Evans, Y Emilio Estrada (1965) *The Early Formative Period of Coastal Ecuador: The Valdivia and Machalilla Phases*. Smithsonian Contributions to Anthropology 1. Smithsonian Institution Press, Washington, D.C.

Meggers, Betty J. (1987) *El Origen Transpacífico de la Cerámica Valdivia: Una Revaluación*. Boletín del Museo Chileno De Arte Precolombino No. 2. Santiago de Chile.

Meggers, Betty J. (1998) *Archaeological Evidence for Transpacific Voyages from Asia since 6000 BP*. Estudios Atacameños.

Meggers, Betty Jane. (2010) *Prehistoric America: an ecological perspective*. 3rd Expanded Edition. Transaction Publishers, New Jersey.

Mejía M., M. Fernando (2005) *Análisis del Complejo Cerámico Pajonal, Proveniente del Sector A, Sitio Chirije, Manabí*. Tesis de Licenciatura, Centro de Estudios Arqueológicos y Antropológicos, Escuela Superior Politécnica del Litoral, Guayaquil.

Melo, Mario. (2008) *Buen vivir, naturaleza y nacionalidades en la nueva Constitución: una lectura esperanzada*. Ecuador. América Latina en Movimiento (ALAI) Available at http://alainet.org/active/26131&lang=es.

Menzies, Gavin (2002) *1421: The year China discovered America*. First Edition. Harper Collins Publishers, Inc. New York, NY.

MINTUR-UEES (2002) *La Ruta del Cacao, Nueva Opción para el Turismo Rural en el Ecuador*. Informe Técnico. Arosemena, X., Burgos, M., Palacios, S., Perrone, A., del Centro de Planificación y Desarrollo Turístico de la Universidad Especialidades Espíritu Santo. Subsecretaria de Turismo del Litoral. Ministerio de Turismo.

Ministerio de Turismo (2007) *Plan Estratégico de Desarrollo de Turismo Sostenible para el Ecuador hacia el año 2020, PLANDETUR 2020*. Empresa Consultora: Tourism & Leisure.

Moreno, Graciela (2012) *Sucre-Bahía de Caráquez Cantón Turístico, Patrimonial, Próspero, Atractivo y Solidario*.

Motamayor J.C., Risterucci A.M, Lopez P.A., Ortiz C.F., Moreno A. and Lanuad C. (2002) *Cacao domestication I: the origin of the cacao cultivated by the Mayas. Heredity*. Available at http://www.nature.com/hdy/journal/v89/n5/full/6800156a.html.

NASA (2002) *Tree-Ring Study Reveals Long History of El Niño*. NASA Earth Observatory. News and Press. Published on December 9, 2002. Available at http://earthobservatory.nasa.gov/Newsroom/view.php?id=22831.

NOAA (2011) NOAA Research. National Oceanographic and Atmospheric Administration, United States. Consulted information on Climate Change. Available at: http://www.oar.noaa.gov/climate/t_observing.html.

NOAA (2012) *ENSO Cycle: Recent Evolution, Current Status and Predictions Update prepared by Climate Prediction Center* . National Oceanographic and Atmospheric Administration, United States "Available at: http://www.cpc.ncep.noaa.gov/products/analysis_monitoring/lanina/enso_evolution-status-fcsts-web.pdf".

Norton, Presley & Garcia, Marco (1992) *5000 Años de Ocupación. Parque Nacional Machalilla*. Quito : Ediciones Abya - Yala; Centro Cultural Artes, 1992. 102p.

Ober, Federick Albion (1906) *Pizarro and the Conquest of Peru*. Harper & Brothers, New York.

OPP (2012) *US buyers told Ecuador is the new number one hotspot*. Overseas Property Professional. Article induced by the Global Property Index by International Living. Published on April 04, 2012. Available at: http://opp.org.uk/news-article.php?id=6407.

Oviedo, G., Zamudio T. and Noejovich F. (2007) *Challenges for the maintenance of traditional biodiversity knowledge in Latin America*. Research report prepared by the authors at the request of the Secretariat of the Convention on Biological Diversity.

Pachamama Alliance (2012) Available at http://www.pachamama.org/about-us.

Pimentel Perez, Rodolfo (2012) *Jose Maria de Villamil Joly*. Accessed in 2011 and available at www.diccionariobiographicoecuador.com.

Pineo, Ronn F. (1996) *Social and Economic Reform in Ecuador: Life and Work in Guayaquil*. University Press of Florida.

Planet Drum Foundation. (2001) *Plan Ecológico para el Desarrollo del Cantón Sucre* (Bahía de Caráquez). Ecuador Dispatches January/February 2001. Aprobado en el Concejo Cantonal en Febrero 15 del 2001. Available: http://www.planetdrum.org/eco_plan_2001_espanol.htm.

Paoletti, Emilio (1999) *Monedas Macuquinas de 8 Reales de Potosí*. Talleres Graficos Chulca Impresora S.A. Buenos Aires. Pp. 232.

Pollard R., Anne (1973) *Pre-Columbian Textile Conference. May 19th and 20th, 1973*. Article of Dr. Jorge Marcos: Woven textiles in a late Valdivia context.

Prescott, William Hickling (1847) *The History of the Conquest of Peru. Book II: Discovery of Peru*. Cosimo, Inc. (2007).

Ramírez, Franklin and Ramírez, Jacques (2003) *La migración en el Ecuador (1997-2003): de la impertinente crisis a la centralidad de las redes.* Informe de la investigación. ALISEI/Quito. Not published.

Registro Oficial (2010) *Code of Production*. Republic of Ecuador. Published in the Registro Oficial™ Quito, Wednesday, December 29th, 2010. Created by the Ministry of Competiveness, Production and Employment. (MCPEC).

Roitman, Karem (2008) *Hybridity, Mestizaje and Montubios in Ecuador.* Research done in Ecuador (2003-2005). Working Paper No. 165. QEH Working Paper Series – QEHWPS165. Queen Elizabeth House, University of Oxford.

Rodriguez, Linda A. (1994) *Rank and Privilege; The Military and Society in Latin America.* Chapter-Authoritarianism and Militarism in Ecuador. Scholarly Resources, Inc.

Rodríguez Pérez, Francisco J. (2003) *Interpretación de las Elegías de Juan de Castellanos.* Universidad de Salamanca.

Saad, Pedro. (2008) *Informe Final "Algunas Consideraciones Historiográficas para el Diseño de una Ruta Spondylus".* Seproyco-Ministerio de Turismo del Ecuador.

Samanos, Juan (1526) *Relación de los primeros descubrimientos de Francisco Pizarro y Diego de Almagro, 1526.* Account of the first discoveries of Francisco Pizarro and Diego de Almagro, from the Codex Number CXX of the Imperial Library of Vienna. [1844].

Saville, Marshall H. (1907) *Antiquities of Manabí, Ecuador. Preliminary Report.* Contributions to South American Archaeology. Irving Press. New York.

Saville, Marshall H. (1910) *Antiquities of Manabí, Ecuador. Final Report.* Contributions to South American Archaeology. The George G. Heye Expedition. Irving Press. New York.

Seproyco Cía. Ltda. y Ministerio de Turismo (2008) *Plan Macro de Desarrollo Turístico de la Ruta del Spondylus.* Grupo Consultor Seproyco Cía. Ltda. Director de Proyecto Patricio Tamariz. Contratación del Ministerio de Turismo.

Simmonds, Norman W. (1973) *Los Plátanos.* Editorial Blume, Barcelona. 539 pp.

Sorenson, John L. and Johannessen, Carl L. (2001) *Scientific Evidence for Pre-Columbian Transoceanic Voyages to and from the Americas.* Paper (extended version) of presentation for conference "Contact and Exchange in the Ancient World", held at the University of Pennsylvania, Philadelphia on May 5, 2001. Provo, Utah: Maxwell Institute

Smith, Bonnie G. (2008) *The Oxford Encyclopedia of Women in World History.* Oxford University Press. New York, NY.

Spain (1680). *Recopilación de las Leyes de Indias Titulo Quince.* De las Audiencias y Chancillerías Reales de las Indias.

Stothert Karen E., Piperno Dolores R. and Andres, Thomas C. (2003) *Terminal Pleistocene/Early Holocene Human Adaptation in Coastal Ecuador: The Las Vegas Evidence.* Elsevier Ltd. and INQUA.

Tamariz, Patricio. 2004 *Perfil del Plan Macro Turístico Binacional "Ruta Del Spóndylus"* .The Spóndylus (Thorny Oyster) Trail. Not Published.

Tamariz, Patricio & Bien, Amos. (2008) *Plan Macro de Desarrollo Ruta del Spondylus.* Consultoría para Seproyco Cía. Ltda. /Ministerio de Turismo del Ecuador. Octubre 2008.

The American Presidency Project. Grover Cleveland's first Annual Message (1885) Available at http://www.presidency.ucsb.edu/ws/index.php?pid=29526#axzz1q9UmLhQh.

Time Magazine (1961) *Fuel & Flame*. Article on Emilio Estrada, on his theory of transpacific contact near Bahía de Caráquez. Edition on January 6, 1961.

Totten, Norman (1988) *Categories of Evidence for Old World Contacts with Ancient America*. In The Book of Mormon: The Keystone Scripture, ed. Paul R. Cheesman. Provo, UT: Religious Studies Center, Brigham Young University.

Tourism & Leisure (2009) *Estrategias para el Mercado Nacional*. Evaluación del Plan Integral de Marketing Turístico del Ecuador 2003-2006. Ministerio de Turismo.

Tourism & Leisure (2009) *Plan de Marketing Turístico de Ecuador – Fase II Síntesis de la situación actual de la Promoción Turística*. Consultoría para Ministerio de Turismo.

Tourism & Leisure (2009) *Evaluación y actualización del Plan de Marketing Turístico de Ecuador - MINTUR Fase III Posicionamiento y Formulación de Estrategias.* (Plan Integral de Marketing Turístico del Ecuador 2011-2015) Mercado Nacional.

Tourism & Leisure (2009) *Evaluación y Actualización del Plan de Marketing Turístico del Ecuador-MINTUR. Fase III.* Posicionamiento y Formulación de Estrategias (PIMTE 2010-2014). Mercado Internacional.

Ubelaker, Douglas (1995) *The Analysis of Human Remains in Chirije, Ecuador inside a Historical Perspective.*

UNDP (2012) *Ecuador Yasuni ITT Trust Fund. Yasuni Ishpingo Tambococha Tiputini Trust Fund. Multi-Partner Trust Fund Office (MPTF Office) of the United Nations Development Programme. Available at: http://mptf.undp.org/yasuni.*

United States Geological Survey (2012) *Preliminary Earthquake Report.* Earthquake Hazards Program/Earthquake Center. Available at: http://neic.usgs.gov/neis/eq_depot/1998/eq_980804/.

Velasco, Juan De. (1789) *Historia Del Reino De Quito En La América Meridional.* Quito, Impr. del Gobierno, 1841-44. Tomo 1 Historia Natural y Tomo 2 Historia Antigua.

Veliz Alvarado, Javier (2012) *La Nave Balsa del Siglo XVI.* Instituto Marítimo de la Armada del Ecuador.

Veliz Alvarado, Javier (2012) *Los Bajos de Santa Marta.* La Ciudad Cara Submergida. Essay.

Wang S, Lewis CM Jr., Jakobsson M., Ramachandran S., Ray N., et al (2007) *Genetic variation and population structure in Native Americans.* PLoS Genetics 3(11): e185. doi:10.1371/journal.pgen.0030185.

Whitten, Norman E. and Quiroga, Diego (1998) *To Rescue National Dignity: Blackness as a Quality of Nationalist Creativity in Ecuador* found in book: Blackness in Latin America and the Caribbean by Norman Whitten, Jr., and Arlene Torres. Vol. 1. Indiana University Press.

Zarate, Agustín de (1555) *Historia del descubrimiento y conquista de la provincia del Perú.* Biblioteca Peruana, tomo 2, pp. 105-413. (1968) Lima: Editores Técnicos Asociados S.A..

Zeidler, James A. y Pearsall, Deborah M. (1994) *Regional Archaeology in Northern Manabí, Ecuador.* Vol.1. University of Pittsburg y Ediciones Libri Mundi, Quito.

The Secret of Paradise

Mysteries of the Pacific Coast of Ecuador

www.secretofparadise.com

PUBLISHER

OneDegree Publishing
333 S. State St., Lake Oswego, OR 97034
www.onedegreepublishing.com

COVER PAINTING

Ruben Martinez

FRONT AND BACK COVER DESIGNS AND MAPS

ZHINO DESIGN
Chino Flores
zhinodesign@gmail.com

GRAPHIC EDITOR

Barry Mack
www.barrymackart.com

COPY EDITOR

Bob Henson
www.borinaldi.com

Patricio Tamariz

www.chirije.com
www.casagrandebahia.com

Patricio is a national and international tourism consultant, and was the main advisor for the Organization of American States for the Andean Region for their program for helping small hotels. Patricio also has held the positions of Director of Tourism for the province of Manabí (2000), Manager for the Coast of Ecuador (2000-2003) and Undersecretary of Marketing (2010) for the Ministry of Tourism. Patricio was also appointed the Executive Director for Ecuador's first Tourism Promotion Fund (2004-2007) and helped place Ecuador for the first time as a sustainable worldwide tourism destination.

He now lives in Bahia de Caráquez, Ecuador with his beautiful family. He helps manage the Chirije Eco Lodge and the CasaGrande Boutique Hotel, which his family has owned since 1994. The Secret of Paradise is his first book and represents the deep knowledge, passion and appreciation for the wonders of the Pacific Coast of Ecuador.

Patricio and his family are related to the indigenous peoples of the Pacific Coast and Andes, as well as the early European settlers of Ecuador. Contained in this book is the unique perspective through his indigenous roots, his European bloodline and his modern day vision of Paradise on Earth.

Bo Rinaldi

www.BoRinaldi.com
www.VeganFusion.com

Bo is a best-selling author, angel investor, sustainability consultant and entrepreneur. Bo is the co-owner of the award winning Blossoming Lotus Restaurants and Vegan Fusion.

Bo first visited Ecuador in 1970 as a botanist seeking new natural plant based medicines from the Amazon and the Andes. Bo immediately fell in love with Ecuador, its people and its rich culture. While developing a sustainable land project on the Pacific Coast of Ecuador in 2011, Bo met Patricio Tamariz and the result of that first meeting is this book, The Secret of Paradise.

The Secret is to live together in harmony with each other, nature, our ancestors and ourselves. The deep and profound nature of this book is felt within every page, as you learn firsthand the rich history of Patricio and his family, their dedication to creating a sustainable world for us all, and the amazing Pacific Coast of Ecuador where surfing, ancient archaeology, organic farming, pure air and a rich and vibrant culture converge.

CPSIA information can be obtained at www.ICGtesting.com
Printed in the USA
LVOW020753190213

320628LV00013B/13/P